Richard Leigh Ha[...]lied the piano and harpsicl[...]isic and was awarded the d[...]ersity.

For nearly three decades, Richard was based in Oxford where he was an Associate Lecturer in Music at Oxford Polytechnic (Brookes University) from 1984–88. Since 1990, he has been a part-time tutor at Oxford University's Department for Continuing Education, as well as being a Visiting Tutor in Composition at the Birmingham Conservatoire.

Over the years, he has worked in duos with guitarists, harpsichordists, recorder players and singers, as well as many solo recitals. He has performed at the South Bank Centre, London, broadcast on Radio 4, appeared on Japanese television and recorded various CDs, including improvised music.

As a writer on music, Richard has contributed articles and reviews to the following journals: *Avant, Classical Music, Harpsichord & Fortepiano, International Piano, Music Teacher, The Musical Times* and *Tempo*.

Compositions include seven string quartets, *encore I–XII* for various solo instruments, *Dark Comes Down, Let Mine Eyes See Thee* for soprano, alto & three clarinets, *Zawn* for two pianos.

In his spare time he enjoys a glass of wine and attempts to play chess and golf.

The Days of Our Vanity

RICHARD LEIGH HARRIS

A MEMOIR

SilverWood

Published in paperback 2012 by SilverWood Books, Bristol, BS1 4HJ

www.silverwoodbooks.co.uk

ISBN 978-1-906236-85-4

British Library Cataloguing in Publication Data
A CIP catalogue record for this book is available from the British Library

Set in Sabon by SilverWood Books
Printed in England on paper certified as being from responsible sources

To the memory of my mother
Grace Jennie Harris (1919–2008)
and to my oldest friend, Roger Prideaux

I have often thought that there has rarely passed a life of which a judicious and faithful narrative would not be useful.
Samuel Johnson

We are largely fictitious, even to ourselves.
Rayner Heppenstall

When I was younger I could remember everything – whether it had happened or not.
Mark Twain

Contents

Prelude

To even consider, let alone attempt writing, what amounts to an autobiography is probably foolhardy at best and at worst a huge egotistical mistake. There – I'm hedging my bets already.

On the other hand, it is also an attempt to order, however poorly, one's own recollections and experiences, such as they are, before old age (or even *middle* age) sets in – the former is, hopefully, some time away, but one never knows…

It is, too, a wishing to share experiences in the hope that they may be helpful, even comforting perhaps, to other people; also, to convey something of the flavour and richness of the decades in which one has lived.

Of necessity, I bring a musician's outlook and perspective to these pages that may be of interest to some and not others. The narrative can be read in order, but this is by no means the only way and I leave readers to sort out the most appropriate choices and method for themselves. Why do we invariably feel impelled to read a book forwards and, by implication, chronologically? Probably the best advice is to dip in and out, leaving out the bits or sections that are of no interest to you.

This possibly ought to be written last, but I am writing this prefatory Prelude (in the first days of February 2005) a month or so after my forty-ninth birthday and a few days to go until my mother's eighty-sixth birthday. Today, the 6th, is a friend's birthday, whilst yesterday would have been the seventy-second birthday of one of my favourite writers, BS Johnson. Were that he was still alive. Alas…

One has to begin somewhere and I thought I would make a start before becoming eligible (perhaps that should read *elegible*) next year for excursions with Saga, the heftily-bejewelled (and that's only the men…), cruising veterans of which I find both slightly cloying and puzzling in equal proportions. A fortnight on a slow-moving ship, for God's sake? Geographically neither here nor there, and all that vastness of water!

Meanwhile, back to the book. (Must make a note to try and avoid these distracting parentheses… holds up the narrative action, etcetera… What narrative, what action…?)

The title may yet prove to be provisional, but seems apt enough and is, perhaps, a kind of warning to us all. Other possibilities that came to mind included *Carving the Runes*, *Moments of Epiphany, Thus Far* and *It Seemed Important at the Time* – this last one may still romp home ahead of the field, who knows?

Talking of provisionality, I suppose that life itself is, to an extent, provisional. After all, at fifty one is, God willing (and all things being equal) two-thirds of the way through one's life, give or take a few years. If you are exceptionally lucky in the genes department, you just *might* be halfway, but that is very unlikely and must rank as a foolhardy thought, one to be dismissed immediately.

I have never been a keeper of diaries, but this could be regarded as a macro-diary spanning events that both seemed (and still seem) to define me in some way over the years, rather than in mere days and weeks – i.e. they were of value at the time.

Also, although I am not a Catholic, this memoir could be regarded (at least some parts of it) as a kind of confession; the admission of failures and wrongdoings that, I believe, are important to confront oneself with. Perhaps then, and only then, one can move on and try to live a better, more decent, life day by day.

Taking my cue from that great man of letters, Dr Johnson, I hope that what follows will be judicious as well as faithful to the people and events that have shaped me.

Candidness and honesty, too, must play their part, although certain things have doubtless been forgotten (consciously or unconsciously), whilst others probably bear too many scars to be related: the equivalent of airing one's dirty underwear in public or finding the proverbial skeleton(s) in the wardrobe – or is it cupboard? 'Whatever', as teenagers are fond of saying.

Structurally, I'll keep you posted – I may yet decide to shape the book into fifty or so fragments/moments – which would be apposite, don't you think? Yes, one for each year of my life, thus far. We will see.

You might be getting the impression that I prefer to keep things open, flexible and ambiguous, with just a hint of procrastination. And you would be perfectly correct! At the very least, I hope that some of this may prove amusing – well, diverting anyhow. Yes – a diversion, if only temporary, from the more pressing issues that routinely beset us and impinge upon our days.

Let's give it a whirl, shall we? Here goes...

BEGINNINGS

Fugue

'Here goes...'

Those words, or something like it (probably stronger, if unvoiced) must have been in her head at the time my mother was giving birth to me, her only child, in Southmead Hospital, Bristol, in the early morning (circa 7.30am) of Wednesday 4 January 1956. (It has subsequently become something of an annual ritual/joke, that when she rings me with birthday greetings, I reply with words to the effect that she must now be feeling better than she was x years ago. Well, it seems funny at the time.)

I seemed to act as something of an early morning alarm call although, given the circumstances, I tend to be a bit hazy about the details. This, however, must have been one of the mornings that Mum did not switch off the alarm, turn over and feel like going back to sleep.

I was placid enough, apparently, once the staff had unwound the umbilical cord from around my neck – an early attempt (the record?) at self-strangulation, but I was underweight and was placed in an incubator for a couple of days. (*Ladieees and gen'lemen, in the blue corner and weighing in at a mere 5 pounds 6 ounces we give you...*) When I emerged from the incubator a few days later, I looked much better.

"Why, you *are* beautiful," said my mother in surprise, after having been warned by my father that I was not the most gorgeous specimen to have emerged from the womb.

"Of course he is," replied the Matron, in a manner recalling those hideous matrons from the *Carry On* films who, nonetheless, seemed to love all newborns however wrinkled and ghastly – in early training to be a Sid James, I suppose.

The birth itself, I imagine, must have been something

of a relief, for Mum had suffered very badly with the effects of toxemia in the preceding weeks. Surprisingly, in the circumstances, she didn't seem to suffer from any bouts of morning sickness.

Altruistically, I arrived ahead of schedule by a full fifteen days (being expected on the 19th). Clearly, I couldn't wait to get out and see the world at large. Then I, or rather my mother, was given the green light, though the eventual landing took a couple of days partially due to inclement weather – i.e. heavy, localised flooding when the waters burst. I was an induced (bribed?) and forceps birth, from which I haven't seemed to suffer any ill effects, so far as I can tell – if I did, no one has told me. (No jokes, please...)

An entry then (or if you believe in reincarnation, re-entry) with no parachute attached... (those last three words might provide an alternative title?)

One other fact which is pertinent, perhaps, and of some interest – indeed, something of a rarity in the 1950s, I would have thought – my parents, although deeply in love, were not married; more accurately and sadly, were not *able* to marry. So – legally (and on paper) – I was a bastard by circumstance if hopefully not by nature.

In terms of strict chronology I am skipping ahead here, I know, but am writing this (wanting to write this) now as it occurs to me and, surely, that's more honest and real, given the slightly unusual circumstances?

What follows is not easy to relate in some ways; but on the other hand and at this distance in time I feel quietly, almost strangely proud of my parents for a) having what was clearly a very loving relationship, even if it did not ultimately survive and b) for their decision to not terminate my life in the first weeks of pregnancy. Given the difficulties, financial and otherwise, many would, I am sure, have done just that.

My father was married to a Catholic who would not countenance a divorce and that was that. He and his wife were both stuck, I suspect, in a wholly lacklustre and loveless relationship. I am certain that this fact was of immense anguish to both my parents, but the situation was unalterable. Up until I was the age of ten or so, my father would visit on as many Saturday afternoons as he was able, before leaving late in the evening to catch his late buses home to Saltford, between Bristol and Bath on the A4. The buses would have been a number 17 or 18 from Clifton to the centre, then a 39 to Bath, most likely picked up from Queen Square or the bus station. He never stayed over until the Sunday, but there were other, albeit rare, occasions when he might join us for part of a holiday or, more likely, a day-trip.

Neither of my parents drove, let alone owned a car, so we relied on public transport – trains from Brunel's imposing Temple Meads station to take us away on holiday or the seemingly sporadic green Bristol Omnibus vehicles, both single and double-deckers, which chugged and toiled their reluctant way up Park Street to Clifton, a prosperous and slightly snooty if beautiful 'village' where I was brought up and remained until I was nineteen. But I digress...

Those short-lived and all-too-short Saturdays must have been both incredibly intense, yet desolate, for both of my parents.

Looking back, I suppose that this business of the absent father was fairly tough for me, but obviously a whole load tougher for my mother, who coped stoically (and on very little money) in bringing me up essentially single-handed. In 1964, when she was forty-five and I was eight, she went out to work part-time, having spent those first years of my life doing a really fine job in providing me with a very loving and secure home life. (This had included nursing me day and night through a particularly virulent ten-or-so weeks of paratyphoid during the summer of 1963 – a real heroine. She must have been completely exhausted. Why did no-one suggest that I be placed in the local Children's Hospital on St Michael's Hill?) More on her jobs and career later on. Meanwhile, back to my beginnings.

From Southmead Hospital, my mother and I were released into the world and headed home to Redland, all of which I do not remember, even vaguely, of course.

After a few months, I think, we moved to a spacious first floor flat at 15 Richmond Terrace, Clifton. There we stayed until I was four years old in 1960. Again, the memories are practically non-existent, but one or two drifting impressions dimly survive, or, more probably, remnants of impressions and sensations of which I must have become increasingly aware as weeks turned into months and I began to take notice of, and adjust to, the necessarily circumscribed world around me; yet a world which we call home.

2

Sleep   mostly   sleep

Warmth   her him   blurry light

Voices   sleep

specks of dust slowly swirling swinging weightless in light

illumined by sun   living room

voices   her voice

his voice   touchings   cheek to cheek

held up   dandled
Momo Dada   yes
Thirsty   drink   warm, yes warm

Now sleep   sleep   sleep

being watched   loved

sensations of love   being loved

a being being loved

baby being

this baby   me

Momo
    Dada

I sleep sleep dream   sleep wake   eat
        always that voice   I turn my head the sounds

                          are nearer
warmth cuddle   sleep again   again

Left: My father at 15 Richmond Terrace, Clifton, late 1950s.
Below: My mother in her flat. Southville, 1990s.

3

A large living room on the first floor of a fairly spacious flat, yes. My mother knew, I think, a lady who worked in the offices on the ground floor, the flat was available so, etcetera, etcetera…

The view from the large windows: to the right, the Kinbourn Hotel and straight ahead, a police station partly shielded by shrubbery. To the left, a small park and the remains of a church, St Andrew's, that was bombed on a Sunday in 1940.

It was from these same windows that my mother looked down one day, to see the hood of my black pram completely obscured by the face of a large Alsation dog, fondly licking my face. To make matters worse, I had both my tiny chubby arms around his neck – a sight guaranteed to raise any mother's heartbeat. According to Mum, her feet had never descended that set of stairs so rapidly until that precise moment.

I ought to explain to any possibly shocked reader under the age of forty-five or so that, in the mid-1950s, it was still perfectly safe to leave a young infant in its pram – in this instance tied to the adjacent railings, where not only my mother, but the office workers could keep an eye on me.

The dog, sensing no fear, was merely being affectionate, but was wisely shooed away, nonetheless.

In my early years the previously-mentioned park would be where I was taken to play, explore and generally toddle about, with or without reins, trying to avoid the seemingly plentiful dog turds. (You never ever see them nowadays, do you? Children's reins, I mean, not the dog turds.) Alas, dogs, their deposits and all things canine will probably never go out of fashion…)

My memories, with some isolated exceptions, are so vague or nonexistent as to be not worth bothering with. These three exceptions are as follows:

1) Long patterned curtains at the windows of the large living room – typically 1950s in its design of asymmetric abstract blocks of red, beige and green. They feature as a prominent background to a photograph of my father who is wearing a blazer with a crested pocket and a gunner's tie. All rather formal looking, but that was probably the nature of the era. He was a formal dresser, bless him, even wearing a dark suit or tweed jacket to the beach on a hot summer's day. He was never very adept at relaxing and, I'm sure, felt guilty if he was not working. My mother asked him about this rather driven attitude and he replied that, when young, he had been so indolent, that he felt that he had to make up, retrospectively, for all the wasted time in his (as he saw it) misspent youth.

2) Me, holding onto the bars of my cot, shaking with laughter, becoming increasingly red in the face, as my mother tripped and fell over. "It's all very well for you to laugh, you blighter," she retorted. Or words to that effect, all of which, apparently, made me double-up with laughter all the more.

3) My first experimental (what else...?) attempt at cooking. I had mixed various cake ingredients in a bowl, including marmalade (I had yet to read and appreciate the Paddington books by Michael Bond) in emulation, presumably, of my mother's baking. She was feeling unwell and had to clear up all the mess, including a heavily-encrusted toddler who had been eagerly licking the spoon of raw and probably unspeakable cake-mix. (My cooking abilities have marginally improved since that day back in 1959.) And those are my only remaining conscious memories of our time at Richmond Terrace.

Oh, yes – one more thing. There was a small newsagent and sweetshop below the terrace which was run by an elderly lady, Mrs Watkins. Here Mum, then I, would buy penny bars of Cadbury's chocolate. I think that I liked the look of the purple foil wrapping as much as the actual taste of the chocolate inside. Indeed, purple has remained one of my favourite colours to this day.

It was Mrs Watkins who once tartly (yet with a touch of zealous pride) claimed that she had never read a single book in her life; nor, furthermore, did she intend to. Clearly, in her book (as it were), reading was merely for idlers and loafers. Perhaps she was a fully paid-up, stiff-as-a-board Baptist?

In 1960, we moved across the road to the garden flat at 7 Lansdown Place, Clifton.

4

A former boss of Mum's and family friend has referred to this flat as 'the cave'! Which was wholly appropriate, because whilst it was full of nooks and crannies, it also had cold, stone floors and no damp course (being built in the 1840s). This meant that we suffered from periodic flooding in bad weather and when this occurred, the flat could become something of a trial for my mother. Yet it was beautifully cool in those hot summers of my boyhood and had a lot of character, even if it did tend to be rather dark and gloomy. No ghosts, though – perhaps surprisingly, given the age of the house. Were so many of those summers really that hot and that idyllic during the 1960s? To be honest, I think that they really were and that I am not just being falsely nostalgic. Tricks of the memory maybe?

The landlady, Mrs Hawkins, lived in Pembroke Road, played golf, drove fast cars and enjoyed the company of even faster men. (It has to be said, however, that she was always very fair and very pleasant in her dealings. The rent was very cheap, even for those days and we stayed there for fourteen years until the summer of 1974.)

Perhaps this was in reaction to her husband Ivor, who had been out in Africa, retired and returned to England to nothing-very-much, except for a horny wife whom he probably could not satisfy. Have you ever known anyone called Ivor who was a bra-ripping, passionate wow in bed? Unlikely, eh?

We felt slightly sorry for him, for occasionally he did the odd job for us, painting and decorating. He always seemed to do these jobs reluctantly and, obviously, at the behest of his wife who liked to take her drinks, as well as her men, in liberal quantities. Ivor had one of those moustaches that succeeded only too well in making him appear even more dejected than he possibly was already.

But he did do the jobs – and for free – unlike Mr Hall who was probably a bit of a rogue decorator, ripping off our landlady, left, right and centre. Perhaps they had a private arrangement…? Don't ask, as they say. (Who are *they*?)

Back to the flat and the house.

Including the basement, there were five floors. Above us in the ground floor flat were a variety of tenants who, over the years, included Heddah and her young son Mark, a posse of noisy students (60s rock-and-roll partying, yeah!) and, latterly, a young buxom couple (well, June was anyway – I have forgotten the husband). On the first floor, at least for the last few years, were our landlady and depressed husband Ivor;

above them, Mr and Mrs Duncan. In common with many men of his generation, Mr Duncan was rarely, if ever, seen without a hat. She was a sweet lady, who would sometimes bake us an apple tart, but who had to put up with his stinginess (he would count the number of sweets in the paper bag and return them to Woolworth's if there were not enough). They would go for their Saturday night drink at a pub near the Clifton Suspension Bridge and make their respective halves of Guinness last all evening. This they did for year upon year, until an increasingly irate publican gave them their marching orders. Last orders, as it were.

She could often be seen leaning out the window, having a crafty cigarette and frantically waving the smoke away from the disapproving nostrils of her husband. To us, gazing up and giving her a cheery 'good-on-you-girl' kind of wave from the pavement below (it would hardly be above would it?), she looked as if she was sending out distress signals in semaphore, which – in a way – I suppose she was. She was full of gossip and what we used to call tittle-tattle, but in a neighbourly, slightly naughty, but not malicious manner – with, perhaps, one exception.

Above them, on the top floor, lived an Irish homosexual – a Latin teacher who taught at St Brendan's College on the A4 road going to Bath. It was reported, darkly, to my mother by Mrs Duncan (with down-turned, pursed lips) that he used to 'entertain' Sixth Form boys in his flat. Conjuring tricks? A monologue or charades, perhaps? Extra-curricular activities, I think it used to be called; either that, or he was just giving them a helping hand – polishing their declensions.

That was the colourful array of personalities that inhabited No. 7 for the best part of a decade or so. They would be glimpsed now and again, usually gingerly descending the steps to the basement to deposit their rubbish in the old, noisy metal dustbins that were kept in an alcove, which also housed one of the most perilous pieces of electric wiring known to man. The cables hung dustily and (if you were a masochist) enticingly from a ceiling which, itself, was clinging on for grim death. Wisely, I was dissuaded from venturing in there – most probably the main reason that I am still here writing this. (You might have wished otherwise? How dare you!)

Inside the basement flat, the layout was as follows: the front door lead straight into the stone-floored kitchen, though at a left-facing right-angle (huh?!) which was long and narrow. There wasn't a lot of room, although enough to house the essentials – table, sink with a Valor gas hot water heater (complete with pilot light), a heavy dresser painted cream with red handles and equally heavy, obdurate stone shelves around the walls.

In these unpromising surroundings Mum, with her usual creative ingenuity, worked domestic wonders. I always remember a chocolate fortress that she made for one of the birthdays (possibly my sixth?) – very impressive to look at and it tasted wonderful!

Beyond the kitchen, you turned left into a large living room/lounge, part of which was screened off to form a small bedroom for Mum. No central heating, but inviting coal fires in the winter and, in the summer, dried hydrangeas (blue turned to lime green) were placed in the hearth in vases. Artistic and elegant – qualities which, come to think of it, absolutely summed up my mother. The lounge had a very high ceiling, too, which would be prodded in the four corners by an extra-long brush during the annual ritual of 'spring cleaning'. Mum would create a kind of turban with which to protect her hair and off she would go, dusting, washing-down, the whole spring-cleaning business, only interrupted by breaks for coffee and a cigarette. Does anyone still do this anymore? Perhaps it's a generational thing – that and, presumably, having the required grit and energy levels.

Coming out of this imposing room, both in breadth and height, you turned into the passage, out of which arose a flight of broad and deep stone stairs, which lead to the ground floor via a door to which we had access if we wanted, but rarely used. (Where would any of us be without doors and stairs? Stymied, that's what…)

Just along from the stairs was an ancient and redundant tall brown cupboard on legs, with a fine mesh 'window' – a kind of cold store, in the years before refrigerators. Old, empty and gathering dust, it sat there eerily – a furniture equivalent of Miss Haversham. It had not been used, I would think, since the first quarter of the century. Next to it, an imposing and large walnut chest-of-drawers with curved corners, in which were stored blankets, sheets, underwear, etcetera. (Especially etcetera…) This, in contrast, looked handsome and almost elegant.

The next room along on the left would have originally been used for storing the wine. We used it to store all the odds and sods such as bits of wood, old pots, irons, saws, etcetera – you name it and my mother probably had it.

I suppose you could have almost termed it bric-a-brac except that, potentially, most of it was useful or might have 'come in handy', an attitude inherited from the scrimp-and-save years of the Second World War.

Continuing down the passage, you came to the bathroom, whose single large cupboard housed a boiler which no longer worked. To have a bath, you had to fill and bring several plastic bucketsful of hot water from the kitchen. It was only a matter of some yards, but seemed a chore, I think, to both of us. The bucket was yellow, by the way. (You really needed to know that detail, didn't you?)

It certainly did not actively encourage bathing; my childhood bathtime was once a week on a Friday night, after I had cleaned the shoes, the one and only task that my mother expected me to perform, except for wiping up the dishes as I grew older. There was no heating in the bathroom. If it was cold, a paraffin stove would be lit whose wick would have to be regularly trimmed. If you didn't, it smelt – it was as simple as that. There was also a lattice window with bubbled glass which, except for the necessity of a pink plastic curtain, looked into my bedroom.

To the right, under the stone stairs was a fairly roomy coal bunker which, to a youngster, appeared to recede a long way back. A mysterious place, from which Mum would periodically emerge with coal scuttle and bucket (not the yellow one, another one...) doing a credible impression of the *Black and White Minstrel Show* – anyone remember that? It was on Saturday nights, yes? And, in those days, yes – it was in black and white. God, it was, in retrospect, unbelievably racist! (If it was revived, it would be required viewing for the whole of the BNP...)

My bedroom was the last room on the left. It was painted pink and my mother painted the interior of the large cupboards bright red. This suited me fine and was where I stored all my toys, books, dinky cars and all the other clutter and paraphernalia that young (and not-so-young) boys collect. As I grew older, the red was incorporated into a striking scheme of black and white gingham check for both bedspread, curtains and chair-covers, whilst red cushions adorned the bed and chairs. It looked adult and chic and I loved it. In todays parlance, it was decidedly 'cool'.

Being a basement or garden flat, my bedroom window looked out onto the garden. From my bed, you turned your head to the right and, in season, a large fit-to-bursting fuchsia seemed to almost come into the room. When I was ill, which seemed to be fairly frequently (mostly bad ears, from which I used to cry out with pain), this was always a source of pleasure and calm.

Down either side of the garden were two lengthy borders, which my father attended to when he came. He was quite a good gardener, with the proverbial 'green fingers', except for the time that he dug up a weed, which my mother had just planted a few days before…

At the bottom stood a laburnum tree with its brilliant gold foliage, various ferns and a rockery which my father had laboriously built, and from which he found a few fossils that were dated by staff at the Bristol Museum. Jurassic period, if I remember. What with the ferns and everything, you half expected a dinosaur to jump out of the bushes… preferably, a herbivore or a vegan who would settle for nut cutlets rather than human flesh.

A square, reasonably wide garden – certainly ample enough to play in, run around and let off steam. Or, sometimes, a space in which to climb inside my wigwam (made from a length of canvas and bamboo poles), complete with Indian headdress to think thoughts – of what? – cowboys? Probably just to dream, I do not remember any specifics; except that I was a very dreamy, quiet child. A dreamy, slightly shy only child, but quietly happy, too; and, most importantly, loved. Loved, but not spoilt, I hasten to add (for any child psychologists among you…) How fortunate never to have needed the dubious ministrations of a psychologist or a social worker!

Later on, an old iron bedstead found its way into the

garden, to be covered by old blankets and sat on. There is a photo, somewhere, of Roger, his sister Susie and me perched on this old bedframe. In addition, there were a couple of brightly-striped pink and green deckchairs, which were reminiscent of Richard Whiteley's blazers on *Countdown*. I can picture this seemingly affable man, but never managed to watch the show.

The walls of the garden were brackish, red-brown. Looking out from my bedroom window on moonlit nights in winter, after saying my prayers, sometimes these walls were topped with snow, reminding me of a rich Christmas cake with crunchy icing.

In the severe winter of 1962–63, this icing seemed to remain for a long time, sometimes brilliantly lit by the moon – either a full, blue-veined circle of stilton, or a thin lemon slice...

A harsh winter, whose snowdrifts seemed to be almost as tall as myself, if not taller.

Returning from visiting my grandmother and Aunty Florence in Trowbridge after Christmas: those oh-so-desolate railway platforms, where my mother and I stood, stamping our feet against the toe-breaking cold.

If you were lucky, there might be a waiting room, not only open, but with a real fire in the grate – a miniature version of the furnace that was stoked in the old steam locomotives. This was just before Dr Beeching took his metaphorical axe to so many of the branch lines and rural, underachieving stations. The thrill and smell of the steam and those hissing pistons! When I was tiny, we went up to an engine at Temple Meads and I was lifted up by the filthy-handed driver or his mate, full of ash and smuts, but I was too young to care – and, to her credit, neither did Mum, although my clothes must have been a sight.

Double-decker buses (green in Bristol, red in Wiltshire) where adults were permitted to smoke upstairs, pressing out the cigarette stub on a slightly raised square of ribbed metal on the back of the seat in front of you, if you see what I mean. The floor would usually be strewn with butts, some of them stained with lipstick, in assorted shades of red and orange.

The red, dinging bell and the separate cabin for the driver seated in his own snug world, but answerable to the conductor; the seemingly huge handbrake whose V-like formation at the top looked like a vicious pair of pliers, or the claws of a long-extinct bird...

Railway stations and buses bring to mind a few of the adverts and products of that era: Bryant and May matches, Tizer, Vernons coupons and those slightly rusting chocolate or cigarette machines, with their metal pull-drawers; the cigarette packets with those cards of racing drivers and butterflies; hoardings advertising Bingo and Premium Bonds...

The smell of stale fag smoke in phone boxes, the press-buttons A and B; the quiet, satisfying whirr-click of the dial as your finger fitted snugly in to dial the shorter number than nowadays. The perceived heaviness of the receiver, at least to an eight-year-old. We didn't have a phone at home – our nearest callbox was outside what was then the police station, about fifty yards diagonally opposite the house.

A conundrum: if you needed the police, did you phone them directly from outside the police station, or did you actually walk the extra few feet and see them in person? ('I would have used the phone, constable, but...') A tricky one there, sarge.

Come to think of it, back in the 1960s, telephones were surely referred to as telephones, never just phones, weren't they? Similarly, some old-timers would still refer to the 'wireless' rather than the radio.

Picking up on the smell of stale cigarette smoke in phone boxes, smells were always important to me. Apparently, I could identify which coins in my pocket-money had been given to me by which family member or relative, even as a late toddler. Not too bad an olfactory function, then. Possibly a bit weird, though.

I also remember the French, bereted onion-sellers – their intermittent visits, wheeling their bicycles unhurriedly from door to door, ringing their bells and advertising their wares along the lengths of Lansdown Place and Victoria Square. Over the years, their appearances became less frequent, faded and died out altogether; to become as obsolete as the motorbike with sidecar – a relic of an age which gently slipped away out of sight (whilst our attention was elsewhere) and remains merely in the memory.

There was a woman who always wore an olive green coat.

The material was thick, possibly wool, but looked homemade. She was sharp-nosed with a short and boyish, but greying haircut. She was, according to my mother, a German-Jewish refugee with a pronounced accent who survived by giving German lessons. I think that she lived in Richmond Terrace, was kindly, but rather fierce in her demeanour and was definitely one of those Clifton characters that seemed to haunt the village for many years. She would, I suppose, have been about as old as the century and was materially poor, but strong in spirit and resilience – as any refugee would need to be.

In the dark, womb-like cave of home, I played, read, dreamed, imagined and was thoroughly content but, doubtless, also sheltered and cocooned. Then, my happy, lazy idyll was abruptly and suddenly shattered. To paraphrase WB Yeats, all was to change, to "change utterly", even if not into a state of "terrible beauty".

In the autumn of 1961, I was sent to that awful detention centre called school, a sentence which was to last thirteen years. And, what is more, with no remission for good behaviour. (Even the guys who suffered the ordeal of National Service only had a couple of years of enforced discipline, come to think of it!)

In later years, we were frequently told (probably by the teachers) that this whole process was 'character building'... To my over-sensitive ears and eyes, it seemed more akin to character destruction, ironing out individual traits into one bland, homogenous mass that could be quickly, efficiently marshalled and controlled. I think that even then I had my doubts as to this supposedly beneficial thing, this reductive system labelled 'education'.

Indeed, it did seem that each pupil was labelled, filed away and, metaphorically, placed in a box to be processed and, eventually, spewed out at the other end many years later. Cynical, moi...? More hypocritical, in all likelihood, for I have myself taught in various ways and at various levels for many years. Perpetuating, indeed, the very system that I used to kick against ! Funny, that – or, at the very least, quite ironic.

But back to myself at five...

SCHOOLDAZE 1

5

Christ Church Junior School was a smallish Victorian school in Princess Victoria Street, built in 1852. As the name suggests, it was affiliated to Christ Church, half a mile away on the edge of the Downs, in Clifton. After 1967, the school moved and the building became Clifton Public Library, whose female chief librarian seemed scary and had a tight mouth, highlighted by a fierce streak of red lipstick.

Structurally, the school contained five large classrooms, three downstairs and two upstairs. The basement housed toilets and a kiln, in which our rudimentary attempts at ceramics were fired by the headmaster Mr Herbert. The playground was rather small and austere, merely a kind of forecourt fronted by a stone wall topped by the usual iron railings.

At either end of the school day, a retired man in a peaked cap and enormous bushy eyebrows would do 'lollipop' duty, safely ushering parents and their offspring across the street. He was a lovely, courteous man, but I forget his name.

The classrooms were large, light and airy and painted in either pale yellow or pale green, with high windows that were opened and secured by long cords. Each of these five rooms housed a large, bulbous grey, vented radiator. Upstairs, there was a very small staffroom accessed by a tiny, curved, outdoor balcony. The staff would have been rendered practically invisible, due to the cigarette smoke.

There were six teachers, including the headmaster: white-haired Mrs Green, already nearing retirement, was the reception teacher; Miss Veasey who tended to shout, wore too much makeup and had pungent halitosis, looked after the next class; Miss Pook, who was always pleasant to me, but seemed to be a bit of a pale-eyed sadist (she hauled some unfortunate pupils to their feet by their hair…). In complete contrast there was firm but kindly Mrs Porter, with her swept-up hair and twinsets and Mr Prickett who had a Jimmy Edwards-style moustache and an irascible temper due, it was said, to his being tortured by the Japanese in the war. He had had bamboo canes inserted into his ears, apparently. I remember his rust-coloured wool ties, his check jackets and his energised manner – a good, solid teacher whom his pupils respected, even if he was rather partial to using the cane. Mr Herbert, the headmaster, red-faced and invariably cross-looking, wore greenish tweedy suits and a similar tie against a white shirt. He didn't, either then or now, seem to be impressive in any way, nor did he appear particularly kind or empathetic. Why he was involved in education at all seemed to be a complete mystery. When he retired (not soon enough for most of us), he moved to Cornwall, I gather, to grow daffodils or mushrooms, possibly both; and doubtless to continue his small-minded, bigoted mode of life. There was no caretaker, as far as I can recall.

My first day at school was, if not a disaster, hardly an unmitigated success. My mother had said that there would be singing and dancing with Mrs Green, which apparently I tearfully denied when Mum came to fetch me at the end of the day.

"There was," said a slightly flustered, but sympathetic Mrs Green, "but he just sat in a corner and was too upset to join in." Oh dear.

I remember the sheer level of noise (amazing how much racket thirty or more children in a reception class can make), which seemed, at the time, quite scary and traumatic. Also, many midget chairs and an area that included a sandpit with brightly-coloured plastic shovels. A desultory simulation of a beach, I suppose? Hardly a holiday, mind you.

We arrived home and, with something approaching relief, I informed Mum politely that I had been to school now, thank you, but that it was pretty awful, as well as tiring – or the five-year-olds' equivalent. Then, an awful moment for her, as she explained that I would have to continue attending school just for a *little* while longer. (Ok, thirteen years longer…)

My face must have been a picture (Munch's *The Scream* or Bacon's screaming pope?), but when Mum explained to me that she might face a jail term if I didn't attend, then I meekly accepted the inevitability of my own prison sentence. Not only that, there would have been no one to feed me. *Quelle horreur*!

Every Friday morning, the Reverend Michael Brettell, Vicar of Christ Church, would visit the school to take assembly, addressing the whole school from an impressive-looking oak lectern.

He was urbane, charming and a good speaker, these qualities being evident even to our young selves sat cross-legged, as we were, under his venerable gaze. Big black bushy eyebrows and slicked-down black hair completed his striking appearance – patrician, but kindly, mixed with a quiet authority and dignity. I consulted Crockford's the other day and found out that he was Vicar from 1962–1973, before moving south to serve in the diocese of Eastbourne.

He was a hard act to follow and his successor, the Reverend (later Canon) Paul Berg, in some people's estimation (including my mother's and myself) failed totally to live up to the previously high standards set by Michael Brettell. I remember vividly his stopping a Family Service to reprimand the congregation for failing to "sing up".

"Don't just sit there like lemons," he admonished, "sing properly!"

His predecessor would never have dreamt of saying anything of that kind. One of the curates clearly loathed him and would always avail himself of the opportunity to take the piss out of Berg on a regular basis. Not very Christian, but the whole process was wittily achieved, was a delight to watch and had the tacit backing and complicity of the majority of the congregation.

6

It must have been when I was five or six that my mother was summoned to see Mr Herbert in his study, as she came to collect me. His opening gambit went something like this: "Mrs Harris, we have been having a problem with Richard. He has been caught urinating in the wellington boots of some of the other children. We cannot have this, you know." No smile, completely deadpan delivery.

In response to this slightly surreal exposition, Mum parried with something to the effect that I was not in the habit of doing this at home and that, perhaps, I had not been able to reach the loo in sufficient time. Either that, or my sense of localised geography was woefully inadequate – probably the latter; geography has never been one of my strong points. Not a good combination, taken in tandem with a bladder that needed emptying… If in doubt, always carry a compass and a bladder emptier on you at all times. Just in case…

Not unexpectedly, Herbert proved to be a completely humourless twat about the whole episode, whilst my mother, in complete contrast, was quietly amused. I think she felt, quite correctly, that Herbert was a shallow, pedantic little man with no breadth of vision. I probably knew this instinctively, but couldn't have voiced it, nor would I have been encouraged to do so in those days. I suppose, if I had wanted revenge, I could have presented the old bastard with a bootful of pee (or two) on the occasion of his timely retirement, but eleven-year-olds tend not to think of that sort of thing, or plan much in advance for that matter.

The matter was dropped and did not, as far as I was aware, occur again. Perhaps I had sought revenge on a few fellow pupils, but think it unlikely (I'm not made that way); merely saw the boots as a useful, temporary place for having a slash, in all likelihood. Anything to miss part of a lesson... Perhaps it was a protest reaction to schooling in general? ('Huh! I PISS on your educational system' – delivered in a French accent, accompanied by a dismissive wave of the hand; think Peter Sellers' Inspector Clousseau here.)

7

One or two things worried me, both consciously as well as subconsciously, in my earliest years at junior school.

I was convinced that the rooms upstairs were dormitories and that I wouldn't be allowed home and would be forced to sleep there. In actuality, of course, they were the teaching rooms of Mrs Porter and Mr Prickett, but no one had bothered to explain that to me – I probably kept it to myself, unvoiced and, therefore, unanswered. But, for a time, this thought haunted me.

The other worry would show up on Sundays. According to my mother, I would be quiet, playing with my cars or small railway layout, after lunch or in the late afternoon, but I would be silently weeping, yet unable to rationally explain the problem to her. This happened regularly enough for her to voice her concern to my teacher. I now think, in retrospect, that this was a dread of returning to Miss Pook's class the next day, but why I am at a loss to tell. As far as I can recall, I was not bullied or anything of that sort, but perhaps picked up on something about the nature of this teacher and her quasi-sadistic attitude to some of the children in the class. These Sunday weepings ceased when I moved up to the next class, so who knows?

I remember nature study lessons with Miss Pook and feeling very tired towards the end of the afternoons, but that is about it. Oh, yes – and not being able to draw at all well and being frustrated by this lack of ability. God, I must have been rather serious and a practised worrier for my age!

The best time of the day was the final half-hour, when we would be read to and could rest our heads on our forearms on the top of our desk. From these late afternoon sessions in Mrs Porter's class, I can still remember Mary Treadgold's *We Couldn't Leave Dinah*, an adventure story about three children being left behind, mistakenly, on one of the smaller Channel Islands at the time of the Nazi occupation, and their going into hiding and eventual escape. A beautifully written book that I still have in my collection.

Absence from school due to illness was a fairly frequent event and I think that I missed out on great chunks of information, particularly Maths, from which I never really caught up. When this happened, Mum would make garishly-coloured jellies (often green or red) in rabbit-shaped moulds for me, plus blancmanges, grapes and all the usual childhood fare. Effervescent Lucozade would be on hand, too, in those ribbed bottles covered in orange cellophane, which always seemed to aid recovery.

My worst, most prolonged illness was in the summer of 1963. We had been on holiday with my Aunty Barbara to Brean and stayed in a chalet bungalow. Whether it was a dodgy ice cream, corned beef or another piece of food poisoning I don't know, but I was seriously ill for something like ten weeks. Para-typhoid was diagnosed and I was very weak with hefty, seemingly unremitting bouts of diarrhoea and vomiting; also temperatures that hit 105 degrees Fahrenheit.

Luckily, or not, it was a hot summer, the windows were open and I could glimpse the pinks and purples of the fuchsias (tiny *art deco* lampshades) directly outside my window. To this day, though, I will not eat corned beef.

I still have a ghost-memory however, vis-á-vis the ghastly smell, as well as how awful the whole episode must have been for my exhausted mother who throughout did a really heroic job of nursing me back to health. Even our normally dour and monosyllabic GP, Dr Miles, congratulated her on her nursing skills. A rare compliment!

I remember him as being always dressed immaculately in a pinstriped suit, a fresh handkerchief in his breast pocket and smelling of aftershave, which seemed to linger long after he had gone. It all added up to giving one confidence in his abilities – that and the neatly trimmed white moustache. A professional! His surgery was in Apsley Road and he suffered the indignities of an alcoholic wife, poor man. He was courteous, reserved and essentially well-intentioned, in spite of his gruff exterior. Fundamentally a kindly and decent man – what we once would have termed 'old school'. *Anno domini...* his kind have now irredeemably vanished, along with the French onion-sellers, the turquoise Austin A40 and the cigarette machines...

One evening, later that autumn, Mum came into my bedroom crying – she had just heard on the radio of President Kennedy's assassination, which marks that evening as Friday 22nd November 1963. I was seven, ill again and, of course, concerned by her evident distress (without comprehending it) but more immediately occupied with imaginary battles in the hills and valleys of my rumpled bedclothes, the kingdom of sheets.

Like most children, I suppose that I was totally wrapped up in my own interior world – sensitive, but a bit oblivious to the real world and all its happenings.

Dream on, young one, dream on...

8

Friendship now.

Although I was an only child, four doors along at 11 Lansdown Place lived the Prideaux family – Joan, Bert and their two children Roger and Susan.

Roger (the co-dedicatee of this book and my oldest pal) was a year older than me, and Susie, as we always called her, was two years my junior (they still are...). I must have known them since I was four or five and they were, in effect, like a brother and sister to me. Unlike the enforced company of brothers and sisters, however, it was always quite pleasing to return to my own quiet solitude when I descended the basement steps to my own home, even though we invariably got on well, racing around the local streets on our scooters. Bicycles were never an option, because the streets in Clifton were, even then, far too busy and congested.

Either Joan or my mother took it in turns to walk the three

of us to school across Victoria Square, under the archway by the chemists, through Boyce's Avenue, across Regent Street (without a zebra crossing at that point) and into Princess Victoria Street. (It was, incidentally, partly due to my mother's campaigning that a zebra crossing was eventually installed at this extremely busy part of Regent Street: by what was then Witts the bakers, opposite the pub with the sign depicting the Sanderman port or sherry man, a silhouette of a mysterious figure wearing a hat and cloak.)

The house where they lived, like ours, was divided into flats. In ascending order: the basement was empty (I think), then on the ground floor were the Skeldings, Liz and Dave (no children), the Prideaux's on the first floor and then the Cuttles on the top floor. Dave Skelding always seemed to be monosyllabic, if not entirely silent and resembled a poor man's version of Sean Connery: good-looking, but slightly sallow and none too healthy. His wife Liz was the chatty one and was kindly towards the three of us, except for the occasional reprimand, when the window would be thrown up and we would be roundly ticked off for making too much noise. When we were older, she would invite us in for a cup of tea. I think that she would have liked children and the three of us were, perhaps, a small substitute for her loss. Reg Cuttle, estate agent, was an obligatory hat-wearer, said little and seemed rather pompous, but had a beaming wife, Phyllis, who seemed to be very fond of us.

After school, at weekends and in the holidays, Roger, Susie and myself would work off our surplus energy on our scooters (Susie had a tricycle in her early years) or play in the park opposite which had big trees and a much overgrown, air-raid shelter which was tempting to explore, yet creepy. The park seemed huge to our small selves, but to adult eyes seems quite small and tame, intimate, even, if not shrunken. Those repeated washes of Time...

As the senior member of our trio, it invariably fell to Roger to organise what we did and we usually acquiesced in his decisions, be it stamp collecting, inventing games or just deciding what we should do. The equation of two boys to one girl, however, did not always make for harmonious playtimes and Susie would often go off in tears and disgust to seek solace and reassurance from her parents.

Over the years we got to know various locals such as old Mr Dix who kept rabbits, but even in the fairly innocent days of the mid-1960s, our parents quietly, but firmly, discouraged us from going into their houses. After all, skulking behind the fond old man, the smiles and the proffered sweets, might possibly lurk a smooth-talking, well-practised paedophile. Possible but highly unlikely.

He did seem, however, to be genuine and very nice. Roger reminded me only recently that Mr Dix papered his walls with articles from the colour supplements of *The Sunday Times* – a cheap and colourful practice that I would associate more with teenagers and students. But, as they say, necessity is the mother of invention; a sentiment that my own mother would have wholeheartedly agreed with.

As we grew older, we explored further and often played on Clifton or Durdham Downs. Those green, open spaces gave us our playgrounds of freedom and we were privileged to have them so close at hand, especially within the context of a large city.

All these things we did until our mid-teens, when the calls of homework and exams became more pressing and the time for play began to diminish. Yes, we were slowly, almost imperceptibly changing and turning into young adults, in spite of ourselves; and our concerns, our hobbies and our hormones were slowly changing, too.

We adapted, as children do, but I think that we occasionally pined for our younger, innocent and uncomplicated years; those long, idle summers of ice-lollies, Airtex shirts and shorts. But these would be private thoughts and memories, not usually admitted to or voiced to each another. We had put aside childish things and whims. Our toys gathered dust in our cupboards, abandoned if not entirely forgotten. To them, we must have seemed like fickle traitors, but all things grow, have their season and then fade away.

9

Christ Church school had no room or provision for a kitchen to provide school lunches, so we had to walk the five-or-so minutes to St Andrew's Hall (the parish hall, but originally attached to the church that was bombed during the war) every day, rain or shine, to be fed. A Noah's ark of gabardine-coated children, two by two. The short journey didn't seem too much of a pain and probably whetted our appetites for what was to come. ('May the Lord make us truly thankful…')

I can still remember my first school 'dinner': liver and bacon (probably rather stringy) with mashed potatoes and, I imagine, overcooked cabbage or greens in the way that they used to be prepared. No concept of *al dente* vegetables in those days! I cannot remember the dessert, but it would probably have been something possibly unrecognisable, surmounted as well as surrounded by thick custard. I am still very fond of both liver and bacon, as well as custard – but not on the same plate, obviously.

Two women served the lunches. One was dark-haired and grim, with a long nose, whilst the other was, in sharp contrast, blond, red-faced (blood pressure?) and jolly. Even at the age of eight, I fancied this latter lady like mad and asked my mother if I could invite her home. This was, clearly, the beginning of my liking for mature women... I think that Mum diffused this surreal request with her usual tact, whilst, in all likelihood, trying to hide her amusement at both my innocence and precociousness. These two qualities are often conjoined facets of childhood.

There were also two other ladies who supervised not only the lunches, but the playtime immediately afterwards. Mrs Elliott (thin lips, orange lipstick) and Mrs Sampson, who was older, a softer personality and to whom I naturally warmed.

The hall was used for all the usual parish activities such as youth groups, bible-readings, scouts and brownies, etcetera. Roger and I firmly resisted the idea of both the cubs and the scouts. We were not antisocial, but neither were we born 'joiners' of group activities, preferring our own and each other's company.

The downstairs hall, apart from being used for our daily lunches, also doubled as the area where we did our (once-weekly?) PE session in singlet, shorts and plimsolls (known locally as 'daps'). This took place later in the afternoon, presumably to allow our lunch to have settled.

I cordially disliked these sessions, never having been remotely talented at any sport. If at all possible, I tried to spend the time hiding behind a small door panel in one of the walls, where my absence, as far as I was aware, was never detected. Or, if it was, it was tacitly and tactfully ignored. Hand in hand with this total lack of sporting prowess went a determinedly non-competitive streak that I must have inherited from either one or both of my parents. I completely failed to see the intrinsic merit or virtue of being first at anything.

My mother, many years later, laughingly reminded me that she had to persuade me to take part in some daft beanbag race at the annual sports day to placate my reception teacher, Mrs Green – that places me as being five at the time. What, logically, was the point in racing to the finishing line clutching a beanbag? I am not made that way and I failed to see it then, just as I still continue to do to this day. Perhaps it was nothing more than fun, like the egg-and-spoon race? I still didn't get it. Perhaps plain laziness was a contributory factor? Maybe the only one? Like much else, it's a bit of a mystery, but I resented the enforced participation and regarded the whole business as a sham.

10

When I was eight, in 1964, five events happened to me that were important and, in one case, actually life-changing: my mother went to work (part-time); I had to wear glasses; I began piano lessons; I joined a church choir; I nearly drowned.

My mother went to work as a part-time secretary in Cotham, at the top of St Michael's Hill, at Oldbury House in the Department of Fashion and Textiles, which was part of the West of England College of Art. Her boss was Robin Thomas who, over the years, became a supportive friend to us both. Tall and elegantly dressed, Robin led the department with both style and distinction until the summer of 1975. By then higher education was beginning to change quite substantially and he possibly felt that he could do with less responsibility. He continued to lecture in the department, but as a part-timer.

Before the whole department moved out to Bower Ashton, Oldbury House was a distinguished, atmospheric and haunted house a stone's throw from the old children's hospital. Aside from Robin and my mother, the staff could have only been in the region of five or six. The department was cosy and small and self-regulating before the advent of the bigger, more faceless polytechnics which were, in hindsight, something of a mixed blessing.

For most of her life, Mum didn't own a car. She had lessons and for a time owned a turquoise Isetta bubble car. This fell victim to the torrential floods of 1968 and gave up the ghost; that and the fact that her test examiner was heavily, wearily sarcastic ("Does this car not move forward?") put pay to a very short driving career. Whatever her shortcomings behind the wheel, she later found out that this particular examiner loathed women drivers and, apparently, marked them accordingly. Misogynistic bastard! The point of this is that Robin never failed to give her a lift in his car and was always kind and considerate, if on occasion an unpredictably tempered boss. His stress levels could be measured in cigarettes and whisky.

After his retirement he was ordained and now lives in Truro. Mary and I visited him a few years ago and he seemed as active and as interested in life as always. He had a prominent black Cornish flag in his garden, so Mary and he talked things Celtic and they got on famously. In a sense this was him coming (returning) full-circle, for he had been born at Porth Navas, near Falmouth. The last time that I bumped into him was in the narrow streets of St Ives. He looked energised and well and had an equally energised small dog on a lead.

In my teenage years, his kindnesses and thoughtfulness were given quietly and generously, without show or fanfare. For example, on at least two occasions, he told me to help myself to jackets and suits that he was discarding. Would I care to try them on? I did and in those days, they fitted me beautifully. He always wore very well-tailored clothes and, crucially, he could *wear* clothes well. There is a difference, particularly in the fashion world.

The other thoughtful gesture was on the night before my interview at the Birmingham School of Music in March 1975: Robin left a note with a good-luck stone from Iona. He didn't ring the doorbell, merely left the envelope on the mat – typically self-effacing and much appreciated by both myself and my mother.

For an adult, he retained a certain sense of child-like joy – watching *The Magic Roundabout*, for example, on his return from work. A good, delightful and escapist way of winding down, I would have thought, particularly before the early evening television news. No worries, as Paul Hogan's Mick Dundee would have said.

The glasses bit now. To be fair, I don't remember a great deal about it (just like the majority of my schooling) except that since the age of eight I have continually worn glasses. When I say continually, I don't mean in bed obviously or for the whole twenty-four hours of each day. Just one pair of spectacles at a time, thus far; not different pairs for different functions. (Presumably you need to wear one pair in order to locate the whereabouts of the other two/three/four pairs that you need...?) I do find increasingly these days, however, that if I attempt to read on waking, then I find problems in focusing with the glasses on – far better for the first fifteen minutes or so to read without them, holding the book fairly close to my face. (I'm rapidly in danger of becoming an ocular bore… I sense a certain amount of coughing and fidgeting going on out there in the auditorium.)

I think that I can recall, very hazily (literally), the blackboard looking very dim and far-off and not being able to do my sums (not a lot of change there, then). No wonder that I fell behind in most subjects. I was probably too ashamed and/or embarrassed to put up my hand to say that I couldn't see. Mum, no doubt, gradually gleaned this fact and took the appropriate action.

I went for an eye test at the Central Clinic in Broadmead (pale green linoleum) where a rather large and slow man called Dr Bannerman sat in a darkened room and fumbled his way through assorted trays of lenses. He asked me to read back letters of the alphabet in diminishing sizes of print. I thought this was a bit strange, as a) I knew my alphabet by then and b) the shrinking size of the letters didn't facilitate reading, especially given that the lighting was so poor… But I kept quiet – after all, what did I know?

In recollection, he resembled some red-faced character from a Dickens novel – which one, however, I could not precisely say. He was in no way alarming, but seemed about as efficient as a senior, senile judge on the point of enforced retirement. All of this was evident, even to a naive, ocularly-challenged eight-year-old such as myself. His daughter is the actress Celia Bannerman. Her career has been more distinguished, I believe, than that of her father.

The necessary prescription was made up and we reported for the fitting to Mr Wiltshire in an optician's that was virtually opposite my junior school in Princess Victoria Street. He seemed nervous and wore a white, linen jacket. I think that he was perfectly pleasant as well as being competent, but it was his fragile, almost bird-like secretary that I remember most. Almost anorexic in her twin-sets with piled-up, bird's-nest hair and typically curvy glasses of that era, she darted and fussed around him – a mother-hen figure who I am sure was a spinster, probably nursing an elderly mother and only too glad to escape the domestic grind to a day-job which entailed working for a nice, polite man. I doubt if there was an out-of-office relationship (as such) between them, although appearances can be deceptive – especially in an opticians. With her spectacles removed, he probably looked quite different – smarter and slightly debonair, albeit in a fuzzy kind of way, with the white jacket of a waiter who had, myopically, entered the wrong establishment.

My first pair of glasses turned out to be incorrect in some details and needed correcting. (I had and still retain a slight stigmatism in my left eye.) The glasses were of the type that most children wore then – of the wire-framed, round National Health species that, luckily for aesthetic reasons, died a natural death in the following decade. They did their job and were efficient, I suppose, but were not guaranteed to wow the girls. The brace that I needed two years later certainly put the tin lid on that ambition...

Wearing glasses might have made one appear erroneously studious, but they were a real nuisance when trying to play rugby or football at my senior school. I was woefully inept at both these games, but by retaining my glasses could, at least, see where the ball was (hopefully, as far away from me as possible). Without them, I had absolutely no hope of even seeing the ball under my nose or feet for that matter. By then, it would have been too late and I would have been buried up to my neck under a scrum of legs and boots, but at least I would have preserved my glasses. These I normally left with Mr Jarvis, the sportsmaster in charge. Come to think of it, it might have been due to my spectacles, or lack of them, that caused my near-demise at the swimming pool. Happy days!

I never learnt to swim and am, I suppose, a little ashamed of the fact. A little, but not a lot. I'm reminded of that old Ronnie Scott joke: "I tried using Tampax – still can't swim, play tennis or ride a bike…"

I did cycle for a while in my late twenties – that is, until the front wheel lodged in a pothole, flipped me up and over, necessitating a few stitches in my left eyebrow. Worse than that, though, was the anti-tetanus injection – a searing warm pain in the arse. After that, riding a bike rather lost its charm, even in Oxford, a city traditionally and veritably besieged by bicycles.

Again I digress – back to the slightly surreal swimming episode.

The nearest swimming baths to our school were situated at the bottom of Jacob's Wells Road, which entailed a few minutes' walk. This was fairly memorable in itself, for we had to descend the very steep and aptly named Constitution Hill. Even worse, of course, was the required ascent (that being the property of hills) back to Clifton after the exertions of swimming.

Children can be very literal in their interpretation of facts. Also, I tended to be a rather dreamy child, very much dwelling in his own mental orbit; actually, parallel universe would have been more appropriate a term. When these two rather naive facets collide in conjunction, the outcome is probably not going to be the happiest of events…

I was a complete novice, a virgin swimmer. My father told me that water was naturally buoyant and would hold me up. At that age, you unswervingly believe your parents. The pool smelt funny and, with all the people in the water, it was very noisy which did not bode well. Perhaps I misheard, perhaps I wasn't concentrating, but when Mr Joyce instructed those who could swim to leap in and those who couldn't to... (WHAT DID HE SAY?)... I did. No messing around – straight in, no questions asked. After all, life was too short (yes, it damned nearly was).

Where's Richard Harris? I thought he was next to you.
He was when I last looked, Sir.
Oh God...

I discovered very rapidly that my father had been misinformed *vis-á-vis* the buoyancy of water. I quickly (alarmingly quickly) sank to the bottom of the pool where breathing became difficult and where it was gradually getting darker, although I can recall lights reflected through the surface of the water...

FALLING   Splashes…

FALLING

                              Shouting children…

        trying to shout   calling

Fading

                              Splashing children shouting…
        trying to

                              Smell of chlorine   noisy

Fading

                              Lungs filling…

        try

Fade

                              Darkening light…

    Flashes.

I cannot recollect exactly how long I was at the bottom of the pool, probably only mere seconds, but the next thing that I was aware of was that I had been hauled up in something like a large net (is that possible? Perhaps I dreamt that) and had been laid out on the side of the baths, the water being pumped out of my lungs. I don't remember how I got back to school (a lift in a car? I couldn't have walked, surely?), but do remember later sitting at my desk in Mrs Porter's class with an enormous packet of Rich Tea biscuits. A consolation prize, I suppose, for having nearly drowned.

A gypsy boy called Dobbin, who was in our class for a few months, asked for some of the biscuits, I remember. He looked perpetually hungry and smelt, poor lad. I gave him some of the biscuits. Quite a morning.

Those swimming baths became obsolete years ago; they are now a dance studio.

The upshot of this event was threefold:

1) I never learnt to swim (too traumatised, I suppose).
2) I escaped swimming, anyway, due to severe ear infections.
3) For some years I was in a near panic state of terror when my hair was washed. Mum was generally very sympathetic about all this, but it tried her patience somewhat after she would get soaked yet again and I would be lashing out and screaming. Incidentally, it took some years before I felt at all comfortable under a shower. The assorted trials of childhood! (I nearly wrote trails – a Freudian slip, perhaps?)

Clearly, I am not cut out for sporty things. As far as water is concerned, I prefer my feet to remain firmly anchored to the bottom, thank you very much. If asked, give me *terra firma* any time. I was not born a Capricorn (goat) for nothing. It's probably just as well that I have never been inclined to try my hand (or feet) at skiing. I could, I suspect, forecast the outcome quite accurately. Perhaps the solution would be to wrap myself from head to foot in bandages *before* I arrived at the nursery slope. Hopefully, the sight of a quasi-invisible, yet paradoxically conspicuous, mummified figure wrapped from head to toe in off-cream bandages would be sufficient to stand out from all that snow.

"Christ, what's that?"

"Don't know. It's not dressed for skiing, whoever it is. Looks as if it's escaped from a pyramid."

"Oi, mate! Get off the slope, you're not wearing the proper gear!"

"Bloody tourists…!"

On second thoughts…

Ok – now for a change of pace and how I started something far less dangerous – namely, learning the piano. (All those octaves – did I say less dangerous…?)

Perhaps it was at my maternal grandmother's, or at the house of an aunt in Trowbridge, that someone spotted a glimmer of potential; perhaps it was in the way that I ran my fingers over the keys, just enjoying the sounds that ensued. Whatever the unlikely genesis, in the autumn of 1964 my mother had found a piano and I began lessons with Ann Maycock in the top floor flat at 11 Victoria Square, which was a couple of hundred yards and at a right angle to Lansdown Place.

Finding a piano, that was the first thing. But, as is so often the case, the chain of necessary events began to fall into place. I entered a competition that was advertised in my mother's copy of *Woman's Realm*, I think it was. Typically for an eight-year-old, I suppose, I naturally assumed that I would win the said shiny upright piano. Mum gently cautioned me that there were, in all likelihood, many other entrants so I must not set my heart on winning. But try telling that to an impressionable child who has set his mind on a piano... As it proved, of course, I didn't; but then a stroke of luck occurred.

A sister of Roger's mum Joan wanted to get rid of her piano. Did Joan know of anyone who wanted a piano for free? Joan did and the piano was duly delivered to our basement flat. This was a Godsend, for Mum would have struggled, I think, to be able to afford to buy a piano. The pieces, as if pre-ordained, were beginning to slot into place.

A child of a colleague of my mother's at Oldbury House had piano lessons with Ann, who was highly recommended by this lady. So, all the elements were lined up and, unknowingly at that time, my life was about to change forever; indeed, it could be said, without much exaggeration, to enter another dimension.

You rang the bell, looked up to the window of the top flat from which would be thrown a key to the front door, wrapped in a foam pocket. A dog was barking loudly. This was Bobby, the Maycocks' loveable Alsatian who would keep barking until you had trudged up three or four flights of stairs and appeared at the door of the flat. When he was satisfied as to your intentions and had all but licked you to death, he would pad away to sit in a corner. Soon after I started lessons, the Maycocks' two Siamese cats, Ming and Sue, gave birth and there was a plentiful litter of little kittens mewing around the room.

Ann was both a thorough and lively piano teacher under whose capable hands I made good progress, taking my Grade 1 examination in 1966. Altogether, I studied with her for eleven years, obtaining all my eight examinations in both piano and theory. For a time, patience was required on both our parts, as I struggled with some of the thornier theoretical problems. But I won through and got there eventually. Actually, that has often been a constant in my life – things and goals only being achieved and secured with some difficulty and often not at the first attempt. A steady ascent – just like the mountain goat! Then, step by sturdy step, eventually attaining the summit and the view at the top.

To this day, Ann and her husband Philip are two of my oldest and dearest friends, whose support has been unwavering for the best part of forty-five years. Without her wonderful teaching, I would have not had the musical foundations for a career in music.

At the end of each lesson, Ann would climb onto the windowsill, open the window and throw down the foam-ensconced key to the next pupil. This always seemed rather risky a manoeuvre, in that the window was a fairly small one and Ann's posterior completely blocked out the light as she leant out. The result of this was an exceedingly local, if temporary, eclipse-darkness at mid-afternoon... Luckily, she always maintained her balance, but it must have been fairly hard on the kneecaps. That key must have had enough of freefall parachuting over the years too. In 1970, they moved to a spacious, high house in Manilla Road where they still live.

The only other music that I was involved with at this time was as a choirboy at Christ Church, Clifton, at the foot of the Downs and within sight of Brunel's famous Suspension Bridge.

The choirmaster and organist was Graham Harris (no relation) who, by 1964, was in his late fifties or early sixties.

He was, on the whole, a patient choir trainer and tolerated my initially out-of-tune singing with good humour. Sunday was far from being a day of rest, as we were required to sing at the Family Service, Matins (with its awful, tedious *Te Deum*) and Evensong. I enjoyed it, in the main, especially the donning of ruff, gown and surplice – the sheer ritual and theatre of it, I suppose, looking back. That, and the stirring music of the hymns. The psalms and anthems remained something of a mystery for somewhat longer.

And then there were the (mainly summer) weddings for which one was paid extra! A welcome supplement to the weekly pocket money. I didn't do paper-rounds, but I sang at weddings – and you didn't have to get up so early! From those first weddings, I have memories of the bride's pink nail varnish and the groom's winkle-pickers, as well as the beaming fathers flushed with pride and, most likely, a stiff Scotch at the prospect of giving away (in a sense, losing) their daughters. Our money was handed to us in small brown envelopes by one of the senior sopranos – the grandmother, in fact, of one of the choristers, Andrew McNab. Is this the same Andy McNab as the famous thriller writer?

Many of these mature lady choristers had a forbidding air, glancing at us boys over the tops of their equally formidable glasses from the safe distance of the opposite choir-stalls. One of the older men had Parkinson's and his hymnbook trembled and shook violently. They were all very loyal to Graham Harris and to the vicar, the Reverend Michael Brettel, who used to solemnly inspect our footwear on Friday evening choir practice. Woe betide any young chorister caught wearing plimsolls ('daps') and not proper shoes. He would be sent home! All this seems another world away from where we are now... Curiously, I remember all these seemingly daft bits of discipline quite affectionately. It certainly kept us in line – and on our toes, as it were.

I have just remembered that Graham Harris used to teach the legendary improvising pianist Keith Tippett when he was a boy – both piano and organ, I assume. Apart from playing for assemblies, Graham would lead class singing once a week – mainly the same old folk songs. This was the only music that occurred in junior school. Not for the first time, my mother and I used to give grateful thanks for my piano teacher. No recorder playing or elementary string teaching; not so much as a sniff of a peripatetic music teacher anywhere within the vicinity. As a result of this lack, I am probably one of the very few professional musicians anywhere who never learnt to play a recorder. Pretty bizarre, really!

The only time that I did try this instrument with very seemingly strange, illogical fingering (perhaps it was just me?) was much later as part of my PGCert Ed year at Reading University. It was dismal, in all honesty. Four Saturday morning classes given by an elderly, uninspiring old fart who achieved the near impossible – namely, making the recorder out to be even more awful than those obdurate, non-recorder playing students would have thought possible. After the first session, I found pressing reasons (shopping, etcetera) not to attend the remaining three. That and the fact that I didn't wish to die from rigor mortis – not at the age of twenty-two and with a treble recorder in my mouth, anyway. Result-wise, it was somewhere on a par, or tied equally, I suspect, between my cycling and swimming. Proficiency was nowhere to be seen – or heard, for that matter…

I stayed in the choir until 1967 or 68, when such things as the increasing demands of homework began to intrude. Coincidentally, my RE teacher from Ashton Park School, Alan

Bullock, used to attend the church together with his wife. Three to four years in this sort of regimen seemed to be enough. I had (mostly) enjoyed the experience and it was, no doubt, good discipline for my burgeoning musical aspirations.

Although I attended church regularly after leaving the choir (occasionally reading the lesson, going to Pathfinder's youth group in the old St Andrew's Hall where we eat our junior school lunches), it would be the summer of 1989, some sixteen years on, before I would become involved with a church choir again – and this next time it would be in Oxford, well-known centre of academia, city of dreaming spires and piles of tangled bicycles.

Looking back on 1964 from my perspective now, it seems as if it was a seminal point in my development. Quite a year.

A young performer,
Summer 1965.

11

What else from those years? Probably not a great deal. Time passed, I grew up, etcetera and so on. Mum was still secretary to the Department of Fashion & Textiles but with two major differences: 1) she was now full-time and 2) the West of England College of Art had been merged into Bristol Polytechnic and the department was moved (you have to say 'relocated' nowadays) from Cotham out to Bower Ashton. This entailed changing buses twice on the homeward leg of the journey: Clanage Road to College Green and College Green up to Clifton. Robin remained her boss, she got on well with the staff and students and was a thoroughly supportive and popular secretary.

For myself, all the usual boyhood things, I suppose – the vast majority of which faded from memory a long time ago. Stamp collecting, inept but often riotous games of cricket and football with Roger and Susie up on the Downs or in the park opposite, sucking on cider-flavoured ice lollies from Roberts' sweetshop in Boyces Avenue, Airtex shirts, miniature balsawood model planes, sherbet dabs with liquorice and crunchy pear drops, tangily acidic and ruinous in equal proportion.

At one point, there were three sweetshops on Boyces Avenue: Roberts' on the corner up from The Albion pub (which was run by a horrible, pompous, slick-haired man who resembled Mr Creosote in Monty Python's *The Meaning of Life*); Jones' almost opposite (always the same litany of "Thank you, ta" from Mr Jones); and the other one – smaller, dingier, more old-fashioned than the other two, run by two ladies (the Davies sisters?), who had trays of Bird's brittle toffee (plain or nut). This last confection was masochistically hard and, after much chewing, eventually gooey enough to probably have destroyed even the teeth of the lions at Bristol Zoo.

This shop, in turn, was next to Victor Kirby's: where cheese would still be cut with a wire, ham and sides of bacon sliced at an angle on a heavy-looking maroon machine; where groceries would be wrapped in greaseproof paper, prior to being slipped into brown paper bags, the price having being hastily scrawled on the outside in biro or felt-tip; where the assistants would wear long white cotton coats – men of a certain age and at a certain stage of hair-loss, who would carefully measure out small bronze shovelfuls (a quarter-of-a-pound, perhaps) of Lipton's loose-leaf tea... At this point, the supermarkets had yet to begin their stranglehold-monopoly.

Our unremarkable, seemingly unimportant childhoods from the mid-1960s. And yet...

And yet they *were* important. After all, they happened to *us*, formed us, moulded our minds and future outlooks. It would be dishonest, foolish and dishonourable even to dismiss them from our thoughts as being negligible and of no consequence. Much of what we knew has disappeared, after all; become a veritable period piece in the era of MacMillan's 'Never had it so good' years.

Roger's dad, Bert, bought a green Morris Minor in 1968. Occasionally, and thoughtfully, he would take me with their family out to Chew Magna reservoir in their new car for a spin on a summer's evening. I think that it had those external orange side indicators that flipped up. In those days, they were pretty much the latest thing and replaced having to give hand-signals (I mean of the directional kind, not the single-fingered "up yours, pal" variety).

Some of that, what I have just written, was totally unexpected. There you are, you see, memories are not predictable. I merely started and then – whump! – a few of them rose to the surface! But why should I be surprised? The very act of writing, typing/word-processing seems to summon forth people, events and places that one had hitherto assumed were wholly buried; absent, forgotten ghosts rise up through the murk and detritus of the years – the majority of them pleasant, welcome even.

Back to music for a moment. I ought to get these bits down whilst I remember them – more accurately, whilst they have surfaced for some oxygen and light; before they return to the depths, perhaps to be lost (or in a state of suspended animation) forever? Cryogenics, yes!

I attended my first piano recital at the Princess Theatre on the Torquay seafront in April 1966. The pianist was Joseph Cooper who, though I cannot be sure, played a mixed, popular programme that included music by Beethoven and Debussy. He was already a well-known musician, although not as famous as he was to become hosting the television quiz show *Face the Music*, notable for its dummy keyboard and special guests, one of whom was the composer Sir William Walton who was his usual droll self. (On his earnings from *Facade*, part of which was used as the signature tune to the show: "Well, it keeps me...") Amongst the regular panellists were newsreader Richard Baker, comedienne Joyce Grenfell, the wonderfully dismissive Bernard Levin, and Robin Ray, whose sense of self-modesty was not, shall we say, greatly evident.

1966 was also the year that the Severn Bridge was opened and that Prince Charles, barely out of short trousers and Cambridge, was crowned Prince of Wales at Caernarvon Castle, much to the chagrin and displeasure of many vocal, vociferous Welsh nationalists. Their welcome for their new prince included the gift of Semtex, but it failed to go off. After all, they regarded their last true prince as Llewellyn, who died way-back-when, some eight hundred years ago. As for Charles, they're still not all that keen on him in mid and north Wales...

In the bitterly cold January, my grandmother died from pancreatic cancer aged seventy-five and her funeral was held at the Haycombe Crematorium near Bath. My mother always remembered the beautiful and calming effect of the brilliant sunlight reflected off the snow-bound hills as seen from the large picture window of the chapel. I didn't attend myself, but was looked after by Carol from the flat above.

My other strong memory from 1966 was going to Bath on the bus and seeing a fairly fresh accident on the dual carriageway just past the Newton-St-Loe roundabout – where you turn up the hill for Haycombe Crematorium, ironically. We were in the front seats on top of the 339 bus and I was wearing a maroon tie. Why I remember this small event, I have no idea. Perhaps I was a bit traumatised by seeing the aftermath of the accident?

Meanwhile, back to Torquay...

We were on holiday with my Aunty Barbara from Bradford-on-Avon, staying in a holiday flat owned by a Pole who drove very fast. It was a very snowy Easter and we skidded our merry way down the A30 (no M5 motorway then) in Barbara's turquoise Austin A40.

"It's not too bad, is it, Aunty?" I chirped up from the backseat, referring to the ice and thickening snow as we gingerly headed our way back to Bristol.

"No, dear," she replied through gritted dentures, hanging onto the steering wheel for dear life as we elegantly pirouetted across the central white line once again. We could have done with some grit on the road, never mind between her dentures. Bless her – she wasn't the best of drivers.

The other memorable concert of my childhood was a string quartet programme given in the Clifton Music Club on the corner of Pembroke Road. The members of the audience were quite elderly and a varied bunch of musical enthusiasts, including my piano teacher Ann (who was decidedly young in her duffle coat and ponytail).

It was she who took along both my mother and myself to many concerts. The one piece, one single movement on this particular evening, however, that opened up new vistas to me was the fugal finale of Mozart's *Quartet in G, K.387* – one of a set of six quartets dedicated to his friend and mentor, Joseph Haydn. This completely and utterly knocked me sideways.

Such, indeed, was its impact that the vivacity and exhilaration of this particular movement has never left me. I was enchanted and thrilled, probably amazed at music's ability to lift one up and to transcend the merely everyday, such as the fading light or the accelerating drizzle on the pavement outside. It transported you, wrapped you in its otherworldly, powerful embrace. Wow! My first experience of a live string quartet, a medium which I still love to this day, both to listen to and to compose for.

I also can picture a lady in that audience of older years with dyed black hair tied back rather severely, which contrasted alarmingly with her white face powder. She wore a black velvet coat and dress and usually sat on a bench to the left side of the platform (from the audiences point of view). I observed this on many evenings, so it was clearly a favourite vantage point of hers.

From about the same period (mid-late 60s), Mum also took me to Colston Hall to see the then elderly Spanish pianist Jose Iturbi (1895–1980) in recital. She said that he looked as if he wouldn't make it to the piano but, once seated, apparently played with some of his old, dazzling magic. Sadly, except for my mother's reminiscence of the event, I cannot recall a single thing about it. I suspect that this was Iturbi's last tour or recital in this country – or, indeed, possibly anywhere.

This misunderstood pianist and conductor died in Hollywood, where he had made films back in the 40s. His reputation suffered at the hands of certain critics who could not, or would not, forgive him for "lowering himself" to become involved with Hollywood and the whole non-culture, as they saw it, of commercial movie-making for which he both played and acted.

I have just watched some of his performances in short clips on YouTube and his pianism, possibly from the 40s and early 50s, was astonishing; indeed, to some degree of an almost Horowitz-like intensity. The playing is cleanly articulated, yet big-boned, full of colour and cleanly pedalled with no due excesses (unlike Horowitz). A so-called 'modern' pianist in the Golden Age of Pianism, he was senior by almost two decades to other such figures as the great Cuban Jorge Bolet and Shura Cherkassky, both born in 1914. Coincidentally, it seems from watching these clips that Iturbi, like Bolet, preferred to play a Baldwin grand piano rather than the usual Steinway or Bechstein.

He studied in Paris with, amongst others, the revered harpsichordist Wanda Landowska – who was, lest we forget, also a very convincing pianist. The reverse can also be true. One of the three clips that I watched was, to my astonishment, of Iturbi playing some Rameau on an old pedal harpsichord. Not only was the playing very stylish, it also had immaculate articulation and execution of the ornaments with which French *clavecin* music of the eighteenth-century is steeped.

At the age of eleven, I must have taken my 11-plus examination and auditioned for a scholarship to Bristol Cathedral choir school. I failed both of these and do not even remember the former – I don't recall Mr Prickett telling us anything about an exam. Mind you, there's an awful lot that I missed, idly dreaming away. Probably thought that it was just another written quiz or something… to be reluctantly completed whilst I was taking my daily trip around the solar system…

I very definitely remember, however, a rather stern-looking Clifford Harker in the choir school of the cathedral, giving me various aural tests at which I clearly was not very proficient. In his retirement he directed the music across College Green at the Lord Mayor's Chapel. In later life, he resembled my father both facially and in the thickness of his hair. He was certainly a dedicated and distinguished musician.

In my last year at Christ Church School, I was made a milk monitor. Ok, so it wasn't quite like being a prefect. Nonetheless, you did manage to miss a few minutes of lessons. Dragging the heavy metal crates of milk bottles around to each of five classes with the aid of another boy was quite good fun, especially if (as we did) you dragged out the whole procedure to its possible optimum. This, hopefully, would be achieved without raising the suspicions or ire of Mr Prickett who, although a fine teacher, was not the most patient of men.

On form and on a good morning, we would probably contrive to knock off about twenty-five minutes to a good half-hour of the lesson. This probably, and hopefully, entailed missing Arithmetic and such classic posers as: 'If a man fills a bath at the rate of blah blah blah, how long would it take three men, one of whom has a severe limp, to fill?' ARRGH!! Cue more milk bottles…

Yes, I suppose you could say that we were milking it for all we were worth. (Sorry – yes, I know, but I couldn't resist it…)

I had been ill again – God, it was becoming a regular habit!

When I surfaced from my bed and weakly walked into the living room for the first time in several days, to my amazement, Mum had acquired a small black-and-white television. A small miracle!

The first two programmes that I watched were the local BBC 1 news with anchor-men Mark Puckle and Jeremy Carrad and *Crackerjack* with Leslie Crowther and his roly-poly sidekick, Peter Glaze. Oh, and probably *Blue Peter*, too. This seemed like magic: a kind of David Nixon, but even better. (In the era before magicians such as Paul Daniels, David Nixon was a very popular and proficient TV magician in the 1960s and early 70s.)

12

This is really a kind of codetta, interlude, or Brahmsian Intermezzo to round off yet link what has just been related through to what is to come.

I finished my first bout of being 'educated' at junior school in July 1967. There was a service in Christ Church for the leavers and we were each presented with a Bible, handed to us by Michael Brettell.

For those that were around at the time, this was the Summer of Love, you will remember. For those readers who were not, it was a heady, idealistic, halcyon time when, in the wake of the American-led Vietnamese war, people thought that they could and would change the world through Love and Peace. A fine and enviable sentiment which, however, proved rather short-lived. "Turn on, tune in, drop out" was Timothy O'Leary's oft-repeated mantra. A statement that only really made sense when apprehended via the psychedelic trips of LSD tablets and the slightly spicy aroma of cannabis. No doubt, had I been aware of such things at the time, I would have been bound to notice the brown, hazy cloud hanging over Clifton that summer.

As it was, I was still remarkably innocent and in short trousers, to boot. As far as I was aware, my family and immediate circle of friends didn't tend to hand around the joints, like After Eight mints. Yes, our parents smoked, but they were Woodbines, Embassy or Silk Cut.

Roger, Susie and myself were just aware of hot weather and freedom for a couple of months before I started at my secondary school, which Roger had already been attending for the previous year. He seemed to be enjoying it and had settled in well. Susie, meanwhile, still had a remaining year to go at Christ Church junior school which, that September, was due to move to Royal Park at the end of our road, Lansdown Place. Not before time, too, for the old site had been outmoded for many years. Indeed, there had been calls to find another location from quite early on in the 1900s.

But – I was talking about the Summer of Love...

This near vista must have seemed, if not secure, at least fairly rosy to the hippies – often literally, as they tended to wear rose-tinted spectacles. The whole apparatus with its beads, swirling and brightly-patterned clothes, the mini skirts, boots and sheepskin coats in a way became, as these things do, another kind of uniform.

Aiding and abetting the fashion of those months was the

experimentation in pop and rock music. Pink Floyd, Soft Machine and Jimi Hendrix were the pre-eminent groups in this area, where heightened sensation, length and loudness was a valid alternative to the highly predictable commercialisation of saccharine pop music with its three-minute ditties. More vitally, these groups and others like them were extending and redefining the three-chord blues and rock riffs then prevalent in the songs of The Rolling Stones and The Who.

Originally this whole movement took off in Haight Ashbury, California and, in retrospect, might seem hugely naive and foolish. But it did bring, I feel, a much-needed breath of colour and fresh air to a staid era where, for example, businessmen in London still wore bowler hats as if time had stood still in the 1940s. The hippies helped to move on (or kill off) this obsolete sartorial dinosaur.

From our perspective now we can see, perhaps, that it ushered in a time where youth was able to have its say (virtually for the first time) and where a sense of altruism and generosity of spirit was in abundant evidence. Deluded? Possibly, but at least they were attempting to change attitudes and things for the better.

These qualities were, alas, to be wiped out in 1979 by the selfishness, greed and general despicableness of the Thatcher era – the 'sod you and anyone else' culture, whose agendas actively and collectively promoted the stamping-on, if not outright elimination of, all opposition and polar, contrary opinions.

Naturally, I had no inkling of this back in those lazy, lemonade days of the summer of '67.

SCHOOLDAZE 2

13

It is now over a year since I wrote that last entry about the halcyon days between the end of junior school and the starting of senior school, which was at Ashton Park in September 1967. I somewhat sheepishly admit that life, teaching, composing, etcetera, has got in the way of continuing this memoir, but hopefully the mind will be jostled into retrieving the relevant memories. (It is mid-August 2010 as I write this and has been a hectic year, including my marriage to Carol, but also the death of her mother, Joyce, in March, and of Carol's best friend, another Carol, in late June.) But back to the old days... not necessarily better, just older...

Going up to the 'big' school seemed, at the time, to open gates into another, quite exciting yet remoter world, where I wasn't at all certain of the boundaries or the rules. Luckily, Roger was a year ahead of me and could (and did) show me the ropes. We travelled together each day, there and back, either on the double-decker bus that picked us up from outside Queens Court Mansions or, during the first term or two, a private minibus that went from The Mall in Clifton, but it became too expensive, as I recall.

Ashton Park had opened its doors in 1955 as one of the first, showcase comprehensive schools in the country. For myself in the autumn of 1967 and in long trousers for the first time, it was more a case of being comprehensively apprehensive.

All the new names, the endless corridors and new room numbers were a challenge, but I suppose that I gradually settled into Fry house and my class, ABL, under the usually genial gaze of a red-faced English teacher, Lesley Blacknell – with whom I acted in my first play in the summer of '68, *Alice in Wonderland*, produced by that indomitable pair of drama teachers, Elizabeth and Dennis Raymond.

This production ran for, I think, three or four evenings and I had an unassuming role as the Fish Footman. One evening, I exited too hastily, slipped on some talcum powder, to be followed with a loud crash off-stage as I slammed into the metal base of a freestanding spotlight. Both the light and I survived intact.

Elizabeth used to walk around the main hall, a suspended cymbal in hand (more effective than the PE teacher's whistle), which would crash resoundingly whenever she wished us to stop our bits of acting and make-believe. Dennis, meanwhile, looked very much the part of a slightly old-style 'ac-tor laddie', padding around quietly in his suede shoes, green tie and matching cardigan, greying hair swept back with a trim moustache and goatee beard. Whenever he entered a room, one was aware of a certain presence; and he could quell a noisy classroom with one long, piercing look, no words being required. The only prop missing from his attire was a cloak and a BBC sound effects record of wind and tempest. Come to think of it, he was absolutely cut out for the lead in Macbeth.

Yes, the Raymond's were a close-knit and very positive presence at Ashton. Looking back from this vantage point now, I wonder if they were really appreciated by the other members of staff for all that they contributed? I somehow doubt it – creative people seldom are. About five years later, Dennis invited me to read a few of my poems on a programme that he hosted on BBC Radio Bristol, which was typical of his quiet and kindly encouragement of young people.

Even in my first year, I think that it was obvious that my talents (such as they were) lay in the areas of Music, Drama and English. Everything else seemed a waste of time and probably went over my head, especially Maths and Science. Although, to be fair, for about nearly two years I did try quite hard at General Science, as it was known. Reader, you want to know why? It was solely down to the fact that I was taught this subject by a gorgeous, sexy lady – Suzy Kendall, who wore a green corduroy miniskirt and had long dark hair. There we are: an eleven-year-old, hormonally-activated time-bomb in long grey flannels.

What was the music like? Pretty good, really. Class lessons were given by Paul Nixon, an extrovert young man who wore corduroy jackets and trousers with bright, floral ties and shirts, as was the prevailing fashion in the mid-1960s.

He persuaded me that it might be an idea to take up a string instrument, besides keeping on with the piano, so I chose the violin. This was both a smaller and safer option to the hideous, gangrenous mouthpieces of ancient tenor horns that had curled up and died in the storeroom, seemingly some decades earlier.

Lessons on the said violin were given once a week in the girls' changing-rooms (yes, honestly…) by a bored old twat called Alexander, who couldn't have given the proverbial damn. There were three of us, all equally nervous, spotty and severely out-of-tune. Aurally, it must have been a complete disaster. Visually, however, there was some compensation in the already busty form of Julane – no small wonder that Alexander seemed to be perpetually perspiring and I couldn't play in tune. He also, unwisely, conducted a local youth orchestra, which once gave the slowest funereal account of Rossini's *William Tell Overture* that has ever been my pleasure to hear – gloriously and unremittingly excruciating, in fact. Both horse and rider sounded as if they were suffering from severe constipation.

Paul Nixon was a good teacher, but left to focus on his doctoral study of Purcell. The next time that I saw him was conducting the Hounslow Youth Orchestra in Clifton in a Saturday afternoon concert that included Wagner's Overture to *The Meistersingers of Nuremberg*. This was new to me and I was bowled over by it, to the extent that I cannot remember anything about the remainder of the programme! It still remains a favourite piece of mine.

My real *bête noir* was sport, at which I think it no exaggeration to say that I was completely and utterly inept. I was quite good, though, at trying to look busy whilst doing bugger all and, simultaneously, shivering on the touchline. By this I mean I met friends such as Bob Guscott.

Failing that ploy, I tried to hide behind the large blue shed where the canoes were housed, only to be summoned out by the stentorian voice of Mr Jarvis enquiring as to whether I might like to participate in the rugger scrum.

"Me, Sir?"

"Yes, you, Harris," this said with a stare that could melt wax at five paces. The sound of the fast-approaching opposition in either football or rugby can only be likened to a posse of thunderous hooves à *la* the Horsemen of the Apocalypse, but more than four... hence, my natural survival instinct.

It was definitely advisable to hand in one's watch, glasses, together with nose and teeth, prior to these sessions. If you were lucky you retrieved the correct watch and glasses... In common with a lot of other things, I got used to it – sort of.

14

Round two, or the second year as it was more commonly labelled, followed on in the autumn of 1968.

My form tutor was tiny Tom Lewis, one of the three Geography teachers. In the classroom opposite him was another Lewis – the asthmatic, huge-bellied English teacher in dark grey tweed, known as 'Puffer' Lewis on account of his wheezing and frequent recourse to his inhaler. Taken together, they resembled some sort of variety double-act, a geriatric version of Little & Large. The larger Lewis taught English, at least nominally, but tended to leave us for long periods; in all likelihood, to spend a rather more enjoyable few minutes looking up the legs of various girls that used to assist him in the nearby stationery cupboard, reaching down items from the top shelves, naturally – alas, not those magazines which most of us still had yet to discover. (We couldn't reach them for a start!) In contrast, Tom Lewis was a pleasant personality, committed teacher and appeared to be a thoroughly upright man.

Some of my fellow classmates were not some of the most motivated and studious of pupils. Indeed, they preferred being disruptive and a general pain in the backside. Oddly enough, nearly all their surnames began with S – Paul Smart, Chris Steynings, John Skinner and Nigel Stick. Yes, Smart, Steynings, Skinner & Stick: it sounds like a firm of dodgy solicitors. Perhaps that's what they became, but I rather doubt it. Dodgy car salesmen, more like. Suffice to say, that over the next three years, they gave me a hard time in the bullying stakes. For the sake of convenience, I'll refer to them as the 'S Club'. Yes, that seems appropriate. Mind you, from their point of view I must have appeared like some alien. Sensitive, quiet, wearing glasses, well-spoken... Bloody hell, it must have seemed irresistible! I was a gift on the proverbial plate, wasn't I? Yes, I had the lot! But, despite all the hassle, they admired my musical ability and, paradoxically, seemed almost proud and quasi-supportive of me on rare occasions.

Our new music teacher was Frank Robinson, who seemed energised, good fun and chuckled a lot. It was to his large music room with views up towards Ashton Court that I often found myself gravitating in the lunchtimes, either playing squeaky violin in the orchestra (lead by a talented Indian boy) or to watch the choir in action. When I wasn't doing this, I would be haring around the school with friends such as Robin Miles or Ian Vowles in various inane games, some of which involved hiding under large stacks of chairs and tables. This was good fun, but it was also partly to escape being shoved outdoors into the rain by bossy and humourless prefects. There also used to be three adult volunteers who had some link with a Christian group and used to patrol around the school in the lunchtimes, being generally friendly and helpful. Two fresh-faced young men and a slightly sour older lady, if I remember correctly.

Some lunchtimes I skipped the school lunch and went off with Adrian Henry for a pie or fishcake and chips at the Robin's Cafe down by the Bristol City football ground. On these occasions, it was lovely just to be able to escape the confines of the school, even if for only an hour or so. Out of the gates, over a pedestrian bridge and through the underpass, out past the pub (forgotten its name), and there was the cafe with its big mugs of tea and red and brown plastic sauce bottles, the contents congealed around the edge.

Adrian used to call me, for some inexplicable reason, by the affectionate nickname of Harry Creamslice. At least, I think it was affectionate; better that, though, than Tosser or Wanker.

He was not, by the way, the famous Liverpool poet Adrian Henri – wrong spelling, wrong place, wrong generation.

I cannot believe the sheer energy levels that we must have possessed back then. It was no wonder that we didn't particularly relish the afternoon lessons or, for that matter, get violent indigestion from rushing around so soon after the school lunch. I hope that Robin, Ian and Adrian have found happiness and luck in their lives, whatever they chose to do and are, hopefully, still doing.

I wonder if the regional BBC1 presenter Ali Vowles is any relation? They both have a similar pointed face.

As for the rest of 1968, there's not anything of significance to report or record on a personal level, as far as I am aware. Globally, there were the two shocking assassinations: of Robert Kennedy (barely five years after his brother John) and that great speaker-out for racial equality, freedom and justice, Martin Luther King. Oh yes – the invasion of Czechoslavakia by Russian troops, too, which provoked worldwide condemnation and justifiable uprisings, especially amongst an entire swathe of students throughout the West. Not that I was very aware of all this happening at the time, of course.

15

After Elizabeth and Dennis Raymond had retired, our new drama teacher was Robert Bradshaw.

Bob was almost elegant, if not suave, and he rather resembled the lead in a slightly outmoded play (farce?) of the 1950s. Indeed, he often starred in musicals performed by the Bristol Light Operatic Society at the Hippodrome. His height and demeanour reminded one of Captain von Trapp from *The Sound of Music*, whilst managing to imply a certain rakishness reminiscent of the actor Leslie Phillips. He was also the possessor of a pleasant, fairly powerful baritone voice.

In the summer of 1970, I appeared in his first production, an ambitious and perhaps slightly unusual choice for a school, Karel Capek's *The Insect Play*, a fable and almost Kafkaesque allegory about insects that gradually assume the less congenial aspects of human behaviour. Or was it the other way round?

Bob was an effective producer who was able to galvanize both his young actors and, of course, through them, the audience. It was a challenging and enjoyable enterprise with which to be involved.

At about this time, I became interested in stage lighting and helped out one or two of the students who really knew what they were doing, technically-speaking. I had virtually no technical knowledge at all, but liked the effects and results of the different types of spotlights, battens, Fresnels and dimmer switches and slides. The smells and the sparks! It's amazing, really, that I didn't electrocute or incinerate myself (much the same thing, I suppose) into an early oblivion. Imagine the possible scenario: 'He was all lit up, Sir. Beautiful it was. A tasteful mix of red and green... then he sort of faded himself out, Sir.' My imagination, it has to be said, exceeded my skill but I did learn a certain amount about stage lighting, all of which has now been forgotten, and it was highly enjoyable and interesting at the time.

These were the days of hands-on manipulation, literally. (No, I didn't mean it like that. It makes it sound like masturbation – far too much like hard work. An art, incidentally, that I could never be bothered to practise or perfect. I suspect that you don't really wish to know any of this.) This was before the era of pre-set systems and computerised consoles. Hands-off was when you accidentally touched a live wire... and quickly learnt not to do that again. Now, which one and what colour did you say it was?

The lighting deck, reached by a fixed metal ladder, was a refuge and safe haven from the boredom, vagaries and unpleasantness of lessons such as PE, Biology, Physics and Maths. That was almost half of the timetable, but never mind. Eventually, after a term or two of this, I was caught and given a bollocking by the deputy headmaster, Norman Bygrave. He had impressive sideburns and was the first teacher to inform us that it was a physical impossibility to strangle oneself; I have never felt impelled to verify this piece of information personally. Oddly enough, he omitted to mention the wisdom of not trying this most finite of practices on others.

On reflection, this would have been useful information vis-à-vis the demise of certain teachers, namely... No, I'm not going to go down that route. If they are still alive, they've probably forgotten who they are, anyway. Yes, but I have not (*echoing sinister laugh*).

So, my little jaunts up to the lighting deck were somewhat curtailed and only sanctioned within the limits of drama lessons themselves, especially when I went on to study for my CSE Drama exams with Bob Bradshaw in the fourth and fifth years.

16

Staying with drama, but out of school, for the moment.

Ever since I was quite young, I had been aware of and been taken to the theatre by my mother. These visits, naturally, tended to be to the annual Christmas pantomime and we invariably went to the Boxing Day matinee. Afterwards, as we waited on the Centre opposite the Hippodrome for the bus up to Clifton, I would be excitedly doing imitations of what I had just seen; the memories would be fresh for some days afterwards. It was a magical two hours and was an integral part of every Christmas.

Even now, the Christmases of my childhood are still punctuated by memories of comedians and 'turns' such as Norman Vaughan, Dickie Henderson, Norman Wisdom (I think) and a youngish double-act called Morecombe & Wise who were still contracted to ATV and had yet to hit their stride on the BBC. Also, the wonderful eccentric dancing of Billy Dainty and the magisterial baritone voice of Edmund Hockeridge. In interludial roles appeared such pop groups as The Batchelors and The Seekers, the last of which included the very pure voice of Judith Durham. They would normally do a spot of about twelve to fifteen minutes, enough for three or four songs.

In Bristol during the 1960s and 70s, visiting the theatre meant three choices of venue: the huge stage of the Hippodrome with its sumptuous red plush seats (we sat in the Upper Circle, which was a long climb up the stairs), the more intimate Old Vic (opened in 1766 and one of the country's oldest working theatres; with green velvet seats), and the smaller Little Theatre, which was located within the much larger Colston Hall but has now closed. As was common in those days, Colston Hall hosted everything from symphony concerts and rock groups to wrestling and religious meetings of somewhat zealous and dubious fringe sects.

By the early 1970s, I got to know the Little Theatre quite well due to the fact that this was the venue which hosted the annual competitive festival of one-act plays. There would be an adjudication on the final night and a cup or cups presented to those groups who had performed especially well.

Mum had joined Drama Group Seven, which met weekly in a house in Redland. Its director was a large, feisty lady, Mary Lavington, who invariably dressed in black and was rarely seen without a cigarette in her mouth. Her husband Johnny looked after the technical side of the productions such as lighting, props and scenery. Mary was secretary to the head of Graphic Design, Dick Taylor, and a colleague of my mother at the Polytechnic site at Bower Ashton. Mum was still secretary to Robin Thomas, head of Fashion and Textiles in the same building. (Mum remembered glancing out of her fourth-floor window and seeing the ghost of Dick Taylor briskly walking across the courtyard below a week or so after his passing) They became close friends and Mary asked her to join her group.

Together Mary and Johnny made a home-from-home atmosphere and were terrifically welcoming, providing a ready-made family for those members of the group who were alone and a little disarray in their lives. Indeed, the most effective amateur actors and actresses often seem to have a raft of personal problems. It is the performing that serves as a release, an externalisation (exorcism?) of their problems and a therapy. I think that Drama Group Seven certainly provided a very welcome social channel and network for my mother, Jennie, aside from the acting.

Apart from my mother and myself (more of a part-time hanger-on), the members included two accountants Charles and Ken, young guitar-playing lads Chris and John, Ralph, Renee, Eunice and Mike. I think that that was the entire core membership, although one or two others probably were drafted in and out as needed. I was soon initiated into this slightly crazy world of fairly intense rehearsals and equally wild and mirthful parties where the booze, conviviality and groan-inducing puns flowed freely.

Also, much to my delight, records by Tom Lehrer received a regular playing. His satirical, subversive songs seemed to absolutely fit the bill for my fourteen-year-old self and, such was the pertinent wisdom of his lyrics, most of them still remain as apposite and as pertinent as ever, some fifty years on. *Vatican Rag*, originally banned by the BBC and most other networks, remains one of my firm favourites. Not only were the lyrics tight and witty, but his piano playing was artful and satirised a particular musical genre, to boot. All in all, his songs were pretty deadly and hit their intended targets square in the face, be it a generally held attitude or the peccadilloes of a particular public figure. More of Lehrer later.

Amongst the various plays produced were ones by David Campton (*Soldiers from the Wars Returning,* etcetera) who specialised in writing taut one-actors, often featuring roles for women, short sketches by the playwriting barrister John Mortimer and the wonderfully dotty, surreal, yet logical inventions of NF Simpson. Simpson's highly individual brand of surrealism stems from the same kind of logic-stretching as *The Goon Show,* yet he always managed to be his own man. With plays such as *One Way Pendulum, A Resounding Tinkle, Was He Anyone?* and *The Cresta Run,* Simpson led the field in this country during the late 50s and 60s with his very individual form of comedy that held up to the light the various idiocies and assorted ridiculousness of bureaucracy and the English variety of 'red tape'.

NF Simpson was a member of what Martin Esslin labelled 'The Theatre of the Absurd'. It was his plays that held my attention and entranced me by his wordplay and his topsy-turvy sense of the illogical that can seem, paradoxically, completely logical. I never acted in any of his short plays, but provided some background music on the harmonium for the one-act version of *A Resounding Tinkle*. (Mention of harmoniums reminds me of Ivor Cutler, more of which later.)

Although firmly rooted in domestic suburbia, Simpson soon turns Bro and Middie Paradock's exchanges with one another on their heads. Conventions of colloquial speech are soon made into quasi-nonsensical *non-sequiturs*. In common with most, if not all, comedy, it is essential that the lines be delivered absolutely straight, with the actors not showing that they think the material is anything other than normal and everyday. If they communicate that they think the text is hilarious, then the whole enterprise is doomed to failure and, in some intangible way, will fail to travel over the footlights. My own personal Simpson favourites are *The Hole, Gladly Otherwise* and *Can You Hear Me?*

As I write this, I'm delighted and surprised to read that Simpson has just had the stage premiere of his first full-length play in thirty-eight years. *If So, Then Yes* is having a month's run at the Jermyn Street Theatre off Piccadilly, having had a read-through three years ago. The author is now 91 and living in Cornwall and was virtually a forgotten name except to a few aficionados who tried to keep the flame of English surrealism burning brightly. There are not many reviews so far, but one or two very encouraging ones saying that NFS, or Wally as he is known, is writing as well, if not better, than in his heyday.

In the summer of 1972, the Lavingtons moved to Norwich with her sister Janet and Johnnie's mother Madge in tow. They had always loved the Norfolk Broads where they had a small boat, but the move was expedient; namely, to escape the unwanted attentions of their son, Keith, who was often turning up and asking for money. They left without giving him their new address and thus, with their departure, Drama Group Seven came to an end.

We went and stayed with them in Thorpe St Andrew in Norwich that summer. Whilst we were there, I attended a wonderful choral concert at Norwich Cathedral, given by the John Alldis Choir. Amongst the items were two that were outstanding: Schoenberg's motet *Friede auf Erden* and Roger Smalley's extraordinary *Missa Brevis* for sixteen solo voices, which came as a complete revelation *vis-á-vis* what was possible for unaccompanied voices. I came out from that concert with my head in a veritable whirl.

I nearly forgot to mention that Mary was a talented contralto and in school vacations I quite often came over to Bower Ashton to accompany her in songs by Hugo Wolf, Richard Strauss and my own favourites Roger Quilter and the bittersweet harmonies of Peter Warlock. This was some of my earliest accompanying experience and proved to be very valuable, as well as being enjoyable. Thank you and bless you, Mary.

Most of the old gang have now died, of course – Ken, Charles, Renee, Mary herself and my mother. John Casey trained as a nurse, Chris Kift returned to Bristol from Norwich (where he had nursed dreams of working with The Temperance Seven), whilst Eunice still lives with her partner Pete in Bedminster. What became of the remaining members, I do not know. It all seems a very long time ago; indeed, almost another lifetime ago, really.

17

It was Mr Everett who introduced me to the songs of Tom Lehrer. It was sometime in 1970 and I was in the third year of my custodial sentence.

He was an English and French teacher, but on this day was substituting for Bob Bradshaw. Known to all the pupils as 'Kenny' (after the DJ and humourist), he had a natty line in waistcoats and expensive-looking, probably handmade, tan shoes. He also had the air of a man not to be messed with, with his broken-looking nose and pockmarked face. In fact, he slightly resembled an older version of the boxer Joe Bugner if truth be told.

Anyhow, he carefully extracted an LP from its purple cover, placed it on the turntable housed in its wooden box with the hinged lid (school issue), lowered the stylus and let us simply listen. Wisely he didn't comment on what we were about to hear, just let us get on with it without preamble then made one or two helpful and astute comments afterwards. Show and tell, in other words; the sound before the sign, the mantra of all good teachers.

It was fresh, slightly naughty and daring in content and unlike anything I had ever heard before. Yes, it was Tom Lehrer, recorded live in 1965 and the album was entitled *That Was the Year that Was*. The piano playing was crisp, well-articulated and accurate, as was the brisk, rather academic (but not harsh) American accent and voice. This was satire with a capital S: hitting its intended victims with an upper cut to the jaw (or testicles) and delivering a punch from which it was well-nigh impossible to stagger up from the floor before the referee had counted to ten. Between each song Lehrer would make a few prefatory comments about the next song he was going to sing.

These 'introductions' were as witty as the songs themselves.

Kenny played us three or four songs, including *Pollution, The Elements* and *Vatican Rag*. What a treat! It was definitely one of the best lessons that I ever had. He was like that – a teacher who could present something, seemingly off-the-cuff, that would both make you think and laugh simultaneously. Amazingly, it all struck a chord with most of us, even the slower pupils. There was an increasing amount of laughter, some of it, I think, of sheer disbelief. But there was no denying it and, indeed, it would not be denied; that laughter welled up and spread around that room, like a joyful infection. And we were, for those few minutes of hearing, a transformed bunch of fourteen year-olds.

A year or two later when he knew that I was trying to write poetry and liked all things experimental, Kenny directed me towards the work of another American whose world-view was celebratory, lateral and outside of the proverbial box: the poet e.e. Cummings. My God, his instinct was bang on and I revelled in the unusual typography, but more importantly the qualities of joy and lyricism that wove their way consistently through the dispersed appearance of those poems.

Thank you, Mr Everett, and thank yous, too, to Tom Lehrer and e.e. Cummings. Or, perhaps that should read:

thank
you

mister
everett

and thank

you

tom

lehrer
because:

cummings
always
preferred
lower-
case words
and letters
see what
I mean?

18

At about this time, my father re-entered my life. It must
have been at some point between my fifteenth and sixteenth
birthdays (either that, or on one of those actual birthdays).
Anyway, he sent me my first razor, a Wilkinson 'manual' one,
as it were, not battery-operated or electric. This was both a
practical as well as a thoughtful present (I can still see it snugly

nestled under the hard plastic lid).

It served to re-establish contact with him, which was good but I would, in retrospect (or even at the time), have preferred more regular contact over the years of his absence. Nevertheless, we did meet up. (Possibly arranged by my mother?) He was working, as he had for some years, as a solicitor's clerk to the colourful and well-known figure of Vivian Jones in the centre of Bristol.

I climbed the old and worn rickety stairs, stepped through a door, the top half of which contained frosted glass or ribbed plastic. There he was, sat in his chair behind a clackety manual typewriter, an ageing father still working at sixty-nine or seventy in an old-fashioned office, in a job that was beneath his intellect and abilities.

He hadn't changed that much, wasn't so different, after all – still the formal attire and the déjà vu of seeing him smoke his omnipresent pipe. I don't recall what we talked about, but he was warm, affectionate and wanted to know all about what I was doing, both musically and at school. I suspect that after the initial awkwardness on both our parts, conversation started to relax and open up. We found that we shared very much the same sense of humour (e.g. The Goons) and that went a long way to cement our newfound, or refound, relationship.

What, exactly, was that relationship? Hard to say really, both then and now some forty years later. Not really a father-son bond; rather, that of a favourite uncle, I think. On my part, I felt affectionate respect, but could not feel that much of a son, in spite of the blood-tie; could not assume or step up to that role. Perhaps this was virtually impossible after the long lacuna of those intervening years. Perhaps he, too, felt much the same of me. A flesh-and-blood boy who was genetically of him, yet had grown to puberty without him. So many Saturdays when we (my Mum and me) felt let down, a faint yet unmistakable taste of betrayal in our mouths. Yet, to be fair, we were not on the phone, so he could not have contacted us vis-á-vis any last-minute changes. Anyway, his work always seemed to come before his family – or, at least, that is how it seemed. I never felt able to tackle Dad about this either face-to-face or by letter (too shy, too embarrassed, not wanting to put him on the spot, I suppose) for, I suspect, that part of him felt torn apart and guilty enough without any further probing from me. Whether his wife, ensconced in Saltford, ever knew of us or about us, I have no idea. Part of me hopes that she did, whilst the other part wishes that she did not.

Having said that, I have just remembered the three-day Cornish coach trip that Mum and I went on. We had just found our seats towards the back of the coach when, to my amazement, Dad and his wife came down the aisle towards us. I innocently greeted him, but his look of shock and surprise propelled him at top speed back down to the front. He looked rather ashamed when he caught Mum's dark beady eyes gunning him down and he certainly made sure that they avoided us for the rest of the trip. With a hint of retributory satisfaction, Mum noted that he was drinking rather a lot of red wine that first evening; Dutch courage in Cornwall, I suppose. It was quite an unexpected start to the holiday. How he explained my "Hello, Dad!" to his wife (if she heard it, that is) I'm not certain.

My mother, to her eternal credit, although often hurt and probably furious with my father's behaviour, rarely ran him down, verbally, in front of me. Indeed, on the few occasions that I raised objections, she acknowledged my opinion, but quietly yet firmly was respectful of him, trying to make allowances if not exactly honouring his absence.

This is a poem about him which attempts to make some

sense of those boyhood feelings all those years ago.

Saturdays

Yes, some Saturdays he would appear
After absences, slightly sheepish –
A dog with its tail between its legs.

The usual sports jacket, flannels
Smelling of his familiarity,
Sat in his usual chair.

I would climb, cuddle the bulk of him,
Feeling the rasp of his five o'clock
Shadow, relishing the tangy pipe smoke.

Then, after what seemed a mere moment
He donned his hat and coat and was off
And out into the night for his buses

Until some future Saturday.
Who was this man, this mysterious
Stranger? Well, yes... he was my father.

We still met occasionally when I was a student and then, for all the usual lazy and stupid reasons, it all faded and slipped away and I ceased to see him in his last few years. Perhaps we had, in a mutually unspoken way, said and seen all that needed to be said?

The next thing that my mother and I heard of him was a solicitor's letter addressed to Mum informing us that he had died a week after his eightieth birthday in March 1982. In the summer of 2008 after my mother had died, I felt I wanted to know more and found that he had spent his last couple of years in a warden-controlled flat in Keynsham, a mere street or so away from Carol's mother, Joyce. Slightly ironic, I felt – so near, yet so far...

Dad was cremated at Arnos Vale cemetery on the Bath Road and his ashes were taken away by his other son, Christopher, who I discovered lived in Cirencester. The past tense is accurate and appropriate for there was no telephone number in his name and, given that he was older than me, he must have died.

So, I had had a half-brother, possibly a sister too? I didn't delve into this issue and thought that I would let sleeping dogs lie, as it were. This unexpected revelation proved to be something of an intriguing shock, but the one was enough!

Jennie and Leigh, my mother and father, first met in 1953. Both had suffered on-and-off post-war stress and had had mental breakdowns, the severity of which I cannot ascertain. But these were areas that I regarded, rightly or wrongly, as private territory which should not be infringed or violated.

On this occasion, however (and perhaps fortuitously?), they were both recuperating in the same convalescent home. Mum had come to Bristol to seek work as a secretary, whilst completing qualifications in shorthand and typing at Everest's, a small commercial college in the Gloucester Road. Dad, meanwhile, was working or about to be appointed as welfare officer at Horfield prison. (He used to tell the story of the prison chaplain, a normally patient man who, driven to exasperation with regard to the limited nature of the prisoners vocabulary, eventually typed a sheet headed, 'These words also begin with F...' which was circulated amongst the populace residing at Her Majesty's leisure. Whether their individual or corporate vocabulary was expanded after the posting of this missive, I do not know.)

After my father's death, Mum passed onto me a sheaf of notes typewritten by Leigh. The contents included memories of his time at Mercer's School, London from 1913–1919 (the year that Mum was born in Chiswick), a transcript of a BBC radio interview given by my father in late January 1957 (*Radio Newsreel* and *The Week in the West*), a one-page précis of his paternal family history (Cornish boat builders) and an article by him headed *After Prison?* written for a Social Services Bulletin in the winter of 1957.

This extract is from the final paragraph of his memories of Mercer's dated 23rd March 1958:

> *I could have stayed until eighteen or more, doing most of the work for Intermediate Arts or Science; but in fact I left after Matriculation. There my troubles began. This note is not concerned with those except to put on record that the capacity to cope with them was formed by several factors. Among them Mercer's is very prominent.*

For me, reading this now, the relevant sentence is "There my troubles began." He doesn't enlarge on what these "troubles" were, but they seemed to be plural, not singular in nature.

Dad was a gifted mathematician and managed to secure a place at the London School of Economics. What happened, I don't know except that he didn't complete his degree, possibly due to an early breakdown. This instability was inherited from his mother, who committed suicide when he was fifteen. Given these awful circumstances (and not surprisingly), his nervous problems continued to blight him to various degrees for the rest of his life.

The only other fact that I have gleaned about my paternal grandmother was that she had been a fairly talented pianist. Perhaps this, coupled to my maternal grandfather (a semi-professional trombonist who played with, and was conducted by, Gustav Holst), ensured that musicality was passed down in the family gene pool to me?

My father took pride in my development as a musician, but found it very hard to listen to me playing the piano for it reminded him all too much of his own mother and her early demise. He did steel himself to listen and offer encouragement, but it must always have been something of an ordeal.

What I have inherited from him is the shape of my face, my grey-blue eyes and the colour of my beard and moustache when I first grew them (ginger with flecks of reddish, fair hair). From my mother, I have received the slightly snub nose, the smallish ears and, until recently, the dark hair, now going grey. A fair division of traits, then, all things considered.

Fathers and sons... perhaps because of my own father, I have never, even remotely, wished to be a parent. This has been a set-in-stone and constant factor even from my student days. Luckily, in their different ways, Mary and now Carol, my wife, were too old to bear children when I first knew them. In another, probably totally selfish sense, I couldn't bear them, either. But... I am jumping the gun and many years, so let's get back to my teenage self.

19

Frank Robinson, our music teacher, was a fairly jovial sort of man, although when he became a father he always seemed to be knackered. Apart from teaching harmony, aural dictation and music history, he was only too happy to divert into talk about the latest episode of Monty Python or whatever – especially whatever.

Quite often he would procure for our O Level music group free rehearsal passes to Colston Hall, particularly at the time of the Bath Festival which was held from the end of May through until about the second week of June. In the early 1970s, this was still under the direction of Sir Michael Tippett (previously the triumvirate of Tippett, and Sirs Colin Davis and Yehudi Menuhin) and, naturally, tended to feature Tippett's own music, although not excessively so. Often these performances would be conducted by the composer himself. The results tended to be idiosyncratic and highly expressive, if slightly odd from a visual point of view. I remember seeing a young Steven Bishop, as he was called then, playing Tippett's *Piano Concerto* (that marvellously lyrical opening!) and, especially memorable, Sir Michael rehearsing his *The Vision of Saint Augustine* just prior to the first recording for the RCA label. This was with the London Symphony Orchestra and Chorus with John Shirley-Quirk as the baritone soloist.

This is radiant, visionary music that poses many challenges for both the soloist and the chorus, as well as the orchestra. It mediates between intensely interior, personal music and much more overtly ecstatic, dancing and joyfully muscular lines. I remember the brilliance and the beauty and also thinking that I had never heard anything quite like this before. It was one of those rare moments when you emerge from the concert hall into daylight and you have been changed. "You are the music, while the music lasts," as TS Eliot phrased it so elegantly.

Tippett was dressed in a black tee shirt, laughed a lot and looked in his early forties, even though he was actually sixty-six. The remainder of the programme was also conducted by him and was devoted to Elgar – the *Introduction and Allegro* for strings and the *Cello Concerto* with Amarylis Fleming as soloist. She was a contemporary of the great Jacqueline du Pre and, thus, tended to be somewhat overshadowed – who wouldn't be? – but was a fine player.

On other occasions we were privileged to see the legendary Italian Carlo Maria Guilini conducting (Beethoven, I think), Sir Colin Davis and a rehearsal of Beethoven's *Fourth Piano Concerto*, where the piano lock became jammed and a hacksaw had to be sent for! (Almost as entertaining as the music…)

The resident orchestra was the Bournemouth Symphony Orchestra conducted, at that time, by that fine Sibelian interpreter Paavo Berglund. We attended many concerts under his baton, the performance I remember most vividly being a highly driven account of Shostakovich's *Tenth Symphony*. This was probably one of the first pieces of twentieth century music that I encountered. Other notable, memorable works that I heard for the first time with Colin Davis and the BBCSO were Gordon Crosse's *Second Violin Concerto* (Gyorgy Pauk, soloist) and Tippett's great humanitarian oratorio *A Child of our Time* with the ravishing Jill Gomez as soprano soloist.

What else? Mozart's *Symphony No 39 in E-flat* (Minuet & Trio, in particular) and probably a whole raft of other pieces that have sunk down and been embedded (eroded?) in the depths of rusting memory. My strongest recollection is that new, contemporary music, whatever the differences in surface style, meant a great deal more to me than works from the eighteenth and nineteenth centuries. To an extent, that still holds true and valid even these days in my mid-fifties, although I do have a broad range of musical loves that embraces music from the medieval period onwards – and equally and firmly-held dislikes, too. This latter category would include a large swathe of opera (particularly of the Italian 19th century variety), ghastly 'hey nonny-no'-type madrigals and Gilbert & Sullivan.

Contemporary chamber music was to be found in abundance at the Arnolfini gallery situated on a corner of Queens' Square, not far from King Street and the Old Vic Theatre. Originally opened in 1961 and housed in The Triangle in Clifton, its far-seeing director, Jeremy Rees, had expanded its national reputation and put in place a musical programme that featured some of the most interesting new composers and players then at work. It was here that I saw The Howard Riley Trio for the first time, with Barry Guy (amplified bass and assorted foot-pedals) and the extraordinary extensions to Tony Oxley's drum kit, such as amplified egg-slicers and other paraphernalia. This trio melded together in quasi-free improvisations, most of which were graphically notated. Fascinating stuff, especially for a musically-hungry, open-eared (probably open-mouthed, too) sixteen year-old. The David Bedford/Lol Coxhill duo appeared there, too, but I managed to miss them. (Both David and Lol had been together with Kevin Ayers and a very young Mike Oldfield in a group called The Whole World.) I also attended a talk by Peter Maxwell Davies on his music. Max was, still is, a natural communicator when it comes to his music, especially to young people. What he said was delivered with a quiet intensity and passion, these qualities reinforced by the laser-like focus emanating from his dark eyes; these eyes were almost, literally, hypnotic. The polar opposite, one might say, to the fractured, splintered and very hyperactive surfaces of his compositions and concerns at that time.

When the Arnolfini moved across the water into larger premises near Canons Marsh, the young composer Jane Wells very ably looked after the musical side of things. I was lucky

enough to see such treats as Maxwell Davies with his Fires of London group performing that seminal music-theatre work *Eight Songs for a Mad King*, Jane Manning & Richard Rodney Bennett, a programme of Satie and the virtuoso sextet, Les Percussions de Strasbourg, thundering out Xenakis and equally relishing the quieter sonorities of music by John Cage (I helped unload their instruments for this gig and Jane let me into the concert for free). She was also encouraging and generous with regard to lending me recordings or getting the technician to record pieces onto cassette. All very illegal, but a great boon to me at the time. Thanks, Jane.

Talking of percussion, I also attended at the Arnolfini a couple of concerts given by the very talented Cirencester School Percussion Ensemble, directed by the composer Elis Pehkonen, who was on the music staff there from 1967–1980. Their wide repertoire included pieces especially written for them by not only Elis himself, but by colleagues such as James Patten, Brian Dennis and George Self. There were also arrangements of medieval and ancient Chinese music used to punctuate, as it were, the modern pieces, all of which were played brilliantly and so professionally by this team of teenagers. I subsequently got to know Elis and his wife Pam in the summer of 1979 and we have remained close friends ever since, visiting them in their lovely cottage near Aldeburgh in Suffolk. Likewise, Jim Patten who lives about an hour away from us in Shepton Mallett, Somerset.

So, all in all, Bristol was a thriving city for all kinds of music – new and traditional, orchestral and chamber. I consider myself fortunate to have had the opportunity to 'soak up' all these multifarious kinds of music at a particularly exciting and eventful period of new music. Mind you, I suppose that every generation says much the same thing, doesn't it?

At about the same time, some of my friends at Ashton persuaded me to go with them to see various rock groups at Colston Hall. In tandem with this, I had become an avid reader of both *Melody Maker* and *Sounds,* which kept me in touch with what was happening (in both senses) in the very different but hugely exciting world of rock and pop music. Groups I saw included Pentangle (tour promoting the release of their *Basket of Light* album), Yes (ditto for their *Close to the Edge* LP), an evening with British R&B bands Chicken Shack and Savoy Brown (who had just released *Hellbound Train*) and Status Quo. The latter gig was very exciting and featured all their hit numbers but was deafening, too. I had a hum in each ear (a semitone apart!) for two weeks after that and I decided, regretfully, that with A Level exams coming up I had better not attend any more rock gigs if I wished to preserve my hearing – which I did, wishing to become a musician myself. It seemed a prudent move at the time – I mean both saving my hearing (pardon?) and becoming a musician. The one implies the other really, doesn't it? Although, come to think of it, I have encountered musicians who seem to be blissfully unaware that they give the impression of being completely stone deaf...

Allied to this, a few of us (Ben, Geoff, Trevor, me) used to meet up in Bob Bradshaw's room in the lunchtimes to listen to new albums by groups such as Fairport Convention, Jethro Tull, Wishbone Ash and Deep Purple on the same turntable that I had first heard Tom Lehrer. This all went well until the day that we got a bit carried away and very noisily started to dance on the desktops. A worried pupil (spoilsport) must have reported us for, without warning, the door burst open (as in a gangster movie) and an extremely irate and red-faced Bob Bradshaw stood on the threshold enquiring, in no uncertain terms, as to what the hell (**** *** ****?!) we thought we were playing at?

"Er… digging the music, Mr Bradshaw, Sir."

"GET OUT, THE LOT OF YOU," he fumed, glaring at me, a pupil whom he had hitherto trusted – at least, up until now. I did feel a bit guilty about that, I have to admit; on the other hand, the music was bloody fantastic and we were having a whale of a time. Yes, in our heads I suppose it felt like our own Newport or Isle of Wight festival, but minus the booze, the drugs and the fags – shame.

If we wanted a lunchtime drink, we just strolled down the path between the two sports fields to The Smyth Arms. It made a change from choir or orchestral practice, but got a couple of us into trouble for missing a practice. Bob Hix was furious and reported us to the resident bastard (aka Head of Sixth Form) upon whom a few of us took revenge later, lacing his mid-morning coffee with laxative and then, prudently, locking the doors of the sixth-form male staff loo. We went upstairs to the library. After a few tense minutes, we saw him dashing across to the main building. He was, we observed, running at quite a lick…

At about the same time (my fifth year) I ordered my first pair of maroon loon pants from the *Melody Maker*. I think that they cost £1.99, inclusive of p&p, and I was delighted with them. In keeping with that anarchic time, I decided that it was a good idea to distribute copies of *The Little Red Book* to first and second years. Yep, no doubt about it, I was a late developer and a bit of a closet hippy – about four or five years too late.

My preferred magazines from this period included *International Times*, *Oz* and non-satirical girlie mags such as *Playboy* and *Peaches*. These last two and their ilk filled me in on any missing gaps in my sex education, provided by courtesy of those revolving magazine stands in certain small shops with dark interiors in St Nicholas Market.

Sartorially, we must have all looked one hell of a sight: in ascending order – flares, tank tops, large-collared shirts with rounded corners and hideously lurid patterns... and then there were the long, girlish hair styles. All this now smacks of a parallel universe where items such as prawn cocktails, Che Guevara posters, Slade, Berni Inns and chicken-in-a-basket were considered perfectly ok, even the norm. Perhaps with hindsight, we all looked like basket cases in the early to mid-70s? If not basket cases, prats of the highest order, certainly.

20

Talking of tank-tops (ah, nostalgia...) that brings me on to Bob Hix, the music teacher who was appointed after Frank Robinson left to become Assistant Music Advisor for Bristol. Hix arrived at the beginning of my fifth year when I was actually beginning to enjoy school. This, in no small part, was due to the fact that the members of the S Club had left that previous summer and I could now concentrate on my studies. To be honest, I was never the most industrious of pupils. But... back to Frank and Bob. Frank's boss was Ronald Smith (not the Alkan pianist) who was kind and helpful, at least to the students. If Ronald had a minus point it was that he strongly resembled Dr Goebbels, Hitler's right-hand architect of propaganda, at least in the areas of face and plastered-down hair.

Bob Hix was a pianist and bassoon player who, at first glance, looked like a cross between Elton John (clothes, platform shoes) and Himmler (round, gilt glasses). Even at second or third glances, actually. I quickly came to the conclusion that a certain section of Bristol's music services were being run by

Nazi lookalikes or, worse still, clones a la the Gregory Peck film *The Boys from Brazil*. Hix was a tougher proposition and teacher than Robinson and really made us work. He could be encouraging and yet managed to be quite scary, too. Under his aegis, however, the music department at Ashton blossomed and I can recall performances of Ives' *The Unanswered Question*, Kurt Weill's *Threepenny Opera* (in which I played harmonium) and Lloyd Webber's *Joseph and his Amazing Technicolour Dreamcoat,* amongst many other things.

One of the other things was delightful. Her name was Linda Richardson, she was a student at Newton Park College, and she came to do her teaching practice at our school. She was a petite blonde, a soprano and liked Delius – all attributes that were fine by me. I sometimes accompanied her and became a smitten teenager. I just hope that my tongue wasn't lolling out of my mouth (like a loyal, panting dog) for the entire time that she was on TP. I visited her at Newton Park and met her parents at the college concert held at Colston Hall (this included a jubilant setting of *Psalm 150* by William Mathias). I suppose that we might have even become romantically attached, even though I was only sixteen at the time.

The next year, however, largely due to her deserved success on teaching practice, Linda was offered the assistant music post and out of professional necessity our relationship had to become more formalised and of the teacher-pupil variety. She looked very smart in her navy-blue suit and I doted on her. I think, for her part, she was fond of me, gave me occasional lifts and was concerned if I tended to skip lunch (usually on the day that I accompanied the junior choir over at Southville).

Back to Bob Hix. He was very supportive of me in my burgeoning interests in contemporary music. He frequently leant me back copies of *Music & Musicians*, and it was through this monthly magazine that I learnt about such figures as Berio, Xenakis, Elliot Carter, Stockhausen, etcetera. I tried to catch as much of their music as possible on Radio 3. In this context, I can still remember vividly the first broadcast performances of Tippett's *Third Symphony* and his *Third Piano Sonata*, both of which completely knocked me for six – despite listening on a small transistor radio (!) in my bedroom.

It was these encounters with new music that led me to be awarded a small bursary that enabled me to attend one of the Composers' Weekends, promoted by the Society for the Promotion of New Music. I think it was something in the region of five pounds, which is nothing now but was a reasonable expense back in the summer of 1973. It was held at the University of Reading in July, it was very hot and, at seventeen, I was the youngest composer (would-be composer might have been a better description!) at the retreat. I felt elated, rather overawed and nervous; but, my God, what an incredible (indeed indelible) weekend it turned out to be! There were lectures, seminars, improvisations, recitals, chamber concerts – a veritable cornucopia of events for anyone fascinated by new music and new ideas in music. The composers who were in attendance that year were a virtual who's who of the most creative minds working in this country in the early to mid-70s: Bernard Rands, Anthony Gilbert, Alexander Goehr, John McCabe, Robert Sherlaw Johnson, the Clap Music Theatre Ensemble from York University with Richard Orton, young composers such as the Australian Alison Bauld, Roger Marsh, Vic Hoyland. The list went on and on. I was in my element, though a bit overwhelmed, and soaked up everything that I could. Highlights included a lecture by Goehr, a piano lecture-recital by Sherlaw Johnson on his *Second Sonata* and *Seven Short Pieces* (both of which used subtly-integrated sounds from inside the piano – plucking, damping the strings with hands, fingers, etcetera), and the high spot: an unforgettably poetic, as well as virtuosic, interpretation of Messaien's song-cycle *Harawi* given by the soprano Noelle Barker and Sherlaw Johnson, her regular musical partner. The recital room looked out over a wide expanse of lawn. It was a very still and humid evening, coupled with the intensity and stillness of Messaien's transcendental music. For me, that performance and its attendant atmosphere amounted to a heightened moment of epiphany. It actually felt like a blessing or a benediction.

I think that I probably returned to the upper sixth that same autumn a different musician. I was still incredibly naive about certain things, from a technical perspective, yet very open to all influences and still very much the optimistic sponge, as it were, soaking up everything and anything that I could.

I left Ashton Park in the summer of 1974 with not enough qualifications to enter any college. I had rather hoped, after the influence of Linda, to try for Newton Park College near Bath, but it was not to be. I then had what would now be termed a 'gap year', where I studied A Level English (Ashton had not allowed me to do it, the bastards) and worked towards a performer's piano diploma with the help of Ann Maycock and Dr Margaret Debley, who supplemented my theoretical studies. In the event, I passed my A Level English (in spite of my dull and uninspiring teacher), but only passed two-thirds of the piano diploma; I got the aural and written papers, but not the playing section. A result which was, in fact, the complete opposite of what I thought would happen. C'est la vie!

Apart form that, I read a lot – mostly American Beat writers such as Jack Kerouac, Allen Ginsberg, the aforementioned e.e. Cummings, and the beautiful and tender lyrical poet Kenneth Patchen, whom I had discovered by dint of hearing one or two pieces by David Bedford who had either directly set Patchen's words or, more often, had used quotations from his poetry as titles for his (Bedford's) pieces. I also spent time with a pal, Andy Fairley, who had much the same, surreal tastes as I had and we used to make slightly bizarre, Goon-like cassette recordings in my bedroom. In some ways, they were probably pastiches of Peter Cook and Dudley Moore. These sessions were always improvised, never scripted and were, I suppose, typical ramblings of two late-ish teenagers, with the addition of improvised music (on piano and percussion). We both smoked at the time, although I didn't inhale (what a waste!), and my patient mother (who was trying to quit smoking at the time) used to bring us mugs of tea whilst fighting through the pall of cigarette smoke, bless her. Everything considered, she was very tolerant of my smoking.

Andy was a very talented artist who painted in the pop art, quasi-cartoon style of Roy Lichenstein. He later studied at the Central School of Art in London, returned to Bristol and did nothing very much. He died from alcoholism in the mid-1980s, being found lying amongst a profusion of empty bottles and his own excrement. This struck me then (and still strikes me now) as a very sad loss of a talented man who had never fully realised his incipient talent.

Amongst the many LPs that he introduced me to was the music of Frank Zappa, Captain Beefheart, and The Fugs. In return I used to play him Ivor Cutler and Spike Milligan. In many ways we were kindred spirits.

21

I discovered Ivor Cutler (1923–2006) by way of a full-page advert in the *Melody Maker*. I was intrigued by the description of this Jewish-Glaswegian harmonium player, singer, and poet as being a cross between the American comedian Lenny Bruce and the actor James Robertson Justice. This struck me as something of a bizarre combination and definitely worthy of investigation. Cutler had just had his LP, *Dandruff,* released on the Virgin label (which this full page was advertising) and I hastened to a record shop near the bus station in the centre of Bristol to listen to some of the forty-five short tracks in one of those soundproof booths with cracked leather seats that have long since disappeared. I laughed so much that I was shaking the booth to the evident disapproval of the guy behind the counter. He was even less impressed when I walked out with a smile and a 'thank you', not having bought the said LP. The smile and the thanks were for free, whereas the album cost money, a commodity that I had very little of at that time. I used to do that quite a lot in those days, especially if the owner of the shop glared at me. The snooty couple that ran Rayner's near the top of Park Street for too many years often experienced this. When they served you, it was with barely concealed disdain, so I often took to very politely asking to hear LPs that I quite enjoyed in their one sound booth with no intention whatsoever of buying. Their single or combined flushed-with-anger faces made it all worthwhile. Such a contrast to the lovely couple who ran the Chapter and Verse bookshop next door where I did buy their stock. But back to Ivor…

The contents of *Dandruff* were eye-wipingly, stomach-knottingly hilarious. Track one set the tone of the album, being an oddball poem about a father having sexual congress with a polar bear in Canada – as one naturally does. There were also songs about eating gooseberries, toadstools, and piranha fish, and finest of all, a series of grimly-observed vignettes about growing up in the Gorbals in Glasgow – tales, as it were, of herring-do... Each episode would be introduced by the doomy, wheezing tones of his small harmonium; sometimes the music would be maintained quietly under the firmly and deliberately enunciated narrative. To my ears, this harmonium sounded like the aural equivalent of an asthmatic sixty-a-day man on the Scottish pipes, only less loud and fearsome. Being a Celt myself, I warmed to these sounds and can rarely pass a switched-on vacuum hoover with its attendant drone without beginning to sing an improvised pibroch in a deep, resonant baritone. It must be the one-eighth Hamish surfacing in me, a wee distant, clannish memory of piping in my kilt in those bleak hills... aye.

Life in a Scotch Sitting Room, Volume Two was the collective title for these darkly surreal tales (there was no volume one, by the way) that threaded their lugubrious way through those forty-five tracks, as rich and heady as a good bowl of Scottish broth.

How best to describe Ivor Cutler? He was slightly gnome-like, stooped, and wore several layers of tartan shirts and caps adorned with a plethora of badges. He possessed an old-world courtesy, preferred to be addressed formally as Mr Cutler and, if real ale was not available, requested tap water. He was also an inveterate hander-outer of sticky labels with various Zen-like aphorisms written upon them. If he thought you were ok he'd be fine, but if not, he tended to be a bit of a piss-taker, particularly if he thought someone was a bit of a square or a humourless twat.

His career was as unusual and as idiosyncratic as he was himself. He had trained as an RAF navigator, but had been dismissed for being too dreamy. Then, in the early 50s, he taught at AS Neill's pioneering Summerhill School near Leiston in Suffolk. After that, his songs and stories were regularly featured on the old Home Service's radio programme *Monday Night at Home*. His humour was very personal and partially observed from a child's perspective (therefore, no filters or hang-ups), but also owed a little to predecessors such as Edward Lear and the dark tales of Harry Graham.

Aside from those slight influences, Ivor was never anything other than himself; indeed, he was unique, a real one-off character. He was possibly the only humourist to be regularly featured on John Peel's programmes on Radio 1, as well as having plays and sketches performed by himself and a handful of mates on Radios 3 & 4. These latter pieces of pure radio were considered eccentric and quirky. For me, they acted like the aural equivalent of much-needed fireworks in a still reasonably (unreasonably?) staid network of such tried, tested and tired offerings as *Just A Minute*, *The Archers* and *I'm Sorry I Haven't A Clue*, the last being especially infuriating with its knowingly smug public-schoolboy guffaws and general silliness. Cutler's all too occasional detonations of off-centre sanity and subtle silliness were, therefore, all the more welcome. Fragments of these programmes would tend to lodge in the brain and cause outbreaks of smiling and/or laughter at amusingly inappropriate times. As that fine (and equally maverick) actor/vaudevillian Ken Campbell used to say, "I'm not mad – I've just read different books… ". A good sentiment and well said, Ken.

My cherished bits of I.C. include the short stories *Gruts for Tea*, *The Beserk Leg*, *Grass Seed*, *Fremsley* and *Big Jim*. Some of these had been published in his collection *Cock-a-Doodle-Don't* (Dennis Dobson, 1966), which incidentally the nice couple who ran Chapter and Verse bookshop ordered in for me. Cutler's endless store of tiny nonsense songs included such gems as *I Believe in Bugs*, *I Worn My Elbows* and *I'm Happy*. Surreal, inconsequent? Most likely, yes. Dull and ordinary? Never! His entire *oeuvre* could be described as deadpan and slightly sinister; he described himself in the *Observer* colour supplement as a "small-time depressive". People either loved his work or cordially loathed it – there were no half-measures or in-betweeners. He remained a small cult, but was admired by diverse figures such as Bertrand Russell, The Beatles, and George Melly, and had the rare fortune of being rediscovered by several generations, both live and on radio.

I was lucky enough to see him a handful of times. The first two occasions were when I booked him to appear at Wantage Hall, Reading University, where I was doing my one-year PGCertEd course (yes, I was certified by a guy called Ed). The first time we couldn't afford for him to come with his harmonium, so he just brought himself plus a temperature and entertained us royally by reading his poems and stories. A few of us met him at Reading railway station in Mark Barzack's car and returned him afterwards to catch his train to Paddington. By this time, he was feeling better and announced that he "ought to do something momentous, like spitting on the platform." With a handshake and a twinkly smile, we shook hands with this diminutive legend and waved farewell as the train pulled out.

It had been a successful evening. My friends Roger and Sue drove over for it and were amazed by Ivor's humour. The only embarrassing moment came as Ivor announced he was going to read a serious poem and some drunken girl staggered into the Common Room where the gig was being held and started to laugh at his appearance. Angrily he turned on her and shouted, "I said that this was a SERIOUS poem!" The audience burst into supportive, spontaneous applause and the ignorant bimbo was led away, doubtless none the wiser that she had momentarily nonplussed a Jewish-Glaswegian harmonium player and humourist of national renown.

The second time that Wantage Hall was able to bring him back, he came replete with his small harmonium. I think that Mark Honan helped to organise that gig. Mark and I also went to see him reading for the Poetry Society at Earl's Court. It was a cold November evening and I rode pillion on Mark's motorbike on the M4 from Reading to London, grimly hanging on to the back with increasingly freezing hands. Somehow I stayed on, but it was a bit scary.

Some while later, we met him in Hyde Park at a peace demonstration, I think it was. We hailed him, but he didn't recognise us. Somewhat apologetically he said with exquisite tact and old-world formality, "I'm afraid that you have the advantage." It was an oblique reply, yet somehow quintessentially Cutlerian, whilst placing the ball in our court, as it were. Once prompted, he did remember the gigs at Wantage and was nice and friendly. It was typical of him to turn up and support a worthy cause that he believed in.

Years later, I saw him in London at the Bloomsbury Theatre, Euston in May 1986 for his evening entitled *Gruts* and on two occasions at the Queen Elizabeth Hall. The last time, I went up with Gervaise, a friend and piano pupil from Oxford, and this turned out to be his final concert (late January 2004). Ivor wore a huge sunflower (real or a badge?) on the side of a cloth cap, check shirts, and a zipped-up puffa jacket that he discarded after a few numbers. He looked more frail, his hands shook when reading, and he seemed disorientated when wishing to exit the stage. The hall was sold out, however, and the woman in front of me was laughing so much I really thought that she was going to wet herself. Ivor would have been quietly pleased on behalf of her possible incontinence. If there had been pads on sale, along with the CDs and small books of poetry, she would, doubtless, have made a purchase.

Yes, Ivor Cutler was a real original, a complete one-off and I was lucky to have caught him live, in print and on LP and CD. In fact, he partially helped to form, if not actually mould, my adult sense of humour. So, Ivor, it's partly your fault...!

The other figure in the equation (and equally to blame) was Spike Milligan.

22

Dear dented, fragile Spike. Although I met him on a handful of occasions, I couldn't really claim to have known him. Probably very few people ever did apart from his long-suffering agent Norma Farnes, co-writers Eric Sykes and John Antrobus, and his wives and children (but Norma, I suspect, had the definite edge).

Yet in a bizarre kind of way, from about the age of seventeen or eighteen, I felt a huge empathy for and with this brilliant, manic, despairing man. Empathy not only with the humour, but with the underlying fragility, the three-skins-lessness of Spike and his interminable suffering. Sometimes when you peeked momentarily through the chinks in the armour, he seemed to roar with the pride of a wounded lion. Yes, I know, a mixed metaphor if ever there was one – but still apposite, I think. Indeed, at times I almost felt as if I *was* Spike Milligan. I don't know what that says about me, come to think of it, but there we are; that's how it seemed at the time.

I suppose that I must have first become aware of Spike and his very special, outside-of-the-box humour in the early 70s from TV programmes such as those that he did based on the seasons – *Milligan in Spring*, for example. Inspired silliness fused with topical satire (can you have non-topical satire?): "The daffodils are out, the miners are out... "

I had read some of his books such as *Puckoon, Adolf Hitler: My Part in his Downfall, A Dustbin of Milligan*, and had seen his and Antrobus' satirical near-masterpiece, the film of *The Bedsitting Room*. Alas, I was too young to see, or know about, the original stage play back in 1963.

In the autumn of 1974, two things of significance regarding Milligan happened to me. Firstly, I listened with shaking head and aching belly to a raft of repeated *Goon Shows* on Radio 4, some of which I taped to sample the delights on future occasions. (I soon became an avid member of The Goon Show Preservation Society after this, keeping up my membership through my student years.) Secondly, I wrote to Spike enquiring if he would be appearing any time soon at the Bristol Hippodrome. To my surprise, he not only replied promptly in person but said that he would be appearing in October, a matter of some three weeks after I received his reply. Equally promptly, I booked a seat for an evening, which turned out to be one of the most memorable evenings I have spent in a theatre.

The show was a two-hander called *For One Week Only,* and featured not only Spike (who was on top form) but the South African satirist and folksinger Jeremy Taylor. Jeremy was a sort of Johannesburg version of Jake Thackeray, playing a sweetly melodic guitar to quite barbed lyrics that tended to rue the many and various hypocrisies then prevalent in South Africa ("Aag, *pleeze* Deddy..."). Like many quality satirists, he had been banned on various international radio and television channels – a sure sign of stature and an indication that the barb has pierced its intended victim. Not hugely known in this country at that time, Jeremy's contributions proved to be a perfect foil for Spike's poems, one-liners and manic gagging. As I recall, they both alternated short sessions of ten to fifteen minutes each.

I still remember the opening of the show: the tabs were drawn back to reveal a series of stagehands frantically hammering and sawing pieces of wood, as if desperate to finish the props and scenery in time for the opening of the show. These guys were all identically dressed in brown overalls (as once worn by men serving behind the counters of hardware stores). One of them turned slightly, peered at the audience, put down his hammer, ran downstage and discarded his overalls. It was, of course, Spike. He then proceeded to set an alarm clock, saying by way of explanation, "Forty-five minutes each way. Anything else is extra time." His whole act had the packed audience convulsed and in tears of mirth; his adlibs were deft, razor-sharp, acidic, affectionate and lightning-quick, all at the same time. Jeremy Taylor's songs were fresh and zingy, too. With Spike, you never quite knew how much of the show was totally, partially ad-libbed or partially scripted.

As teenagers do, I went round to the stage door for an autograph and an admiring few words. I was virtually tongue-tied. He was very pleasant, even quiet, and I was absolutely amazed to hear that he was running a high fever with a temperature of 102F – from his act, one would never have guessed that he was ill, such was the energy of the performance. Whilst he was signing autographs, some passing moron on the pavement called out cheekily, "I'm coming tomorrow, Spike – it had better be good." With an icy glance and equally icy voice, Spike simply replied, "Yes, it is good..." Result: Milligan 1, Moron 0. Or, as Ronnie Scott might have said, a case of a moron *glacé*... No histrionics or losing his temper, just a very firm put-down to an unthinking young man who, like so many, believe that if you are in the public eye you are fair game for this sort of intrusive, throwaway comment.

The next time that I met Spike he was, typically, very variable and on a knife-edge in his ever-changing moods. At a book-signing in George's (now Blackwell's) at the top of Park Street, a man who was in front of me in the queue happened to mention the BBC to Spike. At this perceived affront, Milligan glared at the unfortunate man and positively erupted, spitting out (in capitals), "DON'T MENTION THE BBC TO *ME*!!" The man got his book signed (just) then hastily withdrew. Luckily, Spike was fine with me, as far as I recall. He could erupt and then come down as quickly as he had exploded. At other times, a stray or unthinking word would plunge him into the deepest, gloomiest abyss for hours or even days at a time.

A year or two later, when I was a student at the Birmingham School of Music, the student common room had a television. The college closed at 9pm sharp, but if you spoke nicely to the porters, they would normally let us stay on to see programmes such as Spike's *Q* series. You would have to arrive early in order to get a hotly contested seat for the weekly half-hour showing of *Q6* or *Q7* and the whole room was brimful with hilarity and shouts of howling laughter. In one programme there was a visual *leitmotif* that ran through most of the sketches: all the actors (Spike, Peter Jones, David Lodge) wore blank luggage labels pinned to their lapels – representing, I suppose, a kind of faceless and nameless conformity.

The Monty Python team have acknowledged just how influential the open-ended sketches in *Q5* were to them and it has always surprised me that the complete series of the *Q* programmes have yet to be released on DVD. Perhaps the BBC, in its infinite wisdom, has wiped them all? If you have committed this act of desecration, BBC, you are the ultimate in corporate arrogance and high-handed ignorance as well as being a complete and utter bunch of philistine arseholes...

When the show was over, we would all step outside into the real world until the next time; the real student world usually meant going for a drink at the Night & Day, a pub with magenta faux-leather chairs and, at that time, frequented by ATV technicians and cameramen. All right, then, a version of the real world.

In the mid-1980s, Spike was touring a one-man show again and Mary and I saw it at the New Theatre, Oxford. It was good in parts, contained a mediocre pop group, but was not in all honesty Spike's finest hour. The best bits included a dummy of Margaret Thatcher, which was soundly whacked over the head whenever a joke failed – in fact, for any reason, really. We popped round to see him in his dressing room afterwards, met his new wife Shelagh, talked music with him and had some good white wine from his fridge. Spike was hospitable, well-behaved and seemed to have had a good evening on stage, but we didn't, hopefully, outstay our welcome as he looked tired.

Spike Milligan. What's in a name? God, that man and his multifarious paradoxes! A concerned and caring human being, but mostly for animals and the natural world, not fellow human creatures whom he regarded as cruel and stupid. It's hard to disagree with that, to be fair. But, by so regarding, he himself was far from immune in terms of callousness and cruelty to others. On the other hand, he could be endlessly generous and patient to people whom he encountered with similar experiences, mental problems and unseen fragilities.

Without visible scars or bandages to elicit empathy, millions silently suffer years of inner pain, a fact that Spike knew from first-hand experience all too well.

His magical way with words, his oblique view of life and the resultant, out-of-this-world individuality and surreality – all these facets and gifts proclaimed and reinforced his Irish lineage. Above all, a part of him never forgot what it was like to be a child in his own world of dreams and make-believe; the ever-optimistic, innocent figure of Eccles, popping his head above the parapet and grinning inanely in the face of all the *real* idiots – the besuited powermen who are so convinced that they (and they alone) have the solutions to run this country. Multiply that concept across all the countries of the world and surely we live on a planet far crazier than any *Goon Show* script that even Milligan could have imagined...

STUDENT DAYS:
BIRMINGHAM AND
READING

23

These next entries will probably be shorter and sweeter for my student years were, by and large, very happy, rewarding and fulfilling times. Wasn't it Philip Larkin who commented that "happiness writes white". Perhaps it is, after all, much easier (lazier?) to write and dwell upon melancholia and misery rather than celebrating its polar opposites, happiness and optimism.

A poet who has consistently achieved this latter state, in my view, is PJ Kavanagh. He has by no means omitted to pen the darker experiences of his days (as so beautifully and memorably captured in his autobiography, *The Perfect Stranger*), but he has amply balanced this in his small and hard-won epiphanies of joy. As Thomas Hardy knew only too well, these unexpected, caught-out-of-the-corner-of-the-eye moments often occur through observations of nature – the flight of a bird and how it turns and wheels, for example, or the way in which a tree may seem lit by the setting, reddening sun.

All this is, in a sense, beside the point. This section will relate some of the highlights of my student experiences over four years – three at Birmingham and one at Reading.

Having given up on applying to Newton Park College of Higher Education (why do these titles always look so pompous?), my mother kept an eagle eye out for other music college options. She kept, almost spookily (as Dame Edna Everage would say), coming back to the Birmingham School of Music and its Graduate diploma. After the fourth or fifth reference to this and a chat with Dr John Bishop who was on the staff there, we decided that perhaps something or someone was trying to steer me in this direction. So early one morning in March 1975, I got on a train, destination Birmingham New Street, for an interview at the School of Music.

I carried my battered viola and a briefcase adorned with round and loudly coloured Goon Show Preservation Society stickers. In hindsight (it's all we've got, folks!) I must have looked a bit of a sight, not to say a little eccentric, but there you go; I dare say the staff had (and would) see worse. I received a friendly, helpful welcome from the red-faced Irish porter on the reception desk. I enquired where the interviews were being held. "Follow me, I'll be right behind you," he said, leading the way upstairs. Really, I'm not making this up. It was one of those gems that happens all too infrequently, but is very gratefully received when it does.

I had to play the piano (cannot remember the pieces), which was just as well for this redeemed my awful viola playing. (Circa Grade 4; yes, that ghastly...) I was very nervous and managed to drop the viola on removing it from its case. One of the more highly-strung members of the interviewing panel cried out, "Oh, the poor thing." I think that she was referring to the viola...

Anyway, I felt that I had done so badly that I didn't even stay to look around the college or, indeed, the city itself. I headed straight back to Bristol, thoroughly convinced that I had failed my audition. As it turned out, I had impressed my three auditors enough to gain a place for that same autumn (in spite of not doing the juggling, the jokes or my imitations of Spike Milligan...).

In spite of various efforts, I did not get into the usual hall of residence a mere few minutes walk from the college. Instead (and which turned out to be better in many ways, although lonelier), I rented a large bedsitter on the ground floor of a spacious house in Sandon Road, just off the Hagley Road and a bus-ride from the centre of the city. It was quite a pleasant bedsit, despite the orange walls, but being on the corner of the house with large windows was fiercely cold in winter and a veritable oven in the summer. Despite all this, it seemed to suit me and I stayed there for all of my three years. I didn't tend to cook for myself except for the simplest of toast-based snacks – I ate my main meal of the day in the college canteen. At weekends, after going into college to do a desultory hour or two of practice, I would then eat at one of the various cafes or cheap restaurants in New Street either by myself or with one or two friends. If we could afford it, we'd eat in a Chinese establishment in one of the smaller streets off New Street. On cold winter evenings if I was by myself, I would have my meal and stay reading in the restaurant for as long as I dare to save on my heating bills in the bedsit.

Initially during the first few weeks of term, my main friends were not in my own first year, but older and wiser students who were in their third (last) year. Phillip and Carol were caring and kept an eye on me, a real greenhorn in so many ways. Yes, an innocent abroad in the capital of the Midlands, referred to as the Second City (after London). As fond as I was and continue to be of Birmingham, I would have thought that that honour would have been more aptly bestowed upon the city of Manchester, an altogether more impressive relic of the Industrial Revolution. Phillip and Carol were great mates, but were not a couple as such. Sometimes we had meals together and went to the occasional church service together, too. It was all very companionable and most welcome.

Gradually, almost inevitably, as these things tend to, our bond slackened and was replaced by emergent friendships with people in my own graduate set. There were some real characters amongst this group including: Andrew MacManus, pianist and singer; Nigel Morley, a slim red-haired lad from the wilds of Lincolnshire who was a very able pianist and composer; and Clare Gough, who dressed in twinsets and, in manner and deportment, already resembled a middle-aged headmistress. She was, bless her, the type of person that was starchy and easily shocked – a most suitable candidate, in fact, for the irresistible urge to utter the longest string of swearwords possible.

Andrew used to take a quiet delight in making barely-concealed, quasi-obscene illusions. I don't think that she ever understood the references; she merely blinked and looked rather blankly at him, as if he was some sort of lunatic – which, in a way, I suppose he was. Andrew was great fun, definitely eccentric and something of a teasing piss-taker – mischievous, but affectionate in his pranks and practical jokes. In many ways he was still very adolescent, but everyone adored him, male and female. In the canteen he used to serenade one of the table-clearers, Nellie, a lovely lady who never failed to stop for a chat and a bit of gossip. Andrew, being of the other persuasion, was very partial to a bit of gossip (never heard it called that before…). He could, all too often, be infuriating, too. For example, when a group of us went to buy some fish and chips, Andrew requested a portion and Jim, a Welsh tuba player from Wrexham who resembled Eric Morecombe, went in to place the order for all of us. When he eventually emerged, almost buried beneath a stack of vinegary-papered packages, Andrew had completely disappeared. One moment he was there, smiling and joking, and then – pschhew! – he had evaporated as if by some Merlin-like magic. He was from Wisbech in Cambridgeshire, however, which was known to have the highest concentration of mediums and witches anywhere in the country, apparently. Another student from the same area, Pete Wain, darkly told me that it was a really weird village, along the lines of "I shouldn't go there if I was you, mate."

One weekend, Andrew turned up with a large girl in tow who, it transpired, was a genuine medium. She was very nice, as I remember, but slightly unsettled me by giving me a very straight, piercing gaze and then saying that my aura was very dark – too dark for comfort, in fact. Just for good measure, at that time I was also unable to wear watches for they invariably stopped working or kept slowing down. Perhaps I had a lot of surplus energy or something? I have always been interested and open to such out-of-this-world esotericisms but, unfortunately, Rackham's didn't stock any aura-lightening cream at that time – very remiss. So I was condemned to prowl around the dark streets of the Second City hiding my intensely dark (navy blue?) aura. ("Richard? Oh, yeah. Seems like a nice enough kind of bloke, very quiet, but have you seen his aura? Bloody hell! It's as dark as a Scottish mountain in a thunderstorm, mate...") Perhaps that partially explains my unease and discomfort that I feel on the rare occasions when I am in Scotland?

My other memory of Andrew MacManus is of our one visit to London. He was taking a singing diploma at the London College of Music in Great Marlborough Street, just off the West End, and I was accompanying him. We stayed overnight and took in a concert conducted by Raymond Leppard that featured the soprano Josephine Barstow and the BBC Symphony Orchestra in a radiant and dramatic account of Sir Michael Tippett's *Third Symphony*, a twentieth-century response to Beethoven's setting of Schiller's *Ode to Joy* in his Ninth Symphony. Afterwards, Tippett was presented with the Gold Medal of the Royal Philharmonic Society by Yehudi Menuhin. The whole evening was beautiful, highly charged and memorable.

The only fly in the ointment was the snooty, rude and unhelpful attitude of the staff at the London College of Music.

We got our revenge, however, when we visited the antique toilet in the basement. After washing our hands, we accidentally-on-purpose turned all the cold water taps on, put the plugs into the basins and let the water take its natural course... It could only have improved the facilities – that, or a large bomb.

I haven't seen Andrew since we both left Birmingham, but I know that he taught for a time at Colston's preparatory school for boys in Bristol and then took a job out in Gran Canaria. He would have made a very good and enthused teacher; and, perhaps by now, he has learnt to keep his practical jokes and tomfoolery in check. Anyway, whatever he is doing (and with whom!) I remember him with affection and a smile.

Other mates tended to be either fellow pianists or budding composers who shared the same tutors and/or musical tastes. I suppose that we were attracted to various small coteries, which probably fluctuated depending on whom we were accompanying at the time. Mostly, though, we tended to avoid singers who, all too often, were blessed with good voices but very little in the way of brains and musical awareness and sense of style. Tough, but true.

Lots of friends, then, but as for girlfriends... well, I'll come onto that later.

24

Time for a few words about my tutors at Birmingham.

Well, they all seemed like virtual Gods to this fresh-faced, keen but innocent student. There was my piano tutor Malcolm Wilson (who was only seven years older than myself), my viola tutor Geoffrey Duggan, keyboard harmony tutor Dr John

Bishop, and my personal tutor Tony Cross who was to marry Helen, another student in my year. Tony sadly died far too young in 1999. He was a Bartok scholar and a committed Communist who introduced me to the songs of Hanns Eisler, some of which I performed with another pupil of his, singer Caroline Green. I also remember a tutorial in which he played memorably, and in its entirety, Liszt's *Sonata in B Minor* – a performance which virtually rendered me speechless. He was always tough but fair in his assessments and was particularly helpful, but strict, in his teaching of Palestrina-style counterpoint – quite rightly, too. It was Tony who suggested that Alan Bush would be the ideal composition tutor for me, being both a fellow Communist and a very distinguished teacher who would have been able to pull my somewhat flaccid technique into shape. I didn't pursue this option, however, as I was much more inclined towards more avant-garde composers and their techniques. I have always admired and enjoyed, however, Bush's rigorously constructed music.

The piano was my first study, and although I had talent, I was fairly raw with regard to phrasing and fingering in classical repertoire by Mozart and Beethoven. At that juncture, I felt more confident with such contemporary composers as John McCabe and Richard Rodney Bennett. Much of the problem was my combination of enthusiasm coupled with a highly-strung nervousness that almost rendered me unable to really focus and listen to my own playing. Malcolm was very patient and I gradually began to relax over the course of my first year with tangible improvements – unlike my viola playing, I hasten to add. After six or so futile weeks, Geoff Duggan and I agreed that it might be in my best interests if I abandoned the instrument. I think that his migraines probably ceased from that moment on.

As part of the graduate syllabus, I was required to have a second instrument but didn't play any woodwind or brass, which was problematic. What would I like to play? I suggested the harpsichord which was accepted, although strictly speaking, students were not meant to study two keyboard instruments. But an exception was made for me. It was at this point that it was borne on me just how diabolical my so-called viola playing had been... plenty of scratches and squeaks but very few notes in tune would be an adequate summary.

My harpsichord tutor was the distinguished organist and recitalist George Miles, known in the Midlands for his Bach recitals and broadcasts. Through my next three years of study with him, he unfailingly guided me through the various intricacies and joys of music by composers as diverse as JS Bach (*Musical Offering* and the solo part in the *Fifth Brandenburg Concerto*), Scarlatti, Couperin, the English school of virginalists, plus more recent music by Henze, Peter Racine Fricker, and Ligeti. I also participated in a master class (playing the Henze *Six Absences*) with the more famous George – George Malcolm, this country's pre-eminent harpsichordist of that era. I was asked to page-turn for his lunchtime recital earlier that day and he played very deftly and with great elan, in spite of the whisky fumes that were wafting past my face!

George Miles was invariably dressed in a green corduroy jacket, smoked roll-ups and sported a pencil-thin moustache. He was married to a rather severe Austrian wife whom he met, so rumour had it, in Vienna when he was studying as a young man with an organ pupil of the great Max Reger. On the rare occasions that I needed to phone George at home, the receiver would be invariably picked up by Frau Miles with the peremptory and staccato greeting-cum-military order, "Zis is the Miles' residence..." You got to the point immediately, for she was not a lady to engage in pleasantries. (I imagine that she had been an enthusiastic member of the Hitler Youth movement.) We, his pupils, used to joke that it was little wonder that George sometimes arrived to teach in less than good humour. When he was being particularly dour and stern, he would glare at the music, head raised with his nose wrinkled up with impatience. Yet such was his wisdom and innate niceness that we all revered him and held him in the highest affection and esteem, even when he was being crabby and a pain.

Those lessons with George helped to change my musical life and perspectives. It was from this time that I got to know several pieces by John Bull, the extraordinary fantasia on *Ut, Re, Mi* in particular. I was bowled over and said so. George, with his typical no-nonsense candour, thought otherwise: "Hmm… merely experimental – it's one of his worst pieces," he said, taking a long, elegant drag from his black cigarette holder. So, that was that, then. He was challenging my easy enthusiasm and assumptions, challenging me to think more clearly and critically about music, which I most certainly needed to do at that time. I remain wholly convinced that for George Miles music – great music – was a truth to be constantly uncovered and upheld. That he seemed to achieve this unwaveringly and unremittingly, both through his teaching and performing, was a source of real inspiration to all of us who came into contact with him. Dear George, I revere his memory and still attempt to emulate his rigour and spiritual profundity.

Another staff member for whom these attributes shone out crystal-clear was the Bach scholar Stephen Daw, who was never officially a tutor of mine, but became a guiding light and a dear and valued friend. The first time that I came across Stephen was when a group of us were having a free-for-all improvisation in the harpsichord room, with me playing the harpsichord. Being Stephen, he came and immediately joined in the cacophonous fun. "Gosh," he said afterwards, "I haven't done anything like that since my Royal Academy days!" (Where, after New College, Oxford, he studied composition with Lennox Berkeley.) Stephen was not only an inspiring tutor and figure, but also someone who instilled in me a deep love and reverence for the music of JS Bach. Many students in their teens find both technical as well as interpretative problems with the keyboard music of Bach, and I was no exception. But, by studying the harpsichord and soaking in Stephen's thoughts, I began to acquire some small insights into what helped to bring Bach's music to life in performance – issues of articulation and phrasing, giving the music room and space to breathe, for example. I by no means succeeded, of course, but at least I was beginning to get nearer to a notion of how this music could live and move (in both senses) during the course of playing it.

Indeed, on one or two rare occasions, I felt so at one with the music, as if I had almost *become* the music, that I felt sure I heard a voice speaking in German. It spoke, not so much within the room where I was practising the harpsichord, more within my head. Now, I do not speak German or understand the German language, but these uttered words were most definitely German. They were spoken quietly, as if in encouragement. Maybe the spirit of old Bach himself was gently aiding my endeavours? Whoever the speaker was I felt helped, perhaps even comforted would not be too strong a word. A quiet room containing a young student trying to improve his playing of a Bach fugue in the quiet of mid-evening and, however odd to the reader, he virtually became that music for those few moments or minutes – was so moved by it, that he entered another dimension where time was temporarily suspended... Puzzling and beautiful in equal measure. This has tended to happen when I know a particular piece already quite well. I relax and, almost miraculously, the piece gives the impression of playing itself unhindered by my conscious thoughts – a form of meditation, I suppose. One cannot will this to happen; it always arrives unexpectedly, out of the blue, but I am always grateful and humbled by it. Stephen would understand this, for his attitude to great music has invariably been humble and humane, just like his master JS Bach. When conscious thought intrudes or becomes self-conscious, however, the spell is broken. You have to remain, as it were, in the bubble.

In May 1976, in my first summer term, Stephen, his wife Gillian and I took a train to Oxford for a concert in the English Bach Festival (with whom Stephen had been connected for many years, writing programme notes, etcetera). This was held in the sumptuous venue of the Codrington Library, All Souls College, and featured the first performance of the fourteen Canons appended to the *Goldberg Variations* by JSB, in realisations that a few of us students had been privileged to work on with Stephen. These were the basis for the performance by Trevor Pinnock and The English Concert, introduced from a high pulpit by a young Nicholas Kenyon who would later go on to run the Proms and Radio 3. The interpretations were rather perfunctory, or so we all thought, and slightly disappointing. With the blithe naivety of youth, we felt that we had done a better job of these little gems ourselves back in Birmingham.

Through Stephen, the following years brought annual and memorable visits to the Easter Swansea Bach Week, ably organised by John Huw Thomas, the extramural music tutor at the university. It was situated in Blackpill on the Mumbles and often there would be local delicacies such as laverbread on the menu. Here it was possible to hear fine performances from artists of the calibre of Frans Bruggen and other musicians from Amsterdam, as well as lectures and the latest scholarly research by leading Baroque authorities such as Peter Williams, Handelian Anthony Hicks and Stephen himself. Particularly impressive was an early morning lecture-recital given by Peter on the *Goldberg Variations*. Typically, he threw out provocative ideas and thoughts in his languid manner and yet played with true virtuosity. Of equal benefit and value was the opportunity to do a lot of accompanying, both in small-scale chamber music as well as playing continuo for Bach cantatas, etcetera. I remember an anthem by Zelenka and playing in Bach's *Fourth Brandenburg Concerto*.

Years later, when I had returned to Birmingham as a visiting tutor, Steve and Gill provided unfailing hospitality every single Monday evening for eight years term in and term out, bless them. We usually imbibed Nottage Hill red wine, joked, punned and laughed our way through many a Monday night in Solihull. Occasionally, we would go and eat out at a Balti restaurant. I was referred to as the wine merchant. I used to jest that this particular wine merchant not only delivered the wine, but had the nerve to stay overnight as well! Heady, happy days!

The other tutor who was helpful and supportive during my three years was Andrew Downes. A composer and one-time counter-tenor who had studied with Herbert Howells at the Royal College of Music and sung in the choir of St John's College, Cambridge, under George Guest, Andrew looked after the composition workshop every Wednesday afternoon. Composition was not available as a first-study option in the mid-70s, but there were a handful of us who were dedicated composers who wrote, directed, and played in each other's pieces. It was a very useful and practical platform for a budding composer – what worked, what did not, does that percussion player have time to dash over for that vibraphone solo? Those were the kind of issues that we needed to think about and address in our own writing. Andrew was always encouraging and amusedly tolerant of our wackier conceits (such as my piano piece, written for an April Fools' Day concert, which juxtaposed fragments of Alkan and Noel Coward...).

During my time at Birmingham, I wrote a string quartet (the first of seven, thus far), a miniature piano concerto that recollected various moments from proper, famous concerti (Beethoven's Fourth, the Schumann, etcetera) which is probably best forgotten, plus a handful of other pieces which included *Areas* for a spatially deployed group that included two hocketing trumpeters – me attempting to emulate Birtwistle, I expect. Rather more expressive were two settings of poems by the Orcadian George Mackay Brown, scored for counter-tenor and harp. These were written for Andrew to sing, accompanied by the one-time CBSO harpist, Muriel Liddle (known to all as Widow Twanky on account of her personal, as well as sartorial eccentricities, à *la* Edith Sitwell).

Benjamin Britten had died early the previous December (1976) and I wrote these songs the following March in his memory, having attended (with Andrew) the memorable and moving memorial service held at Westminster Abbey in his honour. Highlights of that service included Peter Pears reading the lesson and the Amadeus Quartet, plus another cellist playing the slow movement of the sublime Schubert *Quintet in C*, one of Britten's favourite pieces of music.

As a singer, Andrew came with the college choir and orchestra to the Dordogne for a fortnight in the baking-hot summer of '76. As I recall, he sang the solos in Bernstein's *Chichester Psalms*, an idiosyncratic blend of Jewishness and Stravinsky, the dryness of the latter serving to mediate the excesses of the former. We were based in St Cere and gave various concerts in chateaux and the imposing cathedral in the medieval town of Sarlat. Apart from the Bernstein, we sang Liszt's setting of Psalm XIII, plus Mendelssohn's oratorio *Elijah*. It was hard work and a very hot, somewhat odd fortnight. We slept in dormitories, where one of our number decided that it would be a good idea to light a fire. We put some wasps into a specially prepared apple pie bed for him and he was fairly subdued after that... as good as gold, in fact.

Homemade greengage jam and the purest white butter with rolls and croissant for breakfast, potent-smelling ripe cheeses and rough red wine at lunch. Wonderful!

What else? A horn player who contracted lockjaw on his birthday; a car which managed to park a wheel on the foot of a cellist; I fainted and fell off a platform; and another student urinated up against a fence which, unfortunately for him, was electrified and sent him reeling backwards. How we all laughed! And so these little vignettes went on, enlivening the spaces between rehearsals, chamber music playing, and concerts.

This trip was also memorable for another reason – I spent its entirety trying to avoid Carolyn, a violinist and (almost) girlfriend. Luckily, for both of us, we were on separate coaches. More on this later.

Obviously our college was trying to economise, for the coaches appeared to be relics from a British film circa 1950. We expected Alistair Sim to pop his head up at any moment, grinning evilly and brandishing a violin case. To soothe our long journey, guitarist Adrian serenaded us with Stevie Wonder's *You Are the Sunshine of My Life*. I can never hear that song without associating it with that trip to France.

It was a happy, if tired and numb-arsed, band of musicians that descended on the little village of St Cere – no, more of an invasion, really. When, some years later, I saw some of those subtle, exquisitely shot Jacque Tati films for the first time, I was put in mind of that welcoming and sleepy little village far down in the snug, rolling hills of the Dordogne.

25

Girlfriends now, or more accurately virtual girlfriends (and I am not talking about on-line computer games). This will be a very short entry, then…

Well, I had two, in effect, during my three years in Birmingham – Carolyn, a violinist, and Ruth, a cellist; both lovely, but a bit bonkers, really. (What's that phrase about like attracting like?)

God, I was so shy, naïve, and nervous that I didn't stand a chance, sexually speaking. Carolyn was a very talented musician from the pink-pavements city of Carlisle, whilst Ruth hailed from Leicestershire. Two pieces that I will always associate with Carolyn's violin playing are Beethoven's *'Spring' Sonata* and the Mendelssohn Concerto, which she played (or as I then thought) to dazzling effect. I had been recommended by another student as an accompanist for her, so that is how we met and started working together. She had a dark, olive complexion and was Jewish (as I found out when I bought her a ham sandwich). She didn't say much, but disdainfully picked out the ham between thumb and forefinger. She was terrific, but I was barely able to talk, so strong was my infatuation for her. When I did talk, I blathered on about music.

There was the occasion when we brought fish and chips back to her flat off the Hagley Road. I was so wound up that

I could scarcely eat them, let alone do anything romantic. Fish and chips is not great before a French kiss – all those bits of batter in the teeth and gums… Yes, I certainly had it bad, as they say. I sometimes found myself standing outside her flat, gazing up at the window, yet not having the courage or gumption to ring the doorbell. I think that I probably needed professional help. Unfortunately, there is no fool-proof guide for the uninitiated in the mysteries of love. So your young, virginal writer had to suffer in silence and make do with the occasional wet dream. (I've never been keen on masturbation – too much like hard work and you know that it is your own hand doing the business. No fun or illusion in that at all.)

Carolyn eventually moved back into student accommodation at Cambrian Hall whereupon we drifted apart. Slightly to my disgust, she gave up music to become a policewoman, although I'm sure that she would have made a very good one.

What about Ruth? (I hear you cry.) Well, she was lovely, too. A good, passionate cellist who had had some lessons with the great legend of her time, Jacqueline du Pre. She did have issues with regard to her own self-esteem, however. Mind you, I suppose that a good many of us did. She was a very warm and special, supportive friend with a nice, lively sense of humour. We were easy in each other's company. I suppose that I was, by this time, slightly easier in my own skin, too. Therefore, there was none of the angst that I experienced with Carolyn.

One particularly memorable time was when we travelled up to London on the coach from fume-ridden Digbeth station to hear Charles Rosen play the last three Schubert piano sonatas in the Queen Elizabeth Hall in March 1978. It was a stupendous recital, full of stillness as well as dynamism, and we were privileged to hear this legendary player who had been a pupil of Liszt's pupil, Moriz Rosenthal. We arrived back at my bedsit in the early hours where we cuddled up together in the single bed. Stupidly, I hadn't had the foresight to buy any condoms, so we reluctantly desisted our explorations and I slept on the floor. We both awoke to a bout of double frustration. Things never quite felt the same after that, but we often referred to that memorable piano recital and still remained good friends. Why I never tried again, I'm not quite sure – probably the sense of an opportunity lost. Sometimes, as we know, circumstances are never as propitious again. After we both left college our rapport faded, perhaps inevitably, and we lost touch. The last I heard (from Stephen Daw some years ago) was that Ruth had married a chef and was living, if memory serves, in North Wales – although memory does not always serve... Yes, she was a good-hearted lass, but quite intense and rather neurotic and, looking back at those years now, she wouldn't have been right for me. But I hope that she has gained in confidence and happiness through the years.

Mentioning my accompanying of Carolyn and Ruth makes me realise that I spent a lot of my time as a student providing accompaniments for others. This was all very useful for honing my sight-reading abilities and provided opportunities to doubtless play music that I otherwise might not have encountered; but there remains the nagging feeling that I was far too altruistic for my own good when I should have been devoting my abilities and practice time to studying more in the way of solo works for myself. All rather annoying in retrospect, but that was how it was at the time. Whatever the advantages or disadvantages, I was grateful for having had my ears opened to such repertoire as the gloriously moving Poulenc solo wind sonatas and songs, piano trios by Mendelssohn and Schumann, various violin sonatas, etcetera. Luckily, perhaps, I never got involved with opera and all the tiresome egos and antics of the singers. (*Tantum ergo* or, as I prefer, tantrum ego when applied to overly histrionic and sensitive singers; by which I mean self-sensitive, of course, for they are a breed who are virtually oblivious to anyone but themselves.)

One singer who I most definitely did enjoy working with, however, was the professional (in all senses) baritone, Michael Rippon. We performed, under Norman Price's direction, Maxwell Davies' extraordinary and moving music-theatre work *Eight Songs for a Mad King*, which depicts the mental disintegration of George III. (Michael had sung many performances of this work under Max's own direction with The Fires of London and was highly effective as well as authoritative in the role.) Harrowing and surreal in equal proportion, this piece is always as draining for the audience as it is for the players. The final moments when the King exits to the words "and he will die howling... howling," followed by the percussionist thwacking a bass drum with whip, must be one of the most chilling and harrowing codas in all music. The percussionist, Clifford, who was a gentle, mild-mannered lad from Coventry, had to be persuaded to thwack his drum with much more aggression and abandon, much to his embarrassment. It was certainly a cracking performance, which kept me busy (not to say fully occupied) playing both piano and harpsichord – although, as I recall, not simultaneously. I wish that we had been able to give more performances of this tough yet tender oddity, which never fails to impact on both player and listener alike.

So much for music with which I was involved. Now a section on memorable concerts that I attended in Birmingham from 1975 to 1978.

26

Concerts in Birmingham for the majority of the city's listeners tended to mean one thing: the weekly orchestral concert given by the City of Birmingham Symphony Orchestra (CBSO) in the Town Hall. At this time, the orchestra was led by Felix Kok and conducted by Louis Fremaux (in his navy-blue tails). Fremaux was versatile in his repertoire but particularly excelled in French music such as Bizet, Dukas, and Berlioz. I do not remember him programming any works by Henri Dutilleux, however, which seems a little strange.

Olivier Messiaen's junior by eight years, Dutilleux has always created a fantastically coloured, as well as delicate, orchestral palette. Aside from his native Frenchmen, Fremaux regularly gave premieres of new works commissioned by the Feeney Trust. Amongst those that I remember were pieces by Nicola LeFanu, John Casken, and Richard Rodney Bennett's *Violin Concerto*, written for Ralph Holmes. Also revived were John McCabe's *Notturni ed Alba* with soprano Jill Gomez, a firm favourite of mine still (the piece rather than the elegant lady, though she was a stunner). Doubtless, there were others, too; to those composers ejected from my memory, my apologies.

There were also moving and very strong interpretations of the two Elgar symphonies (this was several years before Anthony Payne's magnificent completion of Elgar's sketches for his *Third Symphony*) and spine-tingling accounts of works by Walton under the baton of Harold Gray, Fremaux's assistant conductor. Harold, although then elderly, had a wealth of experience, particularly with the works of Elgar, Sibelius, and Walton. Apparently, as a young man he had worked with Elgar himself on certain works of his; this included the great *First Symphony*, which Harold conducted to devastating effect in St Phillips' Cathedral at the graduation concert with the School of Music symphony orchestra in the summer term of 1977. I glanced around the audience at the end of the almost Beethovenian slow movement to find the majority of its members in tears. At the end of the symphony there was a palpable silence, then the audience erupted in a sense of release that mirrored the music. Afterwards, a happy but emotionally-drained Gray smiled and chuckled to various student members. "Ah, my dears – the old boy was with us tonight." As can so often happen, the relative youth and inexperience of the students proved absolutely no barrier to penetrating the emotional heart of this masterpiece. Rather the opposite, perhaps – they sensed that they were unfolding a musical discourse of huge emotional power and responded by playing their individual and collective hearts out, giving it their all. And who knows, perhaps Elgar's spirit was with them all on that summer evening, exhorting them to greater things? Suffice to say, the memory still remains clear (and indeed dear) thirty-three years later.

The only fly in the ointment was that being students we were invariably tired, if not downright knackered, so that even in spite of our best attempts to stay awake and with it, we often nodded off, suddenly coming to with small, forward pitching motions. I tried to hide this, but was often caught unaware; sitting in the cheap choir stalls, it was probably fairly obvious, especially as viewed from the stalls. There was also the possibility of falling forwards into the back of the double bass players, which might have created a not entirely wanted domino effect. Come to think of it, such an extra-musical and dramatic piece of theatre might well have enlivened certain arid stretches of some of those premieres...

Even with the student discount on the tickets, many of us could not afford to attend these CBSO concerts on a weekly basis; we had to be selective in relation to the works being programmed, the soloists playing, and the rarer chance to see a visiting foreign orchestra at work. One concert that fell into the latter category included a beautifully moulded account of Lutoslawski's *Livre pour orchestre* with the Polish Radio Orchestra conducted by Jan Krenz.

The CBSO at the Town Hall was not, of course, the only provider of quality concerts in the second city. There were stimulating events to be heard at the Midlands Arts Centre (MAC) over at Cannon Hill in Edgbaston, the Centre for the Arts at Gosta Green, Aston, and the scruffy, homemade but exciting ambience of the old Arts Lab in Tower Street. This latter establishment which was, in fact, thoroughly experimental and deliciously *anti*-establishment, resembled a building that was somewhere between a brightly coloured, anarchic primary school and a bombsite. Music concerts and workshops were organised by the improviser, tuba player, and composer Melvyn Poore. Audiences were invariably (and perhaps inevitably) small; often no more than seven to ten of us sat in those old cinema seats. But the artists and programmes were always thoughtful and provocative and included pieces by Cage, Cardew, and scenes from *Votre Faust* by the Belgian composer Henri Pousseur, amongst others. Music-theatre performances included *Tuba Mirum* and *Fidelio* by Trevor Wishart, in which Trevor himself was the protagonist surrounded in the latter piece by a tableaux of suitcases – all very Beckett-like.

At the Aston premises, I enjoyed improvisations by such international names as Tony Oxley and Howard Riley, turned pages for Roger Smalley in his two-piano recital with Steven Savage, including Roger's major 45-minute piece *Accord* (nerve-wracking for me as this consisted of fifty-three separate A3 pages), and witnessed the surreal spectacle of a concert which consisted of Baroque pieces played by a student chamber orchestra in the first half and a young and only recently graduated Victoria Wood performing her songs in the second. Not surprisingly, I preferred her fresh and witty songs to the tired regurgitations of staple Baroque repertoire such as the same old tedious and vapid Vivaldi crap.

Concerts at MAC? Well, I can only recall Jane Manning and Richard Rodney Bennett and an engrossing concert by the leading live-electronics ensemble Intermodulation performing pieces by Smalley, Tim Souster, and Stockhausen. Their performance on a snowy February night in 1976 was part of their final tour, so I was lucky to catch them on that one occasion. I also recollect that I had cut my finger whilst shaving and spent most of the concert trying to stem the flow of blood by an inadequate supply of tissues!

What about jazz? (I hear you cry.) There were some events held at the Midland Hotel in Colmore Row and featured music by pianists such as the already legendary Stan Tracey and Mike Westbrook. Stan's quirky, slightly off-centre and richly chordal approach always hits the spot for me. Yes, some of those runs that landed on a thumping chord were akin to a craftily delivered, unexpected punch – a punch that was not without a glint of Monk-like timing and humour.

Oh yes, I nearly forgot. In May 1977, I organised a charity performance of Erik Satie's *Vexations* – the funds raised were donated to the Musicians Benevolent Society. This was held at the Aston Centre for the Arts and involved a relay team of six pianists, including myself, to play the required 840 repetitions of Satie's very slow sequence of chords. These chords were notated rather eccentrically (enharmonically) and you could never get used to them visually, despite the number of repetitions. The whole event was a bizarre and exhausting experience – a kind of 'happening' almost, I suppose. I was very glad to have undergone the whole process (I use that word advisedly and deliberately…), but would not wish to repeat it. The duration is variable and our performance took twenty and three-quarter hours. We all eventually staggered out into the daylight at around 7am the next morning. The performance space had no windows, so if one didn't consult a watch, you quickly lost all track of time. Indeed, for such a mammoth task, it was preferable not to look at a watch too often.

Psychologically, the whole performance was interesting, if not to say rather mind-bending. I have never knowingly taken drugs, but the hypnotic repetitions of this odd but serene (yet slightly disturbing?) music made me feel that I had been on the equivalent of a musical trip. All of us took it in turns to play x amount of repetitions before having a break and/or a sleep. One odd effect of Satie's immobile and static music was that the first couple of hours seemed to tick by painfully slowly, minute by long minute. After this, however, most of us seemed to feel that, as in Indian music, the sense of time passing became very elastic, subjective, and trance-like. The downside to organising the whole thing was that I had to remain awake, or at least semi-conscious, for the entire duration in order to keep an eye and ear on all the play-throughs! To help alleviate any possible boredom, Rod Dunk thoughtfully brought in a barrel of beer, which some bastard thoughtfully decided to remove and presumably consume. We didn't locate the culprit, but I had a fairly good idea who was responsible… I think he played the bassoon.

Strangely enough, though the experience was hypnotic in the extreme, it was (eventually) far from boring or tedious. You felt a sense of becoming one with the sounds, indeed almost entering them – weird but fascinating. Radio 4's *Today* programme came and recorded part of it and it received attention in the local press. The money raised was not a huge amount, but people came and went as they wished and one man did stay for a few hours.

I arrived back at my bedsit practically in a state of hallucination (seeing small rodents running around the wainscoting), switched on the radio for a time-check, and found I was listening to myself playing Satie on the *Today* programme... just what I needed at that point! Then I fell into a long sleep. When I woke up, the rodents had gone. I washed, dressed, had some cursory breakfast, took the bus into town, walked into college, started to play the harpsichord, and within a few minutes fell asleep again. I came to with my head on my arms, primary-school style, on the music desk of the harpsichord.

27

I graduated from the Birmingham School of Music in July 1978 after enduring the usual raft of examinations – piano teaching diploma, keyboard skills, history, harmony and counterpoint (universally known as H&C), choral conducting, orchestration, etcetera. These tended to be punctuated by visits to the local Pizzaland at the top of New Street. (Readers of my generation will remember their logo of the little green man?) In those days New Street was not a traffic-free area; streams of cars and buses continually poured up and down in both directions, making it a highly toxic thoroughfare. Most of the cafes or restaurants that I used to inhabit were either on or just off New Street: the Pizzaland already mentioned; a chips-with-everything type cafe opposite, run by a Greek guy replete with moustache and navy-blue nylon jacket; and, when we could afford it, a Chinese situated up Needless Alley. Other eateries included the Shah Bagh on Bristol Street, a favourite late-night haunt for some of us where they served tasty but mouth-blistering curries for the braver or more masochistic palettes among us.

I had spent an amazing three years at music college and had been opened up to so many new experiences that I could not possibly have foreseen. These encompassed both the personal and the musical – in terms of strong friendships made (less often lost), as well as a multitude of fresh opportunities for composing, performing, and going to concerts and being blown sideways by the new and unfamiliar. I had accompanied (both piano and harpsichord) on countless occasions, organised concerts, and generally had a wonderful time. It was going to be a wrench to leave this heady, safe and, let's face it, fairly privileged environment. Thanks to the generosity of the appropriate financial bodies of Bristol, I had been able to study fulltime on what used to be termed a major grant. This must have been a huge blessing and relief to my mother who, always thoroughly supportive in my endeavours, could not possibly have afforded to pay for my studies.

The question then arose and fairly urgently: what was I going to do next? Various tutors recommended that I obtain the one-year teaching diploma – a useful qualification, even if I wasn't really going to ever use it. I might not set the musical world alight, but with that piece of paper, I was at least nominally qualified to inflict a variety of music on unsuspecting children. Again, Bristol Education Authority came up trumps with another major grant, and as it turned out, three of us from the Birmingham course secured places on the PGCertEd course at Reading University: Clare (the twin-setted headmistress-in-waiting), her friend Gillian from the Isle of Man, and myself. I procured a room to live in Wantage Hall, a redbrick college based on the Oxbridge model of colleges – complete with front quad, Junior and Senior Common rooms, and two or three porters (the nicest and most helpful of whom was Ted). If you had a problem, Ted with his wavy white hair and pipe, would try his utmost to help you. He invariably succeeded, by the way. Yes, we were all unanimously fond of Ted. This was in complete contrast to the weasel-faced Phil, who was mean, unhelpful, and resembled a slick-haired, ageing teddy-boy. Our music group consisted of about a dozen or so students and was based in the education part of the university on London Road which was reasonably near the centre of Reading, which apart from the Town Hall and its occasional concerts, was not by and large a town to set the pulses racing.

Two of the students had graduated from up the hill in Reading's small music faculty, which was presided over by the composer Peter Wishart. The other members of our group had survived and graduated from various institutions such as Royal Holloway, Leeds University, Newton Park College near Bath, Southampton, and Hull, amongst other places. The two main tutors who ran our course were Doctors Tony Kemp and Arnold Bentley (who happened to be an old friend of my geographer uncle Robert Brooker, who lived in Earley, not far from the main Whiteknights campus).

Aside from weekly classes in matters of musical education, both theoretical and practical, we were required to attend lectures and seminar sessions on the history and philosophy of education (perhaps that should be with an uppercase 'E'?) which, on the whole, were tedious and dispiriting. We also received visits from a roster of eminent music education lecturers and practitioners. The majority of these were stimulating and thought provoking however much you may not have been in agreement with the principal being expounded.

It fell (by a short straw) to me to organise the regular series of lunchtime concerts during the autumn and summer terms. There was the usual fare of solos, accompanied sonatas, and the inevitable, dreaded madrigal singing. (Hey, nonny, no, my arse; more likely, Hey, Nonny! NO!!) How can anyone actually derive pleasure from this dreadful, inane repertoire? One memorable recital (more of an event/happening, really) involved myself and viola player Pete Mazur filling an ample part of the performing space with black umbrellas and playing music by Satie and Morton Feldman and others. I think that it was intriguing, enjoyable, and managed to make the more antiquated-minded students among our number blush deeply – an aural equivalent of having one's knickers pulled down with no prior warning, I suppose... At least it wasn't the same old stale repertoire.

There were two downsides to the course. Firstly, if you were a keyboard player, like myself, you had to learn how to play a brass instrument or, at least, the rudiments of it. I selected a cornet and proceeded to conjure from the mouthpiece a series of irregular farting noises, not just for the first term, but more-or-less for the duration of the course. Sonorous and in tune it was not. We had weekly sessions with a glamorous divorcee, but even she failed to improve my embouchure. It was all very embarrassing to the extent that I used to end up practically in tears – more of mirth than frustration, it has to be said; but, on occasion, it could have gone either way.

Secondly, the middle term, the first months of 1979, were spent on teaching practice. I was sent to a senior school in Winnersh in Berkshire whose music teachers, Robin and Ian, were very supportive and – a bonus – the glamorous divorcee was a peripatetic brass teacher there. I suppose the whole experience was rather similar to Christians being thrown to the lions. I survived, but I did not particularly distinguish myself, although there were some glimmers of enthusiasm and teaching ability on my part during that spring term. As so often, it wasn't the music teaching itself *per se*, but the thornier issue of maintaining the requisite discipline in the classroom that was problematic. Suffice to say, I was quite glad when the Easter vacation arrived, after which we resumed our tutorials and seminars back within the more civilised confines of the Music Education department in London Road.

The end-of-year exams were mostly essays and a project which, in my case, explored the educational music of Peter Maxwell Davies, written when he was a young man at Cirencester Grammar School. I visited the school, met composer Elis Pehkonen, attended an evening concert at the school, and interviewed Rosemary Hammond, a delightful lady, then retired, who had been Max's assistant. She very kindly entrusted me with a large sheaf of press cuttings, reviews, and interviews dating from his tenure there from 1959–1962. Max's ideas and practical music making with the children included improvisation and frequent opportunities for the students to write and perform their own and each other's pieces. This was an innovative approach to teaching music at the time and he also introduced the pupils to early English Elizabethan composers such as William Byrd and John Bull, both choral works as well as his own arrangements of keyboard pieces.

We also had a *viva voce* with Tony Kemp and an external examiner that included playing our brass instruments. This was clearly going to challenge my cornet playing to the absolute hilt. Not only predicting, but positively knowing that this aspect of the interrogation would be fairly disastrous for me,

I prudently selected JS Bach's so-called 'Deathbed' chorale. I carefully rehearsed with Gary accompanying on the piano. It proved to be an apt and prophetic choice, as once again I gave a comedic rendition of what should be a haunting melody. The various noises that emerged consisted of fluffed notes strung together with strange, anal-sounding raspberries. It was so bad that I could only bluff my way out of the situation. At the not-a-moment-too-soon conclusion for all parties concerned, I looked into the bell of the cornet and said in a puzzled voice, "Well – that's one way of doing it…" I couldn't help but notice during my performance that Tony Kemp started to shake with silent laughter, turning a deep shade of puce, whilst the elderly external examiner's pallor remained unchanged and his countenance decidedly un-amused.

Despite my attempt to play the cornet like a toddler, I did pass the teaching diploma (PGCertEd). Yes – I had been certified by a large, faceless guy called Ed.

During that year most of my friendships revolved around younger students at Wantage Hall. Gary, organist and horn player, was there, and through the communal dinners I met Nick Drennan who was based in Bray near Maidenhead, the two Marks, and a varied assortment of weird and wonderful people such as Andy, a cybernetics student who preferred exiting his room from the window rather than by the door. This was slightly unnerving as his room was on the second floor. One morning after his birthday celebrations, we silently moved him in his bed and all the contents of his room into the quadrangle. Amazingly, he slept through all this like the proverbial log. On waking, he was in his room but of course minus its ceiling and outdoors. It was a good job that he liked fresh air.

The questions now facing all of us on the course were how

to get a teaching job, begin to earn a living, and keep out of trouble – not necessarily in that order. Posts and positions were advertised on the departmental noticeboard and we were expected to follow these up with various degrees of enthusiasm. ("On a scale of one to ten, how would you assess the possibility of attaining fulltime employment...?") Tony Kemp thought that one post might be suitable for me – a music teacher in the town of Bicester, twelve miles north of Oxford. For some reason I harboured misgivings about this, but felt that I should apply for the job having been funded for the previous year.

I went for the interview in my navy-blue suit (courtesy of Robin) and got turned on by the woman sat next to me on the train, who lifted her blouse to afford me a better glimpse of the generous cleavage thus displayed. Sadly, I had to change at Oxford and, luckily, my erection had gone down by the time I was ushered into the headmaster's study at Bicester School.

By then, I was probably not thinking at my clearest. He explained that they were looking for someone who would re-enthuse and rebuild the music department. This was my probationary year and I was none too sure about the prospect of achieving either of those aims. I learnt that I would be the sole music teacher with responsibility for all the class teaching, including O and A Levels, as well as directing the choir and orchestra.

All in all, it seemed a large undertaking. Both the headmaster and I had our doubts, I think, but... he needed a teacher and I needed a job, so we shook hands and both agreed to give it a go for one year. The school promised to sort out my accommodation and so, in my naivety, I thought that I was all fixed up and ready to go. The only small thing I was forgetting was my total lack of experience. That, coupled to an educational idealism based on my readings of Pestalozzi and the freedoms of AS Neill's pioneering Summerhill School in Suffolk, did not bode well for my ensuing career as a schoolteacher.

And so I became an innocent abroad in deepest Oxfordshire.

THE WAKE-UP
CALL OF THE REAL
WORLD

28

Yes, the school did sort out my accommodation – a mobile home on a small farm at the junction of Skimmingdish Lane to the north of Bicester. The married couple on the farm were nice and welcoming (pint of milk, butter, that sort of thing); their names have slipped my mind, but I remember noting that the wife had small, sharp looking teeth – and I'm not even a vampire – and they had three young daughters.

Bicester (pronounced 'bister') was (and still is, for that matter) a sleepy small town, whose best thing going for it was the parish church of St Edburg. It seemed to be the sort of place where, in Ronnie Scott's inimitable phrase, not only did the residents come out to watch the traffic lights change, but dead people were seen to be not only walking, but smoking as well. One of these lost souls was a depressive shopkeeper who ran a kind of bric-a-brac shop in Sheep Street. His name was Harold and he was something of a nostalgia freak. Whenever you entered his tiny emporium, you were greeted with the yesteryear sounds of Nelson Eddy and Jeanette MacDonald. Until this moment and the writing of that last sentence, I have not given Harold a thought for many years. He is probably pushing up the daisies now, sadly.

Perhaps, not unnaturally, I am heavily biased against the godforsaken place. I arrived at the end of August, met a few members of staff and went to inspect my music room and office (L42, up some stairs). Everything appeared to be in order except for my head, which even now, began to wonder what exactly I had taken on. Some of the staff weren't the most encouraging – "You've got a rebuilding job to do" was just one of the friendly and welcoming greetings. It was also one of those staff rooms where you dare not sit in the Deputy Headmaster's chair. The said Deputy Head swanned around in a grey suit, whose baggy trousers could have contained at least one more occupant. He sweated profusely (at least, he did whenever he saw me approaching…). He resembled an elephant (with all the folds), had a pompous manner and I think that he was also a Mason. All in all, not too promising.

Some of the other staff were not much better, but there were three really fine teachers, who were also good and decent people and stood out amongst all the prats. These rarities were Jim Honeybone (who still seemed to have copious energy at 4pm on a Friday), Andrew Carter, the Head of English and Jo Jannetto, Head of Languages. Jim is still a good friend all these years on and he was a great moral support to me during my time at the school. Andrew organised a memorable evening with the poet Michael Horowitz whom I accompanied on the piano. Michael read, sang, declaimed his quasi-Blakeian visions and emitted some celebratory squeaks on his kazoo. Then we retired to the local pub, where the landlord 'Choppy' Spencer (one-time local councillor and mayor) and his wife Denise looked after us in their usual expansive and generous fashion.

It dawned on me sooner than later that I was not really cut out for classroom teaching, when I found myself almost involuntarily looking out of the windows – probably for several minutes at a time. The kids must have thought that I had gone into a self-induced trance and they would have been not too far from the truth, for my enthusiasm knew no bounds; yes, literally – none at all.

The nadir of my classroom teaching experience was to come back to L42 and find some lad having a crafty cigarette behind the blackboard. A normal, responsible teacher would have been furious and acted accordingly. But I was trying to suppress my laughter, while part of me thought 'good on you, mate' and half-heartedly applauding his chutzpah; perhaps even wishing that he would, accidentally-on-purpose, burn the school to the ground, thus giving himself a head start as a potential pyromaniac? Perhaps he was trying, in his adolescent way, to tell me something? Many of the kids were very trying, truth to tell. If they weren't actively rude and/or hostile, the majority were quite, even exceptionally slow, even the group of CSE/O Level girls, who were more concerned about their make-up, burgeoning busts, nail varnish and their boyfriends' appendages than the rules of four-part harmony. And, in their position and from their point of view, who could blame them, I suppose?

I used to encourage a lot of instrumental improvisation in my classes and, therefore, my lessons tended not to be the quietest, politest or most controlled in the school curriculum. One day, during a particularly extrovert session, the Welsh maths teacher, Tudor Jones, opened the door, looked aghast, probably said something sarcastic and, giving me both a contemptuous and withering look into the bargain (my lucky day), slammed the door shut. I suspect that he then went and reported me without further ado to the Deputy Head.

I survived the first term, but returned in January 1980 still very tired. I had made the classic mistake of throwing myself into the job too hard and not apportioning my time and energies. Not only that, but my command of class discipline was far from commendable. I suppose that I didn't care a great deal, to be honest. Very soon, I was becoming depressed and ill and failing to turn up for work. I took to staying in bed, exhausted, until mid-morning or lunchtime and then roamed out into the town. I think that I got signed off for the remainder of the term by my doctor, but it is all very hazy and vague. If it is hazy and vague now, it seemed akin to a thick fog back then.

To what extent I was really ill I cannot recall, but one or two friends from Wantage Hall (Nick and Mark) who came down to see me, thought that I seemed pretty much 'out of it' in their phrase.

I am still in two minds as to how much of this was self-willed by me, to extricate myself from the situation (not unlike Anthony Burgess quitting his teaching post in Malaysia). In my defence, colleagues like Jim Honeybone did comment that I was definitely not myself. Who I did seem to be, they never said. Whatever the reasoning, I decided that I must quit the school for the sake of my health and sanity (and possibly theirs, come to that) and tendered my resignation on the only possible day, April 1st...

Looking back from my perspective thirty years on, part of the problem was, I think, that I really missed my friends from Reading University. We had a great bond and I felt desolate without their company. I was also probably a very young twenty-four-year-old who was not really prepared, especially mentally, for the hurly-burly of the adult working world; more specifically, the pressures of teaching in a comprehensive school. Needless to say, I left before I had completed my probationary year. After all, I had been cossetted in a luxurious swathe of academic cotton-wool for four years and the wake-up call of the real world came as something of a bombshell, not to say a rude awakening.

At least, I reflected ruefully, as I exited the gates of Bicester School for the last time, I had not had any actual furniture hurled at my head, except possibly metaphorically, by an incensed Deputy Head who didn't know what to do with me. I tended to agree with him, then totally ignore what he said, most of which seemed to be complete balls anyway. I didn't mind taking advice on educational matters, but I was damned if I was going to be told how to run a music department, inexperienced as I was, especially by a bunch of semi-literate, unmusical morons.

I stayed in the mobile home for another few weeks and eventually moved myself and my few belongings out in May. It was soon borne in on me that I was, and entirely of my own volition, now jobless and, more pressingly, homeless. Mum was sympathetic and said that I could always go back to Bristol. I was, of course, grateful but declined her offer. Somehow, I reasoned that this was my decision, my mess, and that I must stand by it and go it alone, however difficult the situation.

Where now, for God's sake? Well, I used to go into Oxford at least once a week on the bus and I knew a handful of people in that beautiful and gracious city. So, that seemed to be the obvious solution, then.

I moved to Oxford in the mid-May and, symbolically, grew a rather unkempt, Rasputin-like beard, probably in the hope that I would not be recognised by former teaching colleagues or pupils. My new life, however uncertain, was beginning and I breathed the air of a man who has been released from an onerous jail sentence which, in a way, I suppose I had, albeit only of six or seven months. Yet, without that odd and unwelcome experience, that *interregnum*, much of what happened to me subsequently, both personally as well as professionally, in Oxford would not have occurred. Only with hindsight and the passing of time, can we see the true, real picture gradually emerging; as slowly and as surely as those old Kodak instamatic prints.

29

One of the few things that sustained me during those six months was becoming a founder member of the Oxford-based contemporary music group, Soundpool. Together with fellow composers Richard Cooke, Helen Roe and Nigel Timms, I was a founder member of this ensemble. We met every Wednesday to discuss, improvise and play each others pieces. Occasionally, we might ask a player in to discuss his or her instrument, such as Andrew Claxton the tuba player, whose exposition was interrupted by a tramp who had wandered in and wanted a blow-go on the said instrument! Due to the monks at Blackfriars, we had a regular rehearsal space which was very welcome; not only that, but they provided it free of charge.

Richard, his then wife Jill, Helen and Nigel had all studied with the Australian composer David Lumsdaine at Durham University. Richard and Jill were earning a living from supply teaching (Richard had come to help me out at Bicester and we talked in our coffee breaks about forming a group), whilst Helen and Nigel were studying for their one-year PGCertEd diplomas up at Westminster College in South Hinksey and were not much enjoying the experience.

Apart from these meetings, which always ended up in a pub, usually the Eagle & Child, we had occasional socials and listening get-togethers in Richard and Jill's basement flat in Polstead Road, just off the Woodstock Road. It was here on those old, now obsolete, reel-to-reel tape recorders that I first heard a handful of David Lumsdaine's pieces which, such was their integrity, power and structure, completely knocked me sideways. After an epiphanic couple of hours listening intently to *Looking-Glass Music* for brass quintet and tape, the mighty fifty-seven minute *Aria*, plus *Salvation Creek with Eagle* for chamber orchestra, I emerged from Richard's flat dazed, dazzled and uplifted in equal measure, barely knowing what had happened to me. God, this music was so powerful!

All three pieces were very tautly organised; but beyond these formal parameters, they also had the confidence and vision to unfold themselves to the listener in a manner that suggested that they (and their composer) had all the time in the world. Their processes and internal workings proceeded logically, organically and unhurriedly. I had never encountered music of such individuality before. It was one of those very rare, but glorious and prolonged moments, when the passing of clock time is virtually stilled and your mind and ears attune (or retune) to an altogether different awareness. This also happened to me, when I first read TS Eliot's *Four Quartets* (Neil Champion, a fellow student at Reading University, alerted me to this masterpiece); that sense of becoming as one with something, his "you are the music while the music lasts". A transient yet transcendent experience that can alter your life; the memory of which remains with you and you carry its cathartic power with you through the years. It becomes etched in your heart and mind, can help to heal you in times of distress and becomes a kind of potent benediction or blessing. Yes, "the unattended moment, the moment in and out of time..."

Whilst trying to find a room in Oxford, I stayed for a couple of nights in a guesthouse on the Iffley Road. Soundpool had a concert up at Westminster College, where I directed a performance of my first String Quartet. This involved a lot of very slow music in which it was difficult to feel and maintain the pulse, hence the players' request for me to conduct it. Although in some ways, it was an inexperienced student piece, it did do its intended job vis-á-vis conveying a sense of almost mandalic stillness, occasionally broken by a more extrovert, dancing refrain. After the concert, Richard and Jill very kindly put me up for a few days in their spare room, a gesture for which I was (and still am) extremely grateful. Your mind is in such a whirl at these times, that I always felt that I had failed to thank them adequately enough. This, therefore, is a very belated signal of appreciation and thanks, thirty years too late, but sincerely felt and given, nonetheless.

OXFORD AS MAGNET

30

After what felt like a small eternity, I found a bedsit above Durhams' the greengrocer on Elms Parade, Botley. The landlord was a nice bachelor called Colin who was a paint-sprayer at the bus depot in Cowley; there was also a young couple who lived in the other bedsit. She was a bossy Northerner, who tended to take over the kitchen. Needless to say, we all shared the one bathroom – which had a green plastic frog peering out between the taps on the bath. But it was a start and at least I had a roof over my head.

Inevitably, with no job, I signed on and remained on the dole for four years – not the happiest of circumstances. I did pick up some piano teaching in Long Hanborough, however, as well as playing the piano at Brown's restaurant at lunchtimes a couple of times a week. The money was not great, but you were fed and watered, which was a welcome bonus (I remember large plates of spaghetti bolognaise). What the management wanted, of course, was background cocktail music, so I played pretty much everything from Satie to Dave Brubeck and Duke Ellington. I tried to provide as wide a range of music as possible. In retrospect, I think that I gave them more cock than tail, but there you go. My own fairly strong aversion to background music for dining probably dates from those years. Later on, I did similar gigs at the Randolph Hotel and a fairly upmarket country hotel-restaurant, The Springs, out at South Stoke, near Goring. Here, I played on Saturday nights and Sunday lunchtimes for three hours per session, with about half an hour for dinner. One of my dinner breaks was spent overhearing (I couldn't help it, they were so brazen) a table of half a dozen men and women animatedly discussing their next porn film – and in some detail. Fascinating, even illuminating, conversation, but it did not particularly serve to aid my digestion. Talking of which, I didn't stay to see what digestif was consumed after their dinner, but I somehow doubted that it was a glass of port that slipped down easily and tickled the tonsils... But I also played to celebrities, such as an appreciative Lulu.

I resided in Botley ('lived' would be too strong a word) for nearly two years, whereupon I moved nearer to the city and took an attic bedsit in Hill View Road. I still couldn't swim, play tennis or ride a bike – or drive, for that matter. I've never trusted Tampax ever since... The owners of the house and their toddlers were Polish and pleasant enough, but the wife had a short fuse and always seemed to be shouting at the children. Her husband was a rather taciturn, put-upon builder, whose back garden (more of a yard really) was littered with concrete mixers and resembled quite a respectable bombsite. I realised, with some irony, that I now really was a near-starving artist in his attic room.

Although not eating very well or healthily at this point, I still managed to find the money to buy myself small packets of cigars. I reasoned that I didn't drink much and that this was my small treat. It was all Anthony Burgess's fault. I had seen him being interviewed by Michael Parkinson about his then new book, *1985*. He had the bearing of a very well-informed Oxbridge tutor; a definite 'presence' who elegantly, almost lazily, puffed on a Schimmelpennick, whilst considering his replies. (I used to think that Schimmelpennick was a Jewish children's programme.) For some reason, probably only known to sad young men (a club of which I had become an involuntary member), I was mightily impressed with Burgess's larger-than-life persona; he was Mancunian-Irish, was as much a musician as a novelist and was, probably, the nearest twentieth century equivalent to George Bernard Shaw. Needless to say, I started to read many of his linguistically virtuosic books and aped his cigar-smoking habit. Pretentious, *moi*? How daft is that? I could have better spent my meagre money on decent food. Obvious now, but it never occurred to me then. Crazy boy!

In that year, Burgess should have, by rights, been awarded the Booker Prize for his massive, weighty and panoramic novel *Earthly Powers*. He was pipped to the post by William Golding's latest offering, *Rites of Passage*. On a whim, I wrote to Burgess at his Rue Grimaldi address in Monaco, to say how much I admired his whole *oeuvre* and, in passing, mentioned that I was a musician. Within a couple of weeks, and much to my surprise and delight, I received a very appreciative postcard from the man himself, informing me that my letter had, as he put it, "lifted a whole load of post-parturitive depression" – i.e. on the completion of the said *Earthly Powers*. He signed off, bless him, at the bottom, with the first bars of the opening melody of the first movement of Elgar's First Symphony, a link back to the Halle orchestra and the Manchester of his youth. It was a kind gesture from a busy writer and from one musician to another and meant much to me at a difficult time. I still have the postcard somewhere, probably up in the loft after all these years. Anthony Burgess also happened to provide a tenuous link between writing, music and journalism, as I was soon to find out, in one of those moments of so-called co-incidence that, of course, do not happen by accident.

Some months earlier, I had come into Oxford by bus from Bicester. The terminus was at Gloucester Green coach station, it was pouring wet and I immediately headed into the steamed-up cafe next to The Welsh Pony pub. The cafe was absolutely full, except for one vacant seat next to an elderly but rather distinguished-looking gentleman. He introduced himself as Frank Dibb, chief arts critic of the *Oxford Times* and proceeded to dive into a diatribe on the merits or otherwise of one of his colleagues on the paper, a New Zealander by the name of Leslie Thompson. This man was clearly a huge thorn (if not a thicket) in Frank's side and this impromptu meeting was to be the first of many occasions to which I had my ear bent over the next dozen or so years, with regard to the seemingly myriad iniquities of the said Thompson. Frank, although very cultured, was also a straight-talking Yorkshireman who had been an actor in his younger days with Sir Donald Wolfit. ("I, Sir, am a thespian, I'll have you know!") If Frank liked you, you were fine; if he didn't, you had better watch your back! Luckily, we hit it off from that very first meeting. He thought that I might have the makings of a good music critic, would have a word with his boss, but don't expect anything too soon, etcetera. And on that note we had another cup of tea, shook hands firmly and departed the cafe which, by now, seemed to be more akin to a very full sauna, it was so hard to see across the room.

Frank was true to his word (he was always a staunch and loyal friend) and he gave me my first review in March 1981. It was the guitarist John Williams giving a solo recital at the Oxford Union. A memorable writing debut, which was the start of a fourteen-year stint on the weekly-published *Oxford Times*. Where I lived in Hill View Road was ideally placed for walking around to deliver my copy by hand to the newspaper which, together with its sister publication, the daily *Oxford Mail*, was situated on the Osney Industrial estate, a mere five minute walk away.

The newspaper staff were a motley crew. Their captain was editor Anthony Price, known for his crime novels. His deputy was a languidly depressed jazz fan, Peter Sykes, who used to have a cigar perpetually hanging from his already-dejected lower lip. In common with many Oxford men, Price and Sykes had, in effect, forgotten to go away after 'going down', such is the allure of this city.

The sub-editors desk consisted of a bunch of hardened South African journalists, some of whom had previously worked on newspapers in Johannesburg. A tough lot, they looked as if they could easily have shot any number of black men, if not for sport, at least for (and before) breakfast. (*"Ach, man, he's oanly a bleck..."*) In that early, unenlightened time of the Eighties, this was still very much the era of Apartheid, with its segregated beaches on the east coast resorts such as Durban. As long as you didn't give these guys too much hassle or grief, copy-wise, they were civil enough, although I have yet to encounter an entrenched, but enthused, non-cynical newspaperman. Pigs, however, may one day fly...

And there was Anthony Price's nice, quietly-bemused secretary, Gillian, whose surprised expression might have suggested that, in late middle-age, she had been made pregnant once again. All these factions were well used to Frank's occasional rages (against deadlines, morons, his editor, the majority of humankind), but began to take a firmer line when he began lobbing typewriters across the open-plan office. I always had the feeling that he was never sufficiently valued, that the journalists were slightly suspicious of an ex-actor, who perhaps, viewed himself as a cut above the others – and Frank would, moreover, have been right in that assumption. In his wide-ranging knowledge of theatre and the arts in general, he left most, if not all, of us standing. Financially, however, he was always on his uppers and was exploited as cheap labour by the newspaper group who owned the *Oxford Times* – shame on them. Due to these circumstances, he rented a small room at the top of a house down the Abingdon Road.

These bits of journalism, although not paid well (a recurring *leitmotif?*), were a good writing discipline for me. (After all, if such a fine and towering novelist as Anthony Burgess could do what some would consider mere hack work, who was I to not try it, work at it and polish it?) Non-negotiable matters included those set-in-stone deadlines (Wednesday, 9am), and the necessity of having to keep strictly to the allotted wordage, as well as having to précis one's own comments. Paring down was the order of the day. However bad the performance under review, I always tried to be constructive and to point out a glimmer of talent, however faint. Usually I reviewed concerts only, but as the years went by, Frank trusted my judgement and sent me off to cover plays as well as art exhibitions. Happy evenings included seeing plays by Beckett, Pinter, John Osborne and a triple exhibition in the Museum of Modern Art (summer of ' 83), which featured small drawings and sketches by Klee, Miro and Braque. All proved to be an eye-opener. Less good evenings involved having to sit through various touring operas at the New Theatre and umpteenth revivals (resuscitations ?) of Shakespeare at the Playhouse. A nude production of Othello set in a brothel was certainly different, as well as being interpretively challenging... Occasionally, though, I predicted a dull or downright tedious evening, only to be subsequently surprised by productions or concerts that were fresh and delightfully presented. It was all grist to the mill and a useful learning curve for yours truly. Not only that but, hopefully, it honed any writing skills that I may possess (please do not feel obliged to respond to that statement).

Frank and I used to meet up regularly for a drink in the Randolph Hotel, a venue which was quiet and elegant, yet probably a bit beyond both our pockets. Looking back we must have appeared an odd couple, this distinguished but ageing and frayed-at-the-cuffs critic with his rucksack and walking stick;

beside him, a young and rather scruffy musician sporting an unkempt beard. Two men with about fifty years between them, yet who shared many artistic ideals in common. Frank could have been my grandfather – indeed, I would have been only too pleased if he had been able to assume that role. We passed the time joking, arranging who would review what concert, whilst over the lagers Frank would periodically return to his *bête noir*, Lesley Thompson, the New Zealander who was as red-faced as a lobster (even in winter) and had trouble stringing two coherent sentences together. Worse than this, however, in Frank's eyes, was the fact that he committed the cardinal sin of being a teetotaller – aagh!

The staff attended to us graciously and politely, particularly the two Irish girls and Roy, the much-loved doorman who had, over many years, worked his way up from boot-boy to braided commissionaire; he was an invaluable source of local information both within and outside of the hotel. Roy was probably the hotel's most loyal servant; he served with dignity and nothing was ever too much trouble. At this point during the early eighties, the Randolph had yet to achieve its national and international fame via the Inspector Morse series. Occasionally, its author Colin Dexter could be seen having a drink in the main bar. Frank and I tended to prefer the more relaxed ambience of the lounge with its duck-egg blue walls and matching furnishings. It provided an oasis of calm away from the throng of students, their assortment of bicycles and their braying dons. If we met mid-afternoon, we would virtually always frequent the tearooms in St Ebbe's, (I've forgotton its name) where the waitresses still wore a smart uniform of black and white, bustling and balancing plates on their forearms, between the ground floor and the basement in the hectic round of serving.

31

Musically, things were rather variable since I had moved to Oxford. As I was living in a bedsitter, I had no piano or harpsichord to practice on. At that time, you could rent practice rooms at both Russell Acott's in the High Street or Taphouses at the junction of Broad Street and I would sometimes avail myself of these facilities. To keep my hand in, as it were, I had had a couple of lessons with the harpsichordist and fortepianist Christopher Kite in London, but these were occasional one-offs rather than regular tutorials.

Luckily, I made friends with David Leigh, also a harpsichordist and fortepianist whose parents Laurie and Wolff ran an antique shop situated on the slow curve of the High Street, just before Queens' College, as you look down towards Magdalen. They specialised in long-case clocks and early keyboard instruments. Laurie had been an actress back in the 60s and had, for a time, worked as Bob Hope's PA in this country. Both she and Wolffie were of Russian-Jewish descent. She was chatty and voluble, whilst he was quieter, possessed a lovely smile and, with his tight crinkly hair and generally cheerful countenance, resembled the boxer Henry Cooper. He was also a fine craftsman, as was his son who restored many old instruments.

This would have been in October 1980. David was giving a harpsichord recital in the historic Holywell Music Room which I attended and they came to a similar event of mine in the same venue the following month. After this, I had a few lessons with him and this was the beginning of a firm friendship with all three of them, but particularly with David. Indeed, we subsequently played two or three recitals of music for two harpsichords together. I often used to pop into the shop for a chat and numerous mugs of tea or take the train to Charlbury and stay overnight with them. They were very kind and welcoming at an isolated period of my life and their hospitality has meant much over the years. Some of these visits would entail both David and myself listening to lots of records and CDs, invariably of pianists such as Horowitz. One such mammoth session was spent in comparing fifteen recordings of Schumann's *Carnival*. Very enjoyable and stimulating, but thoroughly exhausting, too! By mutual consent, we decided that Rachmaninoff's recording was the finest or, at least, the one most suited to our tastes. It is entirely due to David and our long discussions and listening sessions, that I owe my enthusiasm for the older, legendary pianists of the 'Golden Age' such as Rosenthal, Hoffman, Levinne *et al.* That in itself is worthy of thanks and praise.

Casting my mind back to my Holywell harpsichord recital that November, Fate was to play a hand – not immediately, but in its own sweet time and way, as Fate, the Gods (whatever you like to call it) tend to work things out in our lives. A friend and supporter of Soundpool, Mary, brought along another friend, also called Mary, who was her piano teacher in Cumnor, west Oxford. This second Mary's youngest son, Rhodri, was an apprentice with Robert Goble & Son, the leading harpsichord manufacturer. He had persuaded his mother to buy a single-manual instrument and now, aware that one played this differently from a piano, was looking for a teacher. Both Marys (this is getting biblical…) came backstage to see me after that recital and to offer congratulations (always better than condolences). The second Mary asked if I would consider giving her an occasional lesson in the vacations (she was director of music at St Edmund Campion school in Iffley and could not spare the time nor energy during term)? I replied in the affirmative and, after a couple of preliminary letters, I did.

And there began, unknowingly, slowly and unwittingly, in the summer of 1981, the seeding of a relationship that would, after a year-and-a-half, bloom into a twenty-seven year love affair between Mary Howell-Pryce and myself that would only be terminated by her death from cancer in February 2007, a brutal and sudden withering. It was through and with Mary that I was to discover the myriad beauties of mid and north Wales; its landscape and its language conjoined as two leaves on a single stem. But all this richness and sharing would come later in my life, not quite yet; and not for the first time, would I have to be patient awhile.

LOVE, WALES, HARPSICHORDS, ETCETERA

32

It was in March 1981 that I went to see Max Wall's one-man show at the Garrick Theatre – that beautiful and intimate venue almost opposite the National Gallery. I could rarely afford to visit London (had to miss Bill Evans' last appearance at Ronnie Scott's the previous year, indeed), let alone splash out on a London theatre; but I sensed that this would be something special. Not only that but Wall was now getting on in years and it might well be my last opportunity to see him live. So I went and, as a result, had one of the most memorable evenings that I have ever spent in a theatre.

I say one-man show but strictly speaking it was Max supported by the pianist William Blezzard (who had been Joyce Grenfell's accompanist) and Tony Parkinson on drums – a kind of three-ring circus, in the best meaning of that phrase. I am sure that they wouldn't mind me saying that, fine as they were, it was Wall himself whom the audience had come to see. And in common with so many practitioners of his era, the musicians' roles were partly to be the butt and object of some of Wall's gags. Needless to say, the ever-versatile Max not only performed his routines, both utilising those famous legs, but also sang to his own guitar accompaniment ("Alice, where art thou?"), played trumpet (the blues, if I remember correctly), and piano – not simultaneously and not necessarily in that order, to paraphrase Eric Morecombe. Well, he was a marvel, a revelation, and held a packed Garrick audience entranced and enthralled in the palm of his hand, so to speak, for just over two hours. Age had not withered him and he was majestic.

The whole thing was a slow-build, intimate conversation with the audience, which consisted of personal reflections-come-soliloquies, droll, self-deprecatory asides, and a lot of pacing up and down the apron of the stage. In lesser hands, voice and feet, the evening might have seemed self-indulgent, almost inconsequential. But not with this great vaudevillian, whose decades of treading the boards had honed his timing and facial gestures to perfection. Doubtless, he could have read a shopping list and made it into something special – nostalgic, wry and with a liberal dash of innuendo, relished via the twisting, gurning mouth and nose and those slightly mad eyes. All this topped off with a dishevelled pork-pie hat. Theatre critic Kenneth Tynan once memorably described Wall's face as "a condemned playground." The greying pallor and the bags under those eyes proclaimed that Max had certainly lived through some tough times, but his act contradicted this. He relished the old jokes, as knowingly awful as some of them were and delighted at the generous applause and those little sallies of laughter, without which any comedian feels that they have failed. He also offered us affectionate vignettes of some of his illustrious predecessors in the business such as Grock and Dan Leno.

One aspect of Wall's performance centred on relishing, teasing out, and mangling certain words. "My manicurist was sitting on her re-enforced stool. STOO… OOL!," whereupon his mouth would pucker up and distort itself into a gargoyle-like rictus of gross exaggeration. This repetition, highlighting, and savouring of syllables must have partly arisen from his solo performance of Beckett's *Krapp's Last Tape*. Here, Krapp relishes and rolls around his mouth certain words to the full – "spool", for example, becomes "spoo… ool". His anecdote about the manicurist continued inexorably: "I invited her out to dinner. She smiled a radiant smile, ladies and gentlemen, and I knew immediately that this dinner would not cost me very much." A short pause. "No teeth… " This last word was carefully, exaggeratedly enunciated – almost, but not quite, spat out – then the knowing, mock leer. Michael Billington of *The Guardian* (a veteran himself) commented that he would be able to tell his grandchildren that he had seen a genius at work. Max brought this into his act, adding almost wearily and mockingly that "of course, you've all come to see a genius," followed by a gloriously dismissive rolling of the eyes to the heavens accompanied by a grimace. Doubtless, Billington's grandchildren would have been more preoccupied with their computer games, remaining blissfully unaware of this very singular talent.

It was often hard to tell what had been rehearsed and what was adlibbed; indeed, the distinction became irrelevant and something of an absurdity in its own right. Whatever the conceit, the execution was flawless and immaculate. How many other performers (Spike Milligan excepted, perhaps) would have the sheer chutzpah to commence a gag downstage, saunter upstage, examine his trumpet as if he had all the time in the world, then deliver the punch line? That not only betokens a comedian in total command of his material, but one whose comedic instinct is well-nigh infallible. It also takes a lot of guts; in other words, it's flying by the seat of your pants.

On the evening that I was there, a door banged shut at the rear of the stalls. Max put a hand up to shade his eyes and peered into the gloom, no doubt being blinded by the glare of the spotlights. "He's gone to tell a friend to come in," he said after a moment. A little later, he gave a wheezy cough and a distinctly damp sniff. "Must get a room tonight" was his response, addressed to the wings. He then pocketed a none-too-clean handkerchief and flashed his dentures at us in that cod, half-menacing, B-movie manner that he had. A brief recollection of childhood surfaced.

"At the age of six, ladies and gentlemen, my parents left me an orphan." Murmurs and quiet 'aahs' of sympathy from the audience.

"Oh yes. What a card game that was..." A very brief pause. "What in God's name could a six-year-old do with an orphan...?" Wall gestured, opening out his hands in incredulity, rather than dismay.

After the interval, he donned his green waistcoat, black tails, black tights, scuffed boots, and matted wig for his Professor Wallofsky act – a Vladimir or Estragon-like refugee from *Waiting for Godot*, a figure whose limbs are perennially (and perplexingly) at war with one another. When he attempts to play Liszt's *Hungarian Rhapsody No 2*, he finds that his right arm has grown longer than his left, whilst the same shoulder is unnaturally angled. His upper torso now resembles a mid-period Picasso. He tries, in vain, to remedy this situation in a series of flexing jerks back and forth whilst stopping to crack an imaginary flea on his right shin. After a few futile attempts he gives up, tries to relax his arms by aping the gestures of a monkey and, crouching, lopes off-stage. This routine was a bathetic, but organic mime with its unexpected though logical outcome – namely, that the human has turned animal via those flaccid arms and has also signalled that he is ready to give up. In this role as grotesque, Max Wall then went slowly into his eccentric dance routine, prodded and prompted by Tony Parkinson's insistent drum rolls. Out went the head and neck in a chicken-craning parody, whilst Wall's posterior did the same in a surreal play of bodily elongation. He also made the point that whilst he could do all these balletic moves and most of Rudolf Nureyov's routines, the great Russian dancer could not perform any of *his*. ("This is all ballet, ladies and gentlemen, what I'm doing now, oh yes...") So saying, Wall did two or three twirls, attempting to go *sur le pointe* and finished by forlornly revolving his index finger round and round as if to say 'imagine the rest', implying that his legs were not what they once were.

At the end of this extraordinary evening, he received a terrifically affectionate standing ovation. I don't think it an exaggeration to say that there was a palpable feeling of energy and love in that auditorium radiating from the packed house to that lone figure in his tatty tails in the spotlight, humble but basking in the glow of that adulation – the shouts of approval, all those pairs of hands stinging from the enthusiasm of their applause. Then the inevitable downer for him, of course, as any performer knows. After the farewells and the handshakes, the lonely return to his flat and a sense of 'coming down', of real flatness, even desolation – the staring at the photos, that slowly burning cigarette in the ashtray, perhaps another drink, thinking of the reviews maybe, and then the thought of going through it all again tomorrow...

I came out of the Garrick that night in a small cloud of euphoria. I had been privileged to see a legend, a master at work. I caught the coach back to Oxford and walked home to my room in Botley. Amazingly, that magic stayed with me for several days – a distillation, benediction almost, of warm joy. No, they don't make them like that any more. A trite sentiment maybe? Yes, all right, but one that also happens to be true.

33

I continued to give Mary the occasional harpsichord lesson on Saturday mornings in the vacations. Her husband Glyn would thoughtfully drive down to Botley to pick me up and return me afterwards. At this point, I could not drive at all. I was a motoring, as well as a sexual, virgin, in fact. One would have been enough, but in combination... Increasingly, they would ask me to stay on for lunch, although I think that it was Glyn's suggestion initially. As we will see shortly, it was this, or at least in part, that led to Mary and myself becoming closer in our relationship.

As far as I can remember, the pieces that she studied with me ranged from movements from some of JS Bach's French Suites to older music by members of the Couperin dynasty, Frescobaldi, Froberger, and possibly some English virginalists too, such as John Bull and Thomas Tomkins. We both enjoyed the lessons and I noticed that she always dressed smartly (especially skirts and shoes), often in autumnal, rusty colours that echoed and complemented the auburn colour of her hair. After lunch, she would give a piano lesson to the other Mary – the one from Soundpool who had introduced us backstage after my Holywell recital. I was reviewing a regular number of concerts for *The Oxford Times* and, as is still the custom, there would be two tickets waiting for me at the box-office of the concert in question. Rather than going by myself, it was nice to have company, so I naturally and invariably asked Mary to come along. Increasingly, we would be thirsty afterwards and would repair to the Randolph Hotel for a drink or two and a chat. In this way, I got to gradually learn about her life, both as a musician and a mother.

One immediate feature that we had in common was that we were only children – no, neither of us was spoilt, although we were, on occasion, somewhat lonely. She was born in May 1929 on a farm in the sweeping hills of mid-Wales at Kerry, a few miles from Newtown in Montgomeryshire. From a fairly young age, Mary showed an aptitude for music, initially learning the violin then settling down to study the piano. As with all musically talented youngsters in Wales, she was entered annually for the local Eisteddfod and often shared first prize or won outright in her particular class. These annual festivals provided a useful and necessary platform for the budding performer and, in tandem with the raft of Associated Board of the Royal Schools of Music examinations (what a mouthful!), Mary steadily progressed through the eight grades. At the early age of sixteen, she was awarded a scholarship to attend the Royal Academy of Music in London where she studied piano and viola.

One might have thought that a girl raised in the rural farming community of mid-Wales would have, at the very least, been apprehensive and nervous about going to live in the very alien English capitol. Not a bit of it. This was in 1946 and London was strewn with derelict buildings and a massive amount of bomb damage courtesy of Hermann Goering's zealously efficient Luftwaffe. Mary lodged with a lady in Mill Hill whose mother had connections to the St Ives group of painters and who had funded Bernard Leach, enabling him to set up his first pottery. Marjorie Horne had piles of brownish-green Leach bowls stacked up on various surfaces, introduced Mary to various modern painters (in exhibitions, not personally), and they would often go together to concerts at the Wigmore Hall and the Albert Hall. In this way, she saw the legendary pianist Arturo Benedetti Michelangeli making his British debut, as well as attended a recital by Benno Moiseiwitsch who was a regular visitor to London. Marjorie also knew the South African composer Priaulx Rainier who divided her time between London and St Ives, taught at the Academy and, for her first year, gave Mary harmony lessons. Both Marjorie and Priaulx were strong swimmers. They got on well, but Mary reluctantly changed tutors as Priaulx was frequently away composing or on other business. It was Priaulx, however, who encouraged her to attend two concerts where all six Bartok string quartets were played (Bartok had died in America the previous year). Mary was in equal parts impressed and puzzled, as she told me all those years later in the turquoise lounge of the Randolph, particularly by the implicit violence of the string writing and the austere and uncompromising nature of Bartok's harmony. Both of these aspects would become increasingly apparent in Priaulx Rainier's own distinctive music, especially during her works of the early to mid-1960s (e.g. *Quanta* for oboe and string trio). Her compositions were, intrinsically, the aural equivalent of her great friend Barbara Hepworth's sculptures – two artists working away, both refining and in the process, *defining* their respective arts.

Distinguished contemporaries of Mary's at the Royal Academy included: the Welsh harpist Osian Ellis, who would later become a mainstay of Benjamin Britten's music; the violinist Nona Liddell, who would lead the London Sinfonietta with such authority and distinction; and the pianist Ronald Smith, who was an especially effective interpreter of Liszt and Alkan, that half-forgotten French maverick. Mary at an early stage of her student life remembered overhearing Smith practising the Liszt Sonata in the Duke's Hall and being mesmerised by the sounds that were issuing forth. In later life, Ronald Smith was noted not only for his dazzling playing, but also for wearing brightly-coloured jackets and trousers, as well as his enormously thick pebble glasses.

After graduating, Mary returned to live and teach in Newtown and taught at the Priory Girls School in Shrewsbury, going home by bus for the weekends. In the Easter of 1951, she and Glyn, childhood sweethearts, got married in the large and forbidding Baptist church in Newtown. They married earlier than intended, due to the fact that her father John was suffering from stomach cancer and would die in July (the same month as Schoenberg). It was also from this same disease that Mary herself would succumb forty-six years later.

After a period of working as a youth leader in Huddersfield, Glyn obtained a similar post in Oxford at the YMCA and he and Mary moved to Cumnor, a village situated high on the west side of Oxford, in 1956. By an odd quirk of fate, they were looking at houses in Cumnor during the first week of January, the fourth day of which I was born; none of the three parties concerned, of course, had any notion that these events would one day, many years in the future, become inextricably linked.

Their first son, Bryn, was born in 1952, then Sian and Rhodri a few years later. Mary's mother gave up the smallholding at Kerry and moved to Cumnor, where she found a new lease of life and many friends. She died from a stroke in October 1968 and regrettably I never met her, although to an extent, of course, her genes were perpetuated through her daughter and grandchildren. I did see on a couple of occasions some home movie footage which showed Mary's mother walking down Chawley Lane, turning round and stopping to wave at the camera. She looked jolly and full of old wisdoms.

All of these facts I gleaned from Mary over our post-concert chats. There was no doubt, I think, in either of our minds that we were growing closer and forming a bond which was not merely based on shared musical experiences, but on something deeper and much more mysterious – a slowly building, but inexorable force akin to love. That was perhaps the beginnings of attraction and its undeniable corollary – desire. And so our separate, yet increasingly linked lives moved on over the coming months and remained in this close equilibrium for the next year or so until it deepened in the only possible way – into a full-blown romance.

In 1982, I moved out of the bedsit on Elms Parade (had fallen behind with the rent, if truth be told) and moved my few possessions, via a taxi, into one of the two top-floor rooms at 23 Hill View Road, where I shared a small shower (although not at the same time) on the landing with a middle-aged man who had left his wife. We once went for a rather desultory drink together in the pub on the corner. Apart from this, I rarely saw him and after a short time he had left and was replaced by a young, punky girl who mostly wore black leather. She was nice, but alas I didn't share a shower with her either…

I was still signing on, but had my handful of piano pupils in Long Hanborough, plus one or two in Oxford itself; I was also still playing at Brown's Restaurant on the Woodstock Road, whose regulars included a lecturer that had suffered a nervous breakdown and a dodgy geezer-type who appreciated my playing and regularly bought me drinks. After some months, he explained that I wouldn't, in all likelihood, be seeing him again as he had to "go away" for a while. Whether it was abroad or for a long residency at one of Her Majesty's hotels, he did not explain. He warned me off certain types (such as himself), was quite paternal, and in his own way was, I think, "looking out" for me. He probably thought that I was rather naive and callow which, in all certainty, I was in those days.

Within a few weeks of having moved into Hill View Road, I met a vaguely familiar-looking figure who lived on the same street at number six. He had separated from his second wife Eirian, and was now living with a cheery younger woman Brenda, who worked for his publishers at Macmillan and commuted to Basingstoke every day. He was leisurely wheeling his bike and had a hat jammed down on the back of his head. Then it came to me. Of course! He was the poet and novelist John Wain of *Hurry On Down* fame, published before Kingsley Amis' more famous *Lucky Jim*. We exchanged a few words of introduction and general pleasantries. A day or two later, a note was put though the letterbox asking me to pop round for a cup of tea later that day, circa 4pm, should I be free. Well, I was and I did. Thus began a friendship that lasted for twelve years until John's unexpected death in May 1994 at the age of sixty-nine.

34

Seventeen years is quite a long time, but the memories remain sharply etched – Botley or Wolvercote in garden, pub, or sitting room. I think of John Wain (invariably hatted) sitting with a glass of wine or a cup of Lapsang Souchong to hand (depending on the time of day) and relishing in equal parts the beverage, the conversation, and the sunshine.

Oxford always had first claim on John's affection and was his creative and social centre of gravity for the great majority of his working life. The city proved magnetic in a number of ways; it was a lodestar for him, from his student days at St John's College as a contemporary and friend of Kingsley Amis, Philip Larkin and Richard Burton, through his tenure as Professor of Poetry (1973–1978), to his exploration of both Town and Gown. This can be seen in his huge Oxford trilogy *Where the Rivers Meet*, a project that encapsulated all the things that he wished to say and celebrate about the city.

Although prone to despondency like many writers and

artists, John Wain was essentially a celebrator of things, people, and places. His talk was stimulating, anecdotal, and usually full of enthusiasm, especially when the topic of conversation was that of his beloved literary triumvirate – Shakespeare, Johnson, and Hardy. John communicated his knowledge and love of these writers with great affection and a deep reverence for the individual concerned.

I remember, too, his discussion of authors as diverse in style and temperament as George Barker (John reciting with great tenderness the exquisite poem that begins "Turn on your side and bear the day to me..."), BS Johnson, Martin Amis, and Rayner Heppenstall. These observations would often be accompanied by a salty remark delivered *sotto voce*, with a sage-like nodding of the head together with down-turned lips. On the acerbic Welsh poet-priest RS Thomas, for example: "He would curl the ham sandwiches up at any vicar's tea-party..."

Many of these things were touched on over lunch, a socially favourite time of John's day, either in the pub at Wytham or at his local, The Plough at Wolvercote. An especially convivial lunch was held at home, cooked by his third wife Pat in honour of the poet John Heath-Stubbs, a blind yet gigantic presence who talked of the pianist Vladimir Horowitz with approval, his huge bulk like some mighty statue entrenched in a comfy chair. Above all, John had a real gift for friendship and I mightily valued his companionship for twelve years. It is hard to believe that the slightly stooped figure in the hat won't be emerging from his Wolvercote cottage door. For me, the best of him (his humanity) resides in the series of lovingly etched portraits that form the collection *Dear Shadows* (1986); all that was good and precious in the man is revealed there to a heightened degree.

My first meeting with John Wain was in the summer of 1982. We both met in Hill View Road, Botley and discovered that we lived only a matter of some fifty or so yards from each other. *Young Shoulders*, his novel dealing with adolescence and grief, had just been published and awarded the Whitbread Prize, whilst his radio play *Frank* was shortly to be broadcast. We quickly found that we shared places and enthusiasms in common – Reading University, the Lleyn Peninsula extending up to Caernarfon in north Wales, and jazz. John's knowledge and love of jazz tended to desert him, however, after the Mainstream style gave way to Be-bop. His contemporaries, Larkin and Amis, felt exactly the same way. Anything beyond circa 1942–45 was, in their opinion, simply unrecognisable as jazz and therefore beyond the pale.

I vividly remember persuading him to attend a concert given by the Stan Tracey Quartet at the Holywell Music Room; the pianist, bass player, and drummer he could cope with, but the performance by the Coltrane-influenced tenor saxophonist elicited the comment, "I'd pay him twenty-five quid to stay at home..." Needless to say, the performances were inspiring, but John somewhat sheepishly beat a retreat to the safety of The King's Arms and stayed there for the remainder of the concert. Our all-too-few listening sessions together, either in Brenda's house or my bedsit, tended to revolve around an older generation of pianists such as Jimmy Yancey or Art Tatum. He also introduced me to the trumpet playing of his old mate from the 1960s, the Paris-based Bill Coleman, duly celebrated in *Letters to Five Artists*.

A few memories, vignettes that have floated to the surface: John in open clogs and bright red socks in post-siesta mode, ambling around and rubbing sleep from his eyes, trying to locate a book of mine that he had mislaid whilst simultaneously making a pot of tea (freshly brewed, never a teabag). A lot of hand-flapping and 'noises off' from the next room: "Christ! Where IS the cockknocker... piggin' HELL...!" John's CBE lying, forlornly forgotten, in the fruit bowl amongst the grapefruits; meeting John and his sons unexpectedly in the tiny teashop in Aberdaron; recording with him in the Holywell Music Room for his affectionate radio portrait of Oxford, *Pride of Place*, produced by Jane Morgan and then, afterwards, ambling down the cobbled path into The Turf for lunch and a well-earned drink or three.

John Wain's final decade saw the Oxford trilogy *Where the Rivers Meet* written and published – a vast undertaking, especially given that he was suffering from health problems related to his worsening diabetic condition, namely a steady loss of sight. After Eirian's death, he married Pat and she was a great source of support to him both domestically and in terms of enabling him to complete this pet project, which had been germinating in his mind for some years.

Our last lunch together at The Plough saw him at his best – eloquent, witty, and relaxed (he seemed to be getting calmer). We examined his Public Lending Right return for the past financial year. It was healthy and he was pleased, quietly proud that people still valued his work and were still reading him. We talked, too, about his moving monologue on Samuel Johnson's last days in *Johnson is Leaving*, brought to life by the actor Bruce Purchase, another good friend of many years' standing. As it subsequently (and rather uncannily) proved, this was to be John's last piece of writing and is astonishingly appropriate – one Staffordshire author's commentary on the other. This play can now be seen to act as the perfect *coda* to John Wain's acclaimed biography of Johnson – an acute, perceptive, and empathetic homage to a revered master. Indeed, on his last morning, John had written an introduction to the play which articulates Johnson's state of mind during his final hours – a period of increased serenity and acceptance; a sober reflection, indeed, on what his life had been; a soliloquy of personal 'stocktaking'.

John's funeral service was held at the church of St Mary the Virgin on the High Street and the church was packed. I wrote and played a jazz ballad based on his beautiful love poem, *In the Beginning*. I also remember catching a glimpse of a disorientated Iris Murdoch, complete with shopping bag, wondering around the church. This must have been around the time of the onset of her Alzheimer's disease – presumably her husband John Bayley must have been there, too.

This is John's poem, *In the Beginning*:

Now, in our perfect hour,
while the green stem supports the weightless flower,
before the rains, before the blurring mist
disturb the globe of silence where we kissed,
let us be calm and tranquil in its power.

There may be love
as daily and enduring as a glove:
this may be granted when perfection fades,
but never the silken magic that pervades
this first fine tapestry our fingers wove.

Your beauty lifts my heart
to a dimension where time has no part.
It must come down, I know: we take our places
among the normal names and normal faces:
but not in these first hours, not from the start.

This equilibrium,
most rare and perilous balance, leaves me dumb
to say it all, to name the gems and metals
(flame of a butterfly before it settles)
before the troubles and the questionings come.

Before our ship is tested.
before we sail where seas are cold and crested,
for this one hour let lust be pure as laughter:
let your love breathe without before and after,
soft as the hollow where a bird has rested.

As an evocation of the first days, weeks, and months of new love, I find this an extremely affecting and indeed effective poem. Its potent simplicity says all that needs to be said on the matter. To me, it ranks alongside George Barker's already mentioned *Turn on your side and bear the day to me.* After the service, many of us repaired to Brasenose Collage for the reception-come-wake where, for the first and only time, I met John's revered friend and fellow poet, Peter Levi. We talked about the sadness of losing John but, being a Jesuit priest, Levi was quietly philosophical. I explained that I had only known John for a matter of a dozen years. "Well," he said thoughtfully, "perhaps it is the quality and depth of the friendship that matters most, rather than the number of years." Typical of the good and sensitive priest, his response was both wise and comforting.

Perhaps, John, if you are in such a position, you are looking down with affection on your triangle of geographical influences: Stoke-on-Trent, Oxford, and Rhosgadfan. As you would have said, raising your glass, "Let's be lucky!"

English literature and letters were indeed fortunate and lucky to have had such a skilled, wide-ranging, and devoted servant. After all, how many other authors have written an autobiography, a biography, criticism, novels, poetry and plays, particularly in the second half of the twentieth century? He was erudite but without pedantry, considerate but enthusiastic, across the whole swathe of literary endeavour. It would surely be apposite after these intervening years for some of the riches of his *oeuvre* to be made available again. Novels such as the famous *Hurry on Down*, *The Smaller Sky* and *A Winter in the Hills* would be a good place to start. In short, there is probably no author who was more worthy of the epithet 'man of letters' than John Wain. His no-nonsense, north Midlands down-to-earthness and scepticism was tempered by (and tended to mask) an often child-like sense of wonder and naïveté.

As *Dear Shadows* and *Pride of Place* revealed, he was endlessly fascinated by the qualities and foibles that made his fellow men and women tick. Indeed, in his foreword to *Dear Shadows*, John wrote of remembering and writing of old friends, many of whom had already died, by virtue of the fact that "it was always because that person had come and stood beside my chair and said 'Write about me'."

And that is exactly what I have tried to do, remembering and celebrating my one-time neighbour and friend, an old mate – no, more than that. John Wain was also, I suppose, a bit of a father figure, too.

35

By the end of 1982, Mary and I had grown closer still through the two-fold sharing of harpsichord lessons and going to concerts together.

A couple of weeks before Christmas, I conducted the premiere of my *O Magnum Mysterium*, written for the choir of the Oxford High School for Girls. They, plus three flautists and a suspended cymbal player, gave a committed performance, after which Mary and I went for a drink at the Cotswold Lodge Hotel. I think that must have been the occasion on which she came up to my room for a cup of tea and as she was leaving, walking down the short path, I spun her around and gave her a long kiss and wished her a Happy Christmas. She was wearing a cherry-red winter coat, buttoned at the neck. We arranged to meet up on the fifth of January, the day after my birthday. In the interim holiday, I asked her to phone me at my mother's flat in Bristol.

Traditionally, I always went home to spend Christmas, and usually my birthday with Mum. She had retired from work shortly after her sixtieth birthday in 1979 on health grounds and enjoyed the company. In her retirement she kept active, principally by being a member of the St Paul's Players in Southville and becoming a founding member of the Southville Townswomens Guild; both activities she not only enjoyed but positively relished and, over the years, made telling contributions in both spheres.

Christmas, New Year, and my twenty-seventh birthday came and went. Mary, true to her word, phoned me and I returned to my bedsit on the evening of 5th January 1983. I was really looking forward to seeing her again (I had really missed her) and felt that this rendezvous was going to be special in some way, and possibly the coming year, although in what sense I wasn't yet aware.

Come that evening, we fell into each other's arms and it wasn't long before we were making love, our first time. When I have, over the years, replayed that moment back in my mind,

I imagine that the single bed was in the middle of the room. But that is incorrect for the bed was, in fact, tucked into the corner by the desk. The tricks of memory! As one stood in the doorway, the room was laid out like this: on the immediate left an easy chair, then a wardrobe and unit containing shelves and cupboard; panning around, the bed was up against the wall, then the desk and chair in front of the window; continuing round, a washbasin with mirror above it, then a small chest of drawers; then you were back to the door again. Smallish, but quite cosy. In front of the unit on the floor was a small two-ring cooker on which I used to cook simple dishes such as spaghetti with onions, tuna, peppers, and tinned tomatoes.

On that first occasion, although we made love, I didn't, technically speaking, lose my virginity. It wasn't until, I think, the third time that I came. It was joyful, yet oddly marred by the fiery, stinging pain that accompanied the ejaculation. As we lay there afterwards, I reasoned to myself that surely it couldn't always be so painful? Of course, on subsequent occasions that pain was replaced by pure pleasure.

I was a skinny but no longer virginal twenty-seven-year-old; Mary was fifty-three. I could have metaphorically (or in actuality) punched the air for, at long last, I had reached this significant milestone. Moreover, I had had the instinct to wait until the right woman came along; not gone with just anyone for the mere experience, but waited until it really meant something special, which it now did. The age gap didn't worry us for we were very attuned, both mentally and physically, but it was of concern to some of our more closed-minded friends. As our relationship became known, we both lost people to whom our relationship was considered shocking, inappropriate, or both. We didn't so much lose them; rather, they tended to fade away. At least one of my colleagues (one of whom was on my PGCertEd course at

Reading University) informed me that I was making a complete fool of myself. One or two parents in Cumnor withdrew their precious children, doubtless from the suddenly pernicious and morally questionable influence of Mary's piano teaching on their young darlings. Clearly, it was deemed inappropriate to be (to put it crudely) riding a younger man's cock. How this might have altered Mary's ability to be her usual excellent self as a piano teacher (recognised throughout Oxford and its environs), however, continues to elude me all these years later.

And so, for the twenty-four years of our unmarried partnership, the fifth of January was always celebrated as our anniversary. That first lovemaking was certainly the finest birthday present that I could have ever wished for; it was a delightful surprise, and yet everything had seemed to be leading to this consummatory point. After this, quite naturally our relationship became much more intense and moved up a gear, if not two. We hungered for one another, managing to see each other on average two or three times a week and, for obvious reasons, always up in my bedsit. Quite often we would go out for dinner, usually Italian, either at a restaurant in South Parade, Summertown or as regulars at a nice informal pasta and pizza place above Boswell's where we got to know the owner Marco. There we could relax and unwind, and chat freely on neutral ground, for there was always the attendant danger of Mary's husband Glyn finding out about us. As the months passed, he did grow increasingly suspicious, especially as his wife absented herself on a regular basis. There was, even for a musician, only so many concerts that one could attend, after all...

Glyn was an excellent and enthused teacher of History at a secondary school in Blackbird Leys, traditionally a tough and tricky area of the city. He maintained good discipline and respect (something that I never managed in my short stint of class-teaching), was also active as a prominent member of the local branch of the NUT, and was a loyal member of the Masonic brotherhood. He always seemed to be out attending meetings connected with these bodies and, over the years, his drinking increased substantially until it could be said that he was an alcoholic. He was invariably smartly dressed (the first time that I met him, he was wearing a natty pale blue summer-weight linen suit) and resembled, facially, Jack Jones, the then leader of the TUC. The Achilles' heel, the one fly-in-the-ointment of our affair was, of course, the ever-present threat of being discovered. This was far worse for Mary than for me, for she had to creatively lie on an almost daily basis and live with the possible consequences. Probably the worst that might have happened to me was a bloodied nose and a couple of black eyes. But, as anyone newly in love will know, logic is inclined to be entirely absent (indeed, goes walkabout). This all seemed a small price to pay for that unsurpassable feeling which floods the brain with endorphins and happiness – namely, the gift of giving out love and of being loved in return.

The reality, the sensation of this is, I suppose, almost impossible and indescribable, though poets have tried to nail this with various degrees of success down the centuries. My way of putting it would be to say that it is akin to dwelling within the orbit of the beloved one's face. The eyes become a magnet and everything that one could ever need seems to reside there; one is pulled in, both compelled and propelled into that centre of their being. Sexually, too, the act of loving and eventual ejaculation is transcendent, both in terms of the passage of time passed (it virtually stands still and ceases to exist) and taking one, momentarily, into another sphere of experience. The whole, elongated sensation is possibly the nearest that any of us get to an out-of-body sense of transformation. And that is totally appropriate for something as shattering, as life-changingly powerful, as the depth of human love. This remarkable conjoining was what we had found. We had not consciously sought it, but it seemed in some inexplicable way to have sought us out and then taken up residence, bedded down, in both our hearts.

I have mentioned Glyn, but what of Mary's three children? What did they make of it all? No child, even grown into adulthood, can frankly appreciate the notion (yet alone the reality) of having their father replaced in their mother's affections by another man – especially a virtual 'toyboy' and twenty-seven years younger, to boot. If anything was to be remotely in my favour, I suppose that at least I was regarded as a musician. At this point, it was probably the one and only thing as far as they were concerned... Bryn, Sian and Rhodri were all proficient on cello, clarinet, and violin respectively. The fact that they would probably have wished to collectively impale me with their bows is no small wonder and, indeed, a great credit to them that they did not even try. Sian, always the pragmatist, merely commented that she thought that her Mum would end up going to bed with me sooner or later and seemed to be quietly cheering her on. The boys, quite understandably, were not best pleased and took some time to, not exactly come round to the idea, but at least to begrudgingly accept it and to acknowledge that it had happened. Mary and myself, however, saw our by now firm relationship as a mutual rescue – me from my quasi-lacklustre loneliness and she from her unsatisfactory marriage.

Spring turned into summer and Mary had commissioned me to write a cantata for her school choir and orchestra at St Edmond Campion School in Iffley, the funds for which were provided by the school's PTA. The pupils and staff members (who augmented the choir) under Mary's direction worked hard, seemed to enjoy my music, and the first performance was a triumph (it was also repeated in the autumn of the same year). The kids particularly relished the percussion parts, which included the eerie sound of rubbed wine glasses! I selected various texts by Welsh poets Alun Lewis and Vernon Watkins (a tribute to Mary), Shakespeare, Shelley, and Hopkins – all based on the notion of regeneration and the coming of spring. This seemed then (and does now) very apposite and personal, too, as I had undergone a kind of blossoming and metamorphosis myself through the growth of our love.

Term ended and we decided in a fairly impromptu manner to go on our first holiday together. We stayed a couple of nights in Herefordshire and then Mary would drive us on into mid-Wales, her *terra firma*, and then up and north-west onto the Lleyn peninsula, an area of great natural beauty (as I would shortly find out) which was then unknown to me. It was after this week's holiday that Mary thought it would be a good idea for me to learn to drive. At least that way, we would be able to share the driving! (I began lessons that October, generously paid for by Mary.) We drove off from Hill View Road in her red mini (registration number OOM 452R) and headed for the pretty black-and-white village of Pembridge, where we slowly bumped down a longish track and pulled up before a large-looking and quite imposing redbrick house, The Byletts. Two friendly ladies opened the door, were charm itself, and showed us to our flat which was full of low beams and a simple futon to sleep on. It seemed like heaven – our first ever holiday together! I think that it was on the first night that I had to comfort Mary in a thunderstorm. Ever since her days growing up in Kerry, she had seen how lightening could strike down the cows and had always remained frightened of it. We snuggled up and listened to God's percussion section working busily overhead.

It was a gloriously lazy and romantic couple of days, a virtual honeymoon in effect. Just before we went, one of the ladies took our photograph posed outside the door; Mary beamed in a red patterned skirt and navy-blue short-sleeved blouse with me looking almost anorexic in beige slacks and plimsolls beside her, our arms around one another. That was the first photo of us both taken together, and in its own small way seemed to mark yet another watershed.

We leisurely drove on, crossing the border into Wales, along the incessantly winding roads and the oh-so-green hills of mid-Wales until the landscape became gradually harsher, more severe and granitic, sparer – just like the Welsh language itself, really. Aside from *Croeso* (welcome), the first Welsh word that the English are likely to notice is literally laid out in front of them on the road itself – *Araf* – meaning slow. Very useful – no, crucial – around those very tight bends; after a few miles of which the weary English are probably thinking, in their usual superior way, that the Welsh have done this deliberately to tire those English bastards – yeah, too right, bloody *seisnig*... Easy, isn't it? No problem at all. *Dim problem yr cwbl*, in fact. There you are, a handful of Welsh words already and it wasn't even painful, was it? (What ignorant linguistic pillock amongst you said yes? It's the laverbread and Welsh TV for you, mate...)

From the market town Llanlidloes by the River Severn (above its hills Bryn would later buy a cottage), we took the scenic route on the mountain road via Staylittle and Dylife until we lazily wound down to the town of Machynlleth. Twenty-eight years later, as I am writing this, I can still remember that incredible stillness on the mountain road at Dylife where we had a picnic in one of the many prehistoric folds of the hills and where, afterwards, we probably made love in that deserted, still primeval landscape. It was an intensely hot day and the only sound was of the occasional tiny insect chirruping in the long grasses. Chronological, clock time practically ceased to exist. It was a prolonged, very special, and moving epiphany in a very special place – indeed, a place for which I hold an especial fondness and reverence.

The rather alternative town of Machynlleth shook us back into awareness and the present tense as we strolled around taking in the cafe, the bookshop, and assorted craft shops. On the road out of the town, we noticed one of those milk bars from the 60s and 70s and it was still doing a good trade, positively flourishing. Continuing up the A487, past Corris and then on the A470 to Trawsfynydd where, years earlier, there had been several protests about the building of the nuclear plant, but to no avail. Past the lake and then a fairly sharp westward turn and over the causeway at Portmadog, continuing along the A497 until Criccieth, immortalised in that Robert Graves poem about the creatures coming forth out of the caves at low-tide. All that we saw, however, was the nationalistic bookshop, quite rightly proclaiming Wales' independent and very rich literary inheritance; there were also some books in Gaelic and a few IRA flags and banners. I loved it and lapped up all this Welshness as, of course, experienced, shared and explained by Mary. We travelled on along the coast road through Pwllheli, then inland through Botwnnog and Sarn, until we turned off the road and found the track up to the cottage at Brynhunog Bach, run by a tiny but energetic old lady. The first time that we drove to Aberdaron and came down over the brow of the hill and saw the little bridge, it was like arriving in a Cornish coastal village. In fact, with the wide-open vistas of sea and sky creating a brilliant whiteness and purity in the air, the Cornish allusions á *la* St Ives were complete and the place felt familiar.

Wafting through the car windows came the cool, summery coconut fragrance of gorse bushes, sweet and refreshing.

The most creative figure living in retirement within virtually a stone's throw of Aberdaron was the fiercely nationalistic poet and priest, RS Thomas. Thomas, as far as I knew, never did throw stones, but if he had they would have been undoubtedly (and very surely) aimed at the heads and bodies of English tourists who annually snarled up the local roads and, worse, local beaches every summer with their cars and loud Midlands accents. He had a point and although very forthright and vocal about this issue, he was, as he saw it, speaking for and protecting the interests of the local Welsh-speaking villagers. He was exceedingly loyal in this respect as he was, pastorally, to his parishioners.

A couple of evenings later we were having a meal in the local pub at Sarn and were ordering drinks at the counter in Welsh (well, Mary was) and from behind us came the shout of my name, as of surprise, from a familiar voice. It was Ann, my piano teacher from Clifton, with Philip her husband broadly grinning. They had their friend Graham in tow, bringing up the rear. We all had a convivial drink together and then followed their car back to their camp site, to which they had been coming most years, unknown to me, since I was a child. Their own two sons, Paul and Sebastien, would have been small boys at the time. I wanted to take a photo of everyone, but Ann who is rather camera-shy and loathes photos being taken of herself, rushed inside the tent and refused to appear until the offending article (the camera) had been returned to its case.

From their tent, there was a panoramic view along the long stretch of bay, Porth Neigwl, otherwise known as Hell's Mouth. Their tent was pitched at Y Rhiw, almost dangerously close to where RS Thomas lived, as I later discovered. It has always struck me as a wonderful irony that this somewhat grumpy vicar retired to live in the vicinity of Hell's Mouth, where he daily wrestled with his God and his poetry. Doubtless, some locals thought the co-incidence only too appropriate!

Altogether, we had a wonderful time and we felt quite desolate when we arrived back in Oxford and came down to earth with a bump. But as we then knew, this was only the beginning of a long journey together. Within a week or two of returning from Lleyn, I started to write a series of short poems which, originally, were going to be *englynion*, the strict and complex Welsh short verse form (or forms). As in other areas, a little knowledge can invariably be a dangerous thing, so I opted instead to make these poems into quasi-Japanese *haiku*. I hope that I was able to capture something of the sheer delicacy and compact precision of that tradition. More than anything, though, they are intended as a celebration or diary/reminder of those halcyon days, dwelling in a near-magical kingdom. They were published in pamphlet form in 1986 by my friend Mark Heffernen, a John Dee scholar.

Poems for Lleyn

Prologue: Invocation
Valley, beach, fern and mountain:
All humbled by birthplace and mystery.

The Mountain Road to Machynlleth
We stopped, held breath and listened:
A faulted valley lay beneath our gaze.

Brynhunog Bach
Within sight of it: Carn Fadrun,
Primal axis to our sleepy place.

Aberdaron
The plain church sloped down to the blanched beach.
You, gently perched on pink boulders.

Porth Ceiriad
Above all, those spear-tipped ferns.
Both thought of Bryan;
Lay back on wet stalks.

Epilogue: Note to Lleyn
Wild, mist-shifting peninsula:
We can never quite know ourselves,
But your majesty and grandeur has meant much;
A tender, yet sturdy revelation.
Gwyn Thomas was perfectly right:
Your Celtic lights holds us, timeless
In its grasp, enthralled by whiteness.
Draped on our bodies, a cloak of
Ancient, runic wisdom. A sweep
Of hills, valleys and rocks, flung
Mightily down: that tempestuous dawn
When ice and fire flamed the world's floor.
But soon, so soon, the waters flowed,
To cool the very depths of ravaged Earth.

Re-reading those poems again, I'm not particularly convinced by their efficiency or even skill as poetry, but they do their job, I suppose, in a kind of basic picture-postcard kind of way. Gwyn Thomas, incidentally, was a fine Welsh poet. In one of his poems, he talked about light being "full of quietness" and a road that "wound along the face of the world".

You might by now (and quite reasonably) be asking, what

drew me to this remote corner of north-west Wales in the first place? Well, the answer, simply, was one man: the novelist, poet and film-maker BS Johnson (1933–1973) whose last film was made for HTV Wales on the small and isolated beach at Porth Ceiriad, only a matter of weeks before he committed suicide back home in London. This is the 'Bryan' referred to in my poem *Porth Ceriad*. Johnson himself wrote a much finer one reflecting on the same beach, simply entitled *Porth Ceiriad Bay*.

Together, Mary and I climbed down from the small farm car park and descended to this remote beach with its imposing red, stratified cliffs. The scene was beautiful by any standards, but made all the more potent by its association with this writer who had been a seething mass of unresolved contradictions; a Londoner, born and bred, who lived all his life in that city, yet who felt almost inexplicably drawn to this region of Wales, felt akin to its landscape, its sheer ancientness and otherness, and its Celtic sense of mystery. And when you visit this area, that sense of mystery is compelling, undefinable, but most definitely and resolutely *there*.

PS: There is a coda to all this. Twenty-seven years on from that first visit, Carol and I were staying for a few days near Garnfadryn over the Easter vacation in 2010. We decided that it would be appropriate, in all senses, to visit Porth Ceiriad beach again. It was, I suppose, a kind of very personal pilgrimage for myself and a fresh, new perspective for Carol, for whom this region of Wales was totally new. We climbed down to the beach and just lay there for the best part of two hours, soaking up the sunshine, the quietness and the deserted beauty of the place. An occasional dog-walker would pass by at some distance, the dog stopping to sniff at pieces of driftwood before making a quick dash into the sea and, as quickly, coming out to vigorously shake themselves over their owners. Apart from that, there was barely a soul to be seen.

We admired the ancient, stratified cliffs, I thought of Bryan and then we slowly made our way back up the long winding path to the car, shook the sand from our shoes and drove away. We departed from this special place with an almost holy sense of *déjà vu*.

Mary, Aberdaron beach, August 1983.

36

BS Johnson, or Bryan Stanley Johnson to give him his full name (or moniker, as Cockneys would say), was something special and out of the ordinary in English literature during the 1960s and early 1970s. All too often sneeringly chided and derided as an 'experimental' writer, Johnson was certainly influenced by such figures as Laurence Sterne and James Joyce, but always ruefully refuted this allegation by insisting that his work was not experimental, merely idiosyncratic in terms of both literary and visual devices. The form of his books, he insisted, must follow their intended function. He certainly savoured and had probably learnt from some of the French novelists of the *nouveau roman*, but Johnson was invariably his own man. He forged his own path and identity and this, coupled to his rumbustious behaviour towards editors and publishing houses, ensured that BS Johnson was not, by any means, the literary flavour of the month; nor, come to think of it, even the year. Feted by authors from Samuel Beckett and Anthony Burgess to Margaret Drabble and Alan Sillitoe, Johnson's writing essentially occupied a thirteen-year slot. His output was varied (he did not repeat himself; in that respect, not unlike Bruce Chatwin) and each of the seven novels, two slim volumes of poetry, plus film and play scripts displayed what might be interpreted as a slightly schizophrenic balancing (or veering between) down-to-earth, dig-in-the-ribs humour and outright, barely disguised despair.

This sense of despair is probably at its most naked and acute in *Trawl*. Every word that he ever wrote was refracted back through the wide-angle lens of his own melancholic autobiography: his miserable period of boyhood evacuation, the later and seemingly innumerable betrayals by various women (only his darling wife Virginia was, as far as I am aware, exempt from this) and the publishing establishment in this country. This latter group Johnson regarded as ignorant, lazy (both in terms of production, as well as intellectually) and marooned in the literary devices of the nineteenth century. To some extent, he was perfectly justified in these views. Other writers were often included in this category and were, likewise, scolded and lambasted. My own awareness of his *oeuvre* began with a regional screening of his last and highly personal television documentary, *Fat Man on a Beach*. Directed by Michael Bakewell, this forty-minute programme is, in effect, a series of reflections or soliloquies addressed to camera. Whilst roving around portions of the beach (amusingly echoed by fluid camera work), Johnson shares his thoughts, reads poems, sets off a few low-key fireworks and cracks some knowingly lame jokes. The whole thing, though scripted, has the relaxed feel of an old mate chatting to you, sharing his thoughts and, at the end of the day, having a bit of a laugh into the bargain. *At the end of the day.* So ironic that phrase isn't it? Particularly potent with respect to this author, too. Yes, at the end of the day... at the end of his day, indeed... until this metamorphosed into the end of his tether in mid-November 1973. This screening was broadcast exactly one year later. I watched it almost by accident and as Jonathan Coe (Johnson's excellent biographer) found, responded to the quirkiness of it, but more so still to the hypnotic monologue which seemed both laidback, jovial and yet somehow rather rueful, sad and vulnerable all at the same time.

What was it about this man that drew one's attention, drew you in to share his thoughts? What was certainly and abundantly clear, above all else, was his undisguised passion for this part of Wales. Three years earlier, BS Johnson had been appointed the first Gregynog Arts Fellow in the University of Wales, where he was required to be in residence for a portion of each year. This was pure pleasure and far from being a penance for Bryan, who loved the area (not far from Newtown and Kerry, where Mary was born). Here he was free to write, give readings and generally be around to encourage and stimulate the students. He also fished and felt able to relax and recharge his creative batteries, too.

The next day I hurried down to the Central Library in Bristol to borrow any books that I could find by this man. Already, certain of his novels had seemingly fallen victim to that anonymous breed, long-term borrowers – i.e. thieves. But there under the J's was his last, posthumously published novel, *See the Old Lady Decently.* Something about the cover photograph of the author and the injunction on the back cover, as well as the black and white on the pink background (like a thriller!) served to welcome the reader in – well, this reader, at least. If I recall correctly, there weren't too many date-stamp entries and, best of all, it hadn't been stolen. Again, in common with the documentary, the structure of *See the Old Lady Decently* appeared, initially, to be highly random. As Michael Bakewell explained in his Introduction, however, this was far from being the case. In fact, Johnson had, as always, given very careful thought to every element of this book – from diary entries, letters from his maternal grandfather to fictional episodes and thoughts on the Mother Goddess. The net result? A novel that was amusing, moving and thoroughly idiosyncratic in a highly effective treatment of form and content, the one satisfactorily echoing and shaping the other. It also had the feel of turning the pages of a family scrapbook. This volume was to have been the first in a trilogy whose full title (running across all three spines) would have read *See the Old Lady Decently Buried Although Amongst Those Left Are You.*

Ever since that screening, I have retained a devotion to the writings of Bryan Johnson. In 1982, I contacted Melvyn Bragg about the possibility of doing a South Bank Show programme devoted to Johnson. I went up to the headquarters of London Weekend Television for an interview with Bragg and he commissioned me to write an outline synopsis. Unfortunately, due to my proposal to film on location (Lleyn, in fact), the whole project was deemed too expensive for a dead author. After all, the South Bank Show was devoted to living artists. I then wrote to the writer and broadcaster Frank Delaney with a view to writing a programme for radio. He replied with enthusiasm and one or two suggestions; but, as is so often the case, these fell on stony ground and failed to bear fruit. In researching this potential project, however, I did meet and interview BS Johnson's widow Virginia, his agent Diana Tyler and corresponded with Michael Bakewell. All three gave willingly of their time and reminiscences.

Twenty-two years later, in 2004, I gave a paper on *See the Old Lady Decently* at the first international conference on Johnson in London. This was subsequently published in *Re-reading BS Johnson*, ed. Tew & White (Palgrave Macmillan, 2007). In the autumn of 2009, I gave another paper at the second international conference also held in London, but this time at the British Library. My subject on this occasion was humour in his novels. 2013 will mark what would have been his eightieth birthday – so, watch this space, as they say. His flame is still being kept alight... If you are new to BS Johnson, by the way, a good place to start would be his deadpan penultimate novel, *Christie Malry's Own Double-Entry*. It is short, brutal and mercilessly funny. If one reads the novels again (not so easy with the first and last being out of print) and, more pertinently, the two collections of poems, you can assemble a not inaccurate picture, I think, of BS Johnson's descent into a veritable black hole from which there could be no escape. The signs are already there in such poems as *The Short Fear* and *Distance Piece* where, in the former, the author fears that it has all been said; in the latter, that he would, in effect, try to go on living – Johnson's use of the word 'resolve' seems to be loaded with implication and resonance, here.

The Lleyn peninsula acted as a significant geographical context and crucible for Johnson. He had first come to the area (hitching lifts by lorry) to seek casual summer labour before going to visit Dublin in the late 1950s. These experiences form the backbone of his first novel *Travelling People* (1963). In what could be viewed as a piece of almost eerily neat symmetry, Lleyn in general and Porth Ceiriad Bay in particular is the focus, the prism through which the author's experiences are reflected in his last piece of work, *Fat Man on a Beach*. I am sure that he was only too aware of this macrocosm himself, possibly superstitiously so. That this documentary, in retrospect, was a summing up of BS Johnson's life was, I believe, no accident. Earlier that same summer, his collection of short prose was published. Prophetically, in the circumstances, it was entitled *Aren't You Rather Young to be Writing Your Memoirs?* More worryingly, the publisher's blurb on the inside front cover referred to the fact that "...he has collected here all his shorter prose *which he wishes to keep in print*" (my italics). This sentence has a final and posthumous ring to it, or so it seems to me.

In the first couple of weeks of November 1973, Johnson was clearly of the opinion that he had run dry, come to the end of himself. For such a purely, almost solely autobiographical and egotistical writer (I do not necessarily use that word in a pejorative sense), he would have feared that he had said it all; that there was nothing of himself remaining, *ergo* no material with which to furnish the remaining two volumes of the projected trilogy. Bizarre, yet strangely, hauntingly logical – honest, too. BS Johnson was always honest and laceratingly candid in his writing. That *lacuna,* that immeasurable, unmeasurable black hole was over and within his head, waiting to pull him in, in that final, massive and irrevocable gesture; that final and largest of betrayals.

The Dark Hour

to Diana Tyler with many thanks
In memoriam B.S. Johnson

Had it all been said?

That new beginning
Unobtainable?

No greater truth
Reached you that day:

Your uncertainty
Broke loose the dark hour.

Stilled by that gentler hand,

Bryan be calm, now.

I wrote that towards the end of 1982, or early 1983. It doesn't really matter does it? Whenever and whatever, it remains a heartfelt homage to a writer who has always been and continues to be on my wavelength.

37

In the early summer of 1984, Mary decided that she had had enough of her domestic situation in Cumnor, at least temporarily. She decamped to a room in Headington, sharing the house with an elderly widower called Harry Badger who, ironically, like Glyn was an organ-playing Mason. He was a nice, slightly wizened man in his mid-eighties whose larder was full of evil-looking bottled fruit, which Mary prudently avoided in spite of frequent offers. From a distance, these bottles resembled those gruesome, pickled specimens found in science labs or museums. It had to be said that Harry himself seemed to suffer no ill-effects after ingesting these peculiar-looking items that no longer bore any resemblance to their original shape or, presumably, taste.

This was an immensely tense, stressful, and uncertain time for Mary and this manifested itself in severe palpitations which continued unremittingly for several days. Through all this, typically, she kept resolutely on, continued teaching both at St Augustine's school as well as her private and numerous piano pupils. It must have been a huge strain for her, which was (and could only ever be) partially relieved when we met up in the evenings either in my room, her room in Harry's house, or eating out. I felt both inadequate and impotent in my ability to really help her in this situation.

It was a weird, surreal summer. Mary and I decided to earn some extra cash by playing the organ in the two chapels of the Oxford Crematorium. Inevitably, these services took place on a conveyor-belt like system, albeit with as much dignity as is possible under the (not very propitious) circumstances. There were the usual electric organs, upon which we took it in turns to play the usual hymns. Occasionally, the resident minister would require us to press a button, thus drawing together the curtains and, often distressingly to the relatives, obscuring the loved one's coffin from view. This curtain-closing finale had the potential, in the wrong hands or fingers, to become something of a Morecombe and Wise routine. Fortunately, as far as memory serves, neither of us got it wrong. There was, however, no escaping those Masons for practically the entire crematorium was staffed by them, doubtless doing dodgy deals with equally dodgy undertakers, some of whom in their dark glasses and gloves looked highly sinister. One individual from this latter club was, indeed, prosecuted for falsifying ashes of various dearly departed, much to the understandable disgust and fury of their families.

After a few weeks of doing this, we had both had enough – more than enough, in fact. We decided that we were in need of some fresh sea air, preferably of the Welsh variety, and headed back to the calming balm of the Lleyn peninsula. This time we stayed in a bungalow whose owners were a farmer and his wife. The weather smiled on us once again and we spent a few lazy days in this beautiful scenery. We drove around, ate leisurely pub meals, and generally regrouped. I am sure that it was on this visit that we took the north, coastal road up to Caernarfon, stopping off at Nefyn and then Clynnog Fawr where we found the church open and the organ unlocked. This was too good to miss, so I drew some stops and started an improvisation. Within moments of doing this, we heard a huge rumbling that appeared to not issue forth from the organ. In true Hollywood 'B' movie style, there was a substantial earth-tremor in the vicinity just as I was unleashing a series of *fortissimo* chords on the organ. I assumed, not unnaturally, that it was the power and resonance of the pedals. Rather amused by the whole event, we made our way up to Caernarfon. It was only when we returned to our B&B at Bryncroes later in the day that we found out what had really happened. Our farmer had been sitting on his wall talking to a neighbour when the wall began to shake and wobble and he was thrown off. Lleyn does not, it has to be said, usually see this level of excitement, although the occasional tremor is not unknown in this area.

We returned to Oxford refreshed and more relaxed, I think, but of course as is the nature of these things, Mary's problems still remained. Part of her very much wanted to leave home and get a divorce, but any relationship is embedded with deep memories and shared experiences that are not so easy to merely wipe clean and start again; neither should they be. She was very much in two minds and being pulled this way and that, which did nothing for her stress levels. For a while it was a topsy-turvy world for both of us. I had also moved out of my bedsitter in Hill View Road by this point and found another one on the eastern side of the city in Rose Hill. Here, the owners of the house in Annesley Road were a pleasant couple, Maurice and Fiona who had a young toddler, Matthew, and a daughter, Emma, who would arrive in a couple of years hence.

That autumn (1984) I started a new job as a part-time Assistant Lecturer in Music at what was then Oxford Polytechnic, now Brookes University. I really thanked God for this as I could now come off the dole (after four years!) and get back a modicum of self-respect and esteem through employment in my chosen subject. I was still playing cocktail piano and also had a handful of pupils both privately and at St Augustine's, the Catholic school in Iffley, where Mary directed the music. (The staffroom there was one of the friendliest and most relaxed that I have ever come across.)

But back to Oxford Poly…

The post, although full-time, was split into two halves, 0.5

of a post each. This had become available, due to the previous occupant having been suspended for interfering with girl students – not just one, but several. Therefore, I and my other musical half, a bubbly Greek girl called Yva (who had been a lecturer at Hatfield Polytechnic) were, I think, especially welcomed by the students if not by all the staff, one of whom straight away took a dislike to Yva and seemed a little uncertain about me. Due to my predecessor's unenviable reputation, for the first few weeks some of my one-to-one piano students opted to take a chaperone with them into their lessons – and who could blame them? Gradually they relaxed and their chaperones disappeared. Apart from piano teaching, my other duties included giving a series of lectures on the history of keyboard instruments – harpsichord, piano and organ. This was my first lecturing experience and it was initially fairly nerve-wracking, but I eventually settled down and almost began to enjoy it. Wednesday afternoons were devoted to me leading and organising a module on Performance, directed towards enabling the students to be able to perform as effectively as possible in their annual end-of-year exams. I also had the responsibility for organising student lunchtime concerts, thus affording them playing opportunities. This was particularly valuable for the shyer students.

Whilst Yva had her office in one of the portacabins on the Gypsy Lane site, my office (my predecessor's, in fact) was out at the Wheatley campus, ensconced within the Business Studies faculty. Travel between the two sites was provided by free buses. This was a blessing, as I still didn't drive. I had a bike and used to cycle around town and up to the Poly. I was, however, having regular driving lessons with a terrific instructor and a real character, Bert French, who was based in Kidlington. Mary had started me off brilliantly, but she recognised that I needed some professional lessons. Bert proved to be ideal – we got on well and got a lot covered in our two-hour sessions (he refused to countenance hour lessons; his demeanour implied that those were for bloody sissies). He was also an HGV instructor and examiner and had been in the Army for years. This was reflected in a kindly, but nonetheless stentorian manner, accentuated by his ruddy cheeks. With such a man, one did not argue and get off lightly. I think that his ruddy cheeks were caused by blood pressure due to being cooped up for hours on end with erratic and neurotic pupils, rather than healthy living; he had quite a penchant for Yorkie bars, as I remember. I also remember with affection his admonitory but encouraging and oft-repeated shout of "Mirrors!" After I'm not quite sure how many lessons, Bert deemed me ready to take the test. Due to his expert tuition I passed first time. Only afterwards did he tell me that the man who examined me was the Chief Examiner. I was glad that I didn't know that fact beforehand! My first car was a slightly battered-at-the-seams beige Renault, whose front windows had the odd habit of slipping down in their frames. But it was sturdy enough and sufficed for a couple of years until I bought a bright green Mini whose windows stayed in place.

1985, in general, passed fairly smoothly and uneventfully except for two personal mishaps. The first occurred whilst we were flying to Venice during the Easter break. I hadn't, perhaps surprisingly, flown before and didn't quite know what to expect, yet wasn't nervous either. All went well until we began a rapid and steep descent from the French Alps down to sea level on the approach to Venice. Mary was pointing out the red, terracotta-coloured roofs, while I was struggling to refrain from shouting and swearing as my right ear was undergoing a steady but undeniable twenty-five minute *crescendo* of increasing pain. A stewardess was called, who was sympathetic but couldn't help; I tried sucking sweets, but to no avail. I realised that I would just have to suffer this, tough it out and emerge at the other end. We landed, disembarked and caught a vaporetto to near our hotel. Either later that day or at the earliest opportunity the next morning, we visited the hospital (not planned on our itinerary) and a doctor grimaced and shrugged in the usual Italian manner and informed me of what we suspected – that I had suffered, yes, a large perforation in the right eardrum. Also, the scars from numerous childhood ear infections had also blown. As a musician, I was slightly alarmed by this unexpected development. I was prescribed some powerful antibiotics which was good, but as a result I was unable to drink which was not good. So, there I was on my first trip to Italy not able to drink any red wine. What a bitch and a bastard! I could and did, however, smoke my small cigars which when I lit up, due to all the accumulated gunge being forcibly extracted from my ear, made me practically jump in the air every time I struck a match. It sounded like a small bomb going off. As had the pain in my ear, come to think of it.

We had, in spite of that, a lovely four days. We took in various churches, including the ornately gilded St Mark's which seemed doomy and oppressively dark, as well as short trips to Burano, Murano and Torcello. (I always think of Pinter's *Betrayal* at the mention of Torcello...)

Fearful for any possible further damage to my ear, I saw Mary off at the airport and opted to take the train back, in effect travelling the Orient Express route for a fraction of the price. The single ticket cost me eighty-nine pounds and I had most of an extra day so, although it was a bit of a bind, it wasn't all bad. I sat at cafes listening to the water lapping the stonework in St Mark's square and thought of Benjamin Britten who loved this place and of Stravinsky who was buried a mile or two over the water at San Georgio. On the overnight train,

I was looked after by a veritable guardian angel in the form of a jovial, but not too jovial, Frenchman. We talked, amongst other subjects, about astral travel and dreams. I think that he was some sort of research scientist. An interesting companion who, I am sure, was sent at the right time to keep an eye on me. If I hadn't, on a sudden whim, changed compartments we would have never met. I thought of that Biblical quote which says something about being alert and open for sometimes we entertain angels, unawares. On this occasion, I had the fortune to be entertained by one, I am sure.

A few weeks later, on the recommendation of Mary's daughter Siani, we both visited a medium, a Mrs McKeever who lived in Cowley. We were all going through what was, in effect, a rough patch of churning waters. Siani, who has always been very open to this sort of thing, paid this lady a visit and was so impressed by the results (what she had to say about Siani's forebears) that Siani urged us to go. We went separately and, though Mary was slightly sceptical, I found the lady marvellous. I approached the session with as open a mind as possible and I was rewarded with a stream of detail about my maternal grandfather (who this lady 'channelled') who had died in 1937 (the same year as Gershwin and Ravel). Perhaps I was especially receptive, I don't know, but an hour passed very quickly even though I had only paid for half an hour. I left this woman's house with a spring in my step as if I was on air, my head feeling both calmer and clearer than when I had entered. A few days later, I relayed as many of the details as I could remember to my mother who had to sit down with shock at some of the observations that Mrs McKeever told me; many of which, incidentally, were unknown to me but proved to be entirely accurate. Other matters also arose in that session and she warned me that I might suffer a minor head injury at some point in the not too distant future.

About six weeks later, this proved absolutely correct. The evening light was fading into dusk and I was cycling into a garage to buy a pint of milk. As I rode over the not-too-well illuminated forecourt, my front wheel lodged itself in a pothole and over I went. The next sequence of events occurred, as people testify, in a gentle and freewheeling slow motion where time seemed to be elongated. A mere few seconds or moments passed, of course. My head hit the ground (which I did not feel) and my glasses broke, flying off into local orbit somewhere along the Botley Road. I groggily came to, picked myself up, and gingerly walked into the garage (nothing had been broken) where a large, kind girl behind the counter rang Mary and instructed me to sit down. "You're going nowhere, my lad, except hospital," she said affectionately. Who was I to argue? At that point I hadn't looked in the mirror to see a profusely bleeding cut on the corner of my left eyebrow. When I did look in the mirror I resembled a boxer who, to all appearances, had lost. Mary appeared, rather surprised and slightly shaken, drove me up to the John Radcliffe Hospital where a Scots lady did a fine job of stitching me up, as it were. "Lucky for you that I'm a good seamstress," she said in a broad Glaswegian brogue, grinning. That was nothing compared to the tetanus jab in the bum that rounded off the evening's entertainment. This was far more painful than being pitched face-forwards and describing a small arc towards concrete (the nearest that I have come to free-fall parachuting...).

So that turned out to be my predicted minor head injury. That particular prediction, if you'll excuse the pun, turned out to be bang on... Oh yes – the medium also mentioned that my eardrum was being healed by the spirit doctors, which was good news. Quite an eventful few weeks...

38

In 1986, Mary summoned up her courage (of which it must have taken a great deal) and filed for a divorce. The usual legal wheels turned not too 'exceeding slow' and by the autumn we were free to live together. This was wonderful and, to be honest, a day that I thought might never come. We had survived the interim period (an odd and not quite real no-man's-land), neither of us had been attacked by Glyn, and now we could face the future and whatever it might bring or, at worst, angrily hurl at us. There was still guilt, of course, on Mary's part for leaving her husband and on my part for, effectively (only too effectively...), breaking up their marriage of thirty-five years. But, as we know, love is all-consuming, all-powerful, maddeningly illogical and irrational. It also takes no prisoners and is as strong as gravity.

At huge personal expense, Mary had purchased a small, detached 1930s house at the top of Ferry Road, New Marston. This was achieved by means of an exorbitant bridging loan. Despite her full-time earning ability, neither her bank nor building society deemed it appropriate to give her a mortgage... By the time she moved in October, she had one pound to her name, bless her. She had really put herself on the line for both of us, both emotionally and financially, and I just hoped and prayed that we would be able to live harmoniously together. The majority of me (say, ninety-five per cent) did not doubt it for one moment, but there is always that tiny, persistent, nagging five per cent, isn't there? We need not have worried. For the first time since I had moved to Oxford, I now had a proper home – not just somewhere to put my head down, not merely one cramped room, but space and a study of my own; best of all, I had a bed to share every night with the woman I loved, plus regular home-cooked meals. We both treasured one another and felt very lucky and blessed.

We also had a tiny and fairly basic kitchen, plus a wide and reasonable-sized garden that looked out, beyond the railings, to the sports ground that was shared by two of the Oxford colleges. In the summer months, we admired, from a distance, the curious ritual of several men dressed in white making contact between leather and willow known as cricket – a game for which neither of us had any understanding nor enthusiasm. To watch this game was rather akin to watching a group of hyperactive ghosts performing a bizarre ballet in which we, as spectators, had no clue as to what the rules were.

There had only been one previous set of occupants – a couple who had moved in just prior to the outbreak of World War Two. They had spent all their working lives there and, now that they had retired, wanted to move to Southampton to be nearer to their daughter. He had been a stonemason for one of the colleges. Clearly, over the years there had been little or no real improvements made to the house and even the garden didn't appear to have much growing in it. There was, however, a few dog graves under the lawn marked by raised bumps in the ground, which didn't worry us unduly. In the succeeding years and with the initial help of our opposite neighbour Hilda, Mary established a fine garden that was veritably stuffed full of exotic flowers and plants.

As with everything that she did, Mary gave her all and didn't do anything by halves. This dedicated, committed and uncompromising attitude was applied, particularly after she retired from the school in 1987 (with a wonderful send-off concert given by her many talented pupils), to various hobbies such as: learning Latin for eleven years (this helped with the plant names!); Egyptian dancing (which to her delight, slightly shocked a few friends!); and undertaking the not inconsiderable task of studying Welsh, her native language.

As a teenager, her Welsh teacher at Newtown Grammar School had been the distinguished Welsh language poet and short story writer, T. Hughes Jones, who later taught at a college of higher education in Wrexham. (On one visit to Aberystwyth, we found two of his first editions in a second-hand bookshop, much to Mary's surprise and delight.) With this latter language, Mary achieved a level that enabled her to have the distinction of twice being admitted (by examination) into the Gorsedd of Bards at the International Eisteddfod. On the first occasion, she was elected in the company of the then Archbishop of Wales (and of Canterbury elect), Dr Rowan Williams. We knew Rowan slightly from his visits to our church, All Saints', in Lime Walk, Headington (when he was Regius Professor of Divinity at Oxford University, one of his doctoral students was our curate). Dr Williams' first visit was to preach at the three-hour service on Good Friday, where his penetrating meditations on the Passion were a real breath of fresh air. Subsequent visits and sermons were no less illuminating, and I remember feeling that the last time that he visited, he had left a spiritual 'stain' within the church that remained for at least a couple of weeks – a definite feeling of holy echoes, if such a thing there can be. At this particular Eisteddfod held near St David's in Pembrokeshire, we congratulated him on his appointment to Canterbury. Conspiratorially and under his breath and behind a hand, he admitted that this particular honour (the bardic one) meant more to him than the forthcoming appointment at Canterbury! (I felt that he was only half joking.)

Mary was always ready to actively engage in promoting and publicising the Welsh language. In this role she became the secretary of the Oxford branch of Cyd, a group that met on the first Saturday of every month for coffee and conversation in Welsh in the back bar of The Mitre on the corner of The Turl and the High Street. This monthly gathering comprised two professors of History (Sir Rees Davies – medieval; and Robert Evans – modern), plus assorted people from all over Oxford and its environs. Each session lasted for about an hour, before individuals started to drift off; the only stipulation was that Welsh alone should be spoken, a requirement that was not always enforceable!

In the year prior to her retirement, at the encouragement of our friend Andrew Claxton, Mary and I decided that we would like to study for an M.Mus in Performance at Reading University. The course was part-time over two years, requiring us to attend every Friday afternoon and alternate Thursday afternoons. Mary's school kindly let her teaching timetable accommodate these external activities (though they would not contribute financially), whilst my mother very generously paid my fees for me. Naturally, we both chose the harpsichord as our instrument. I had accompanied Andy for his M.Mus tuba recital (quite an event in itself and a marathon of breath control), which he passed with flying colours, and he thought that the degree course would suit both of us. We applied, passed the auditions, and after the prescribed course, were duly awarded the degree. Mary's harpsichord tutor was Virginia Pleasants, based near Victoria in London, while I received lessons from the other harpsichord Virginia – the much-admired player Virginia Black, who was based in Harlow, Essex. Alas, she no longer performs but was an excellent and very dynamic interpreter of Scarlatti and Soler, in particular. She was also a wonderful, joyous teacher and I remember her sessions very fondly.

I think, looking back, that the Music department at Reading University rather regarded us as an odd couple – this young(ish) man and this older lady. I suppose that they were all slightly embarrassed. Apart from our dissertation tutor Dr Christoper Kent, an organist and Elgar scholar who supervised us both very supportively, we felt that the staff were far more interested in the undergraduate students – which, in one sense, is how things should be. Mary's dissertation was on the eighteenth-century composer Thomas Roseingrave's keyboard music, and mine was on the virginalist John Bull and his twelve keyboard settings of the plainsong incipit, *In Nomine*. As reading, these dissertations were dry, pedantic and tedious (they certainly did not constitute gripping page-turners), but they did do their required job of completing the course requirements.

That summer, Mary had a phone call, then a visit from an old colleague and associate that went right back to the late-1950s. The Reverend James Cocke had been appointed Vicar of All Saints', Highfield, Headington in the February of 1957. When Mary was a music teacher at Headington Middle School, the pupils used to crocodile their way down to All Saints' for the annual carol service. Now all these years later, as Jim patiently explained to us, he was in a tricky situation. His then organist, a brilliantly-gifted recitalist, was becoming more and more reluctant to direct the choir. The summer was something of an interregnum and would Mary consider taking up the post of Director of Music at All Saints? Mary's enthusiasm was not immediately evident on this occasion, but she took a deep breath and said that she would consider the proposition – which she then did after a matter of few days. She accepted the post on the basis of doing it for six months. She eventually stepped down from it seventeen years later, having built up a more than reasonable parish choir.

It wasn't easy. Some of the choir members were supporters of the organist and left as a mark of protest. As is so often the case, Mary was, on at least two occasions, rung up by interfering busybodies who gave, in their opinion, valid and very strongly-voiced reasons why Mary should not accept the post. She was icily polite, but firmly in her own charming way, told these so-called Christian meddlers where to go and how – which presumably they did as we didn't hear from them again.

Jim Cocke, amazingly, is still Vicar there as I write this. He is eighty-five and going strong, leading his congregation both enthusiastically and firmly and chairing his various committees in like fashion. He is a marvel of sustained perseverance and an object lesson of remaining loyally steadfast to his calling and his parishioners over many decades. All Saints' celebrated its centenary last year (2010), and Jim was at the helm and fully in command of all the various celebrations.

39

In 1989, we jointly decided to buy a double-manual harpsichord, expensive though it was. Mary already had the single-manual instrument, a Flemish copy, built by Robert Goble & Son whose workshop was in Headington on the edge of Shotover. The Gobles were a natural choice, for not only were they local, but their consistently high level of craftsmanship and reliability ensured that their harpsichords were exported worldwide. Over some twenty-seven years, incidentally, Andrea unfailingly provided me with beautiful copies of German and Parisian instruments for my many recitals in the Holywell Music Room in the centre of Oxford, often at very reasonable rates. What with performing and reviewing, the Holywell (the oldest purpose-built music room in the country, opened in 1748) often seemed to be a second home.

Andrea informed us that our order would be ready around Easter time of 1990. To house this larger harpsichord, however, required an extension to our lounge. This began on the Good Friday by a family group of builders, the Robertsons, who were based near Didcot and were members of an exclusive religious sect. The good thing about this was that they were quiet (no blaring transistors) and hard workers with good skills. They had built a very good extension to Hilda's bungalow opposite and she recommended them. After about six weeks, the project was complete – the floor laid and varnished and the harpsichord ready to take its place in its new home. Andrea delivered the instrument. In its duck-egg blue with gold inlay (a copy of an authentic 1768 Taskin), it looked gorgeous and over the years has matured to sound likewise. Like fine wine, good instruments need time.

By now, my part-time lecturing at Oxford Polytechnic had finished (in 1988, due to a golden handshake paid out to my groping predecessor), but I was now giving piano tuition in two independent girls' schools in Oxford. In the autumn of 1990, this was further supplemented by two further part-time academic appointments – as a Visiting Tutor in Composition at my old college, now renamed Birmingham Conservatoire, and as a Tutor in the Extramural Department of Oxford University. I was still continuing to teach some private pupils and write reviews for *The Oxford Times*, but had stopped playing as a cocktail pianist. Eight years of that in three different venues had been ample, I think. Experience is one thing but masochism is yet another, and I had suffered enough. Musicians are well used to picking up bits and pieces of employment where they can. I have grown so used to this that I would now more-or-less shudder at the prospect of a nine-to-five job in one location.

Awful! Mind you, the money would be a lot better, but you cannot have everything. Or can you? That's a poser.

So, life sweetly ticked on with its usual demands and routines for us both – pupils and lots of them for Mary, different pieces of teaching, playing and lecturing for me. And, with two harpsichords (the small one upstairs in my study and the new, big one in our lounge) we were able to practise individually. This was particularly useful when we were planning our recitals of music for two harpsichords, which we did on a few occasions, each time in the Holywell. There is much more of a repertoire for this combination than one might imagine – mostly Baroque, granted, but rich and beautiful nonetheless. We played pieces by three members of the Bach dynasty (JS, WF and CPE), French repertoire by Francois Couperin, Armand-Louis Couperin and Gaspard Le Roux, plus Concerti by Padre Antonio Soler and pieces by early English composers Giles Farnaby and Thomas Tomkins. Twentieth-century pieces included Peter Maxwell Davies, as well as the first performances of two works by composition students at Birmingham, Sam Parker's *8 + 8* and Andrew Price-Jones' *Cerulean Blue*. In these recitals, Mary and I felt very attuned to one another and this togetherness seemed to come across to the audience. Various friends commented that it was an intimate, almost erotically-charged, experience hearing and watching us play; two people almost sounding as one unity. This was gratifying to us both. I felt that the whole performing process between us was rather akin to watching a pair of butterflies dancing and flying together in the air, conjoined in a series of celebratory, wheeling arcs. I remember on all those precious occasions feeling a sense of beauty, tranquillity, and genuine music-making.

All those same facets were present, too, in performances

with the guitarist Raymond Burley. Again, something special used to occur, particularly in the slow movements of Trio Sonatas by JS Bach. Originally these Sonatas were written for organ; Ray would take the top line and I would play the left-hand and pedal parts on the harpsichord. It made the counterpoint very clear, proved effective and very moving. Our duo lasted for some twelve years and then, as it happens, we ran out of repertoire as well as opportunities to play. This also happened with my colleague at Birmingham Conservatoire, virtuoso recorder player Ross Winters. Again, we played regularly in Birmingham and at festivals over, roughly, a dozen years. These associations, these things tend to be finite; they have their time (their sell-by date, perhaps?), then lessen, fade, and fall away. A natural cycle, like the seasons. They did provide, hopefully for all parties concerned, some treasured memories.

I came into contact with saxophonist George Haslam through us both teaching at the same two girls' schools. George, who also runs and owns his recording company Slam Records, is mainly known for his stentorian baritone sound – gnarled, grainy, and sounding as if the QE2 is leaving Southampton. Knowing that I was interested but also virtually a jazz virgin (in terms of performing), George and I got together, rehearsed a few tunes, and developed the beginnings of a duo together. In this format we appeared opposite Stan Tracey (with bass players Dave Green and Malcolm Creese, respectively) on two occasions at – where else? – the Holywell Music Room. We also did a series of quartet gigs with players including pocket-trumpeter Janusz Carmello, saxophonist Bobby Wellins, and trumpeter Henry Lowther – fine and respected soloists all. Not so fine, however, was my own inexperienced playing and soloing; therefore, for me (personally speaking) these sessions are best forgotten and consigned to oblivion.

More to our tastes, however, were free, or what George terms 'natural' music – i.e. totally spontaneous playing whereby the participants listen and react, passing ideas between one another, sometimes in accord, sometimes in opposition to what they have just heard. Down the years, I have been blessed to play in the company of such esteemed figures as Lol Coxhill, Howard Riley, Paul Rutherford, Evan Parker, Pat Thomas and others. Each time is a different, wholly unique experience for me and also, hopefully, for the audience. Some of these collaborations were truly inspirational and each time included, besides myself and George, the esteemed bass player Steve Kershaw, who is unfailingly creative and sensitive in his interaction with other musicians.

From 1997 to 2002, I was also the pianist in George's ten-piece band Meltdown. This was a collective whose main premise was to commission and perform new pieces, both by band members and from more established figures such as pianist Mal Waldron (with whom George also had a duo) and one-time bass player and late band leader Graham Collier. We did at least two or three concerts of Graham's own music, and here the band veritably leapt into life and flame. My pal Andrew Claxton was the tuba player, and the most distinguished musicians amongst us were the trumpeter Steve Waterman and alto player Tim Hill. Pieces that I wrote for the band, which were regularly performed, were *Jacqui's Chorale* and the refrain-based *Our Days Were a Joy, and Our Paths Through Flowers,* whose title comes from the last line of Thomas Hardy's poem *After a Journey* (dedicated to his late wife) and is also the title of a painting by David Inshaw. Its mood is of nostalgia and melancholy, and those attributes seemed to be caught by audiences. In the band's lifetime, we played some important concerts including The Stables at

Wavendon in Bedfordshire (the Dankworth's home) and at The Vortex, as part of the International London Jazz Festival.

We broke up for the usual reason – lack of funding. Even the greatest players in the business find that trying to sustain a medium-sized or large band is a mightily fraught venture (and not just financially speaking); so, on reflection, I think that George did a very credible job.

40

This might be a timely moment to mention my compositions that are *not* jazz-based or, more accurately, a selection of them. (If you are not a musician, you might wish to skip this section and go out and make a cup of tea, or pour a glass of wine or a beer.)

One of my favourite instrumental mediums is the string quartet. It is a sound world that is, curiously, both public yet private. My first quartet, completed during my last year as a student at Birmingham (1978), is I suppose still very much an apprentice piece. Yet many of its concerns, particularly in the slow stretches of music, still seem relevant to that sense of stillness that is a constant in my compositions through the years, almost regardless of the medium. (Hence the reason for including it in my list of proper or 'real' pieces.)

This stillness pervades the majority of my second quartet. Its subtitle, *Parakeelya*, refers to a delicately-blooming, purple Australian flower that only appears briefly after heavy rains in desert areas. It might be considered a metaphor for those rarely-achieved moments of epiphany or transcendence. The viola player also plays a wood-block both at the beginning and at the end of the piece, providing a ritualistic 'framing' gesture, whilst the cello's lowest string is detuned (*scordatura*) to provide a deeper and darker sonority.

Quartet No. 3 is in several small sections, all played without a break. Stockhausen's "moment form" was the principal influence (if not the sound) behind this work that contrasts, often quite rapidly, different kinds of music which succeed as well as interrupt one another (solos, trills, a rocketing homophonic line, a vigorous fugal section, etcetera). The initial impetus was Flann O'Brien's quotation about how an author might start a book with several varied openings – a multiplicity of possibilities.

The fourth quartet, dedicated to the memory of my composer friend David Gow, is a different animal altogether; it is very elegiac and full of dark beauty. It's structured in four hymn-like verses; two freer interludes serve to relax the sustained tension of the verses. The piece manages to achieve a mere few bars of radiance towards its conclusion before finishing with a few solo cello gestures, which are highly ambiguous, almost dismissively uncertain and bleak.

Quartets Nos. 5 & 6 are, again, totally contrasted. The single-movement fifth is based upon (and eventually moves towards a full statement of) the Irish folk-song *Boolavogue*. The composer and pianist Mark Lockett and I had played Cornelius Cardew's two-piano piece of the same name. This tune had haunted me for ages and I wanted to use it as a basis for one of my own pieces. In the original song appear the lines:

God grant you glory, brave Father Murphy,
And open heaven to all your men;
The cause that called you may call tomorrow,
In another fight for the green again.

This became the motto for my work, which is dedicated to Father Murphy who lost his life fighting for and protecting his parishioners in one of the earliest and bloodiest of Irish uprisings. After a fraught and violent climax, the cellist surreptitiously pulls out and then blows, *fortissimo*, a police whistle. An uneasy silence ensues, followed by a quiet statement of the folksong, after which the piece begins to stabilise around the note D. The last mysterious sounds are the two violinists striking high crotales, also on D.

Quartet No. 6 is more expansive and in six movements. Although completed in 2009, its origins date back to the summer of 2003, specifically when I was in bed with a bout of food poisoning and an alarmingly high temperature. I was delirious and repeating to myself (as a comforting mantra) the words of the Greek Orthodox *Jesus Prayer*. Simple and powerfully effective, the sentence (intended to be memorised) is: 'Lord Jesus Christ, Son of God, have mercy on me, a sinner.' Oddly enough, I had attended a lecture only a few days before on this very subject given by Bishop Kallistos Ware, a figure whom I had seen for years striding out in north Oxford in his flowing robes and generous beard. He always looked every inch the venerable, but kindly, patriarch. This did, indeed, seem Heaven-sent at the time of my illness. The speech-rhythms inherent in this phrase soon found themselves turning into a Stravinskian hymn, which eventually became the fourth movement *Unceasing Prayer*. Other movements include canons, cadenzas, an homage to Paul Klee in the fifth, and the work ends with a spacious, serene chorale.

The most recent quartet, the seventh, also dates from 2009. Its single movement is roughly of ten minutes duration and consists of fragmentary utterances projected over long-held drone notes. This piece also employs digital delay, thus sending out variously-timed echoes to create an elaborate texture.

Aside from string quartets, I continue to add to an on-going cycle of short pieces for (mainly) solo instruments with the generic title *encore* that was begun in 1996. The first one, for soprano solo, sets an incredibly short but resonant poem, *Dieppe* by Samuel Beckett, whilst the second in the series is a slightly elaborated version of the soprano solo but given to a clarinet. *encore III* is scored for a luminous ensemble of flute, clarinet, viola, cello, piano, and percussion. It is a delicate, spacious sound world that, perhaps, owes something to that incredibly subtle composer, Morton Feldman. Numbers four and five are for harpsichord and recorder, respectively. I have jettisoned six and seven (flute and tuba) for being weak. *encore VIII*, however, is a substantial piece for cello (based on a phrase from James Joyce); *encore IX* for alto saxophone takes its subtitle *The Mouth of Flowers* from the beautiful valley in County Cork where Michael Collins was assassinated in the mid-1920s. *encore XI* is for solo harp, whilst numbers ten and twelve are scored for vibraphone and accordion. Both of these are influenced by a visit to the Dordogne in the summer of 2010, when Carol and I were on our honeymoon in Le Bugue. There may yet, who knows, be a final (ensemble) piece to balance out *encore III* and may employ all the previous solo instruments.

What else? There are a few pieces that have been influenced, directly and indirectly, by Japanese *haiku*. I have, for some years now, been intrigued by the seeming dichotomies that pervade the Japanese arts, particularly poetry and painting. Placed alongside images of great delicacy (cherry blossom, tea ceremonies, etcetera) are the equally traditional images of violence (samurai) so effectively depicted in the films of Kurosawa. My cycle *Kuro Haiku* for guitar and harpsichord are based on seventeen *haiku* by the great writer in that form,

Basho. Everything from note durations to silences, both within and between the pieces, is governed by the pattern of 5-7-5 syllables. Hopefully, the aphoristic pieces mirror something of the tightly-constructed Basho originals.

Another cycle, *Objects, Orbits and Haiku* for recorder(s) [one player] and piano, is more playful in its effect. The first movement of the three presents fourteen tiny sections and returns to the 'moment form' scenario of the third quartet. Much of the music is deliberately referential, akin to picking up pebbles or found objects on a beach.

Musical allusions here include plainsong, Britten, Stravinsky, jazz 'scat' singing, and even a transformation of a well-known tune by a certain glam-rock band (!)... I had a lot of fun writing this and, after all, why shouldn't composers have a bit of fun sometimes? This work was written for Ross Winters and myself to play and we certainly did have a lot of fun rehearsing and performing it.

The Japanese word *Karumi* (lightness of being) provided the title for a short seventieth birthday tribute to the composer Anthony Gilbert, written for sopranino recorder, which was first performed by John Turner. Another influence behind the piece was the exuberantly coloured, whirling paintings of Gillian Ayres, seen at the West of England Academy of Art.

Paintings, this time by a handful of St Ives artists, lay behind my seven-movement work for two pianos *Zawn*. *Zawn* is a Cornish word meaning a cleft or a chasm in a rock. There are three homages to painters: Patrick Heron, Peter Lanyon, and Wilhemina Barns-Graham, and a fourth to the composer Priaulx Rainier who (as I have already indicated) was a close friend of the sculptor Barbara Hepworth. Another piece connected to St Ives is *Four Moons* for percussion and organ, commissioned and first performed by Keith Fairbairn and Malcolm Pearce.

This is based on a painting by the late Sir Terry Frost, *Five Black Moons* (2000–01), which I saw at a retrospective of his work in the Innocent Gallery in Clifton, Bristol.

One of my performing hats is as a jazz player (of the free, avant-garde variety). In a handful of my own pieces, however, I have used jazz satirically, although (usually) affectionately. A fast unison be-bop line appears in the first movement of *Objects, Orbits and Haiku,* whilst the urine is extracted, if I may put it that way, with nods to Gershwin in general and Walton's *Facade* in particular in the *Crucible of Sea and Sky* movement of *Zawn,* where a short but rumbustious blues boils up in unsuspecting circumstances. Rightly or wrongly, I have never been a fan of Gershwin, a couple of pieces excepted. His music seems to me innately brash and full of vulgar showing-off, much like his own over-the-top improvisations. More recently, blues harmonies (of an almost big-band richness) occur in my transformation of Liszt's *Vallee d' Obermann,* and in Chopin's bicentennial year (2010), I made a ragtime version of one of his *Études.* All of this must sound sacrilegious. Far from it – my intention was to pay homage to these two giants of nineteenth century pianism. The ragtime transformation of the Chopin was already implicit and lurking in the original – specifically, the left-hand part. There are also other bits of his *Études* woven into this piece.

That's probably more than enough on that topic, but it might help to give you some idea of what influences have lain behind some of my music. What unifies the greater majority of them is the Jungian notion of moving, however slowly, from a state of darkness to light and illumination – a journey of growth and awareness, in other words. Technically, I often employ the Fibonacci series (1, 1, 2, 3, 5, 8, 13, 21, 34, 55, etcetera) for durations and lengths of sections, while pitches are partially dictated by cipher and numerical aspects.

41

We had travelled to Orkney before; the first time was as part of a Scottish coach holiday in the summer of 1989. Apart from seeing a Russian submarine docked in Ullapool (its crew waved, beamed sunnily, and gave us the thumbs up sign) and the red sandstone glories of St Magnus Cathedral in Kirkwall, I cannot recall very much. Except for being very sick in the gents' (the bowels, as it were) of the P&O ferry *St Ola* as we bumped our way through, if not exactly over, the Pentland Firth's colliding currents towards Stromness. Not only was I very sick, but I was being so to a recording of pungent bagpipes being piped through the loudspeakers in the loo. I emerged pale and groggy (as much from the bagpipes as the vomiting), although, in the time-honoured tradition, as soon as I set foot on dry land I felt a lot better instantly. On our subsequent trips to Orkney, we always made

The author composing.

sure that we stayed on deck where we kept our eyes glued to the horizon, even if it was bobbing up and down and from side to side. To be fair, it was fairly calm on one or two occasions.

The farmer's wife from South Ronaldsay introduced us to a young man. "Say hello to him," she urged and placed into four pairs of hands, in turn, a 5000-year-old skull. She spoke in the present tense and with an affection which suggested that this was just one of many such ancestor friends. For her, the thread of history was a seamless, unbroken narrative. We each weighed the small man's skull in our palms – an intense moment of marvelling silence. We dwelt, for a fraction of time, in the remote Neolithic past. Skull, sea, sky, and stone – it could almost be a poetic rune inscribed at Maeshowe.

That occurred in July 1993 on our third visit to Orkney, yet that experience at the Tomb of the Eagles left an indelible impression on both Mary and myself. It is typical of the way that this landscape and its people affect one's own sensibilities. There is time and space in Orkney (not one landmass, but seventy islands) to unwind and relish the cleansing effect of sea and sky; to feel genuinely welcomed by communities who value visitors and who are possessed of a natural courtesy, yet who are not intrusive nor too eagerly inquisitive. Things do not change very much in these islands or, if they do, it happens slowly, almost reluctantly and with a sense of sadness. A great deal of their beauty lies in these very qualities of continuity and stability: the repeating seasonal cycles of crofter and fisherman unchanged through the years; the skills (and dangers) that are ritually repeated through the generations. Yes, a slow dance is Orkney's living history, yet one that transcends mere chronology.

We left hot and sticky London, taking the sleeper train from Euston to Inverness, then the local stopping train and cooler temperatures right up to gaunt Sutherland and the end of the line at Thurso, which feels like the end of civilisation and the known world. The final leg of this long journey is the two-hour ferry crossing, as already mentioned, from Scrabster to Stromness. This crossing is only six miles as the crow (or artic tern) flies, but this is a watery crucible of surprising and capricious vehemence where the conflicting currents and tide races of both the North Sea and the Atlantic meet head-on.

Orkney's special spell takes hold as the *St Ola* passes Hoy, the high southern isle. Guarding the island is the stern presence of the Old Man of Hoy, a sheer pillar of red sandstone much beloved amongst intrepid climbers. The ferry docks in the port of Stromness, whose main flagstone street snakes its way between houses, closes, and piers. Each house overlooking the harbour has its own 'noust' or jetty; above the town hangs the delicious smell of peat smoke, for fires are still essential here even in the summer months.

Some places have a magic all their own. So, too, is it the case with Orkney. Even the place names fire the imagination – Birsay, Quoyloo, Shapinsay, Orphir, Egilsay, Yesnaby – a ritual litany that quickens heart and mind. Everywhere you turn, history breaks over you in a wave that carries within it a potent past: Maeshowe with its runic graffiti, the burial chambers scattered liberally among the islands; and the most imposing of them all, St Magnus Cathedral in Kirkwall, dedicated to the memory of the pacifist Earl whose axe-fractured skull can be seen in Tankerness Musuem. His bones resided for many long years in the thick sandstone pillars in the cathedral itself.

Magnus, whose martyrdom occurred on Egilsay on Easter Monday 1117, is absolutely fundamental to both the past and the present in Orkney. His life and legendary death have been repeatedly brought alive through the writings of the great Orcadian poet and novelist George Mackay Brown. Since his own death in April 1996, George himself has, likewise, become the stuff of legend. Mackay Brown's death was a personal sadness for us, for he always welcomed us into his Stromness home where the conversation would range over mutual friends in Oxford, the music of Messiaen, and the novels of Martin Amis and Ian McEwan. Whatever people sometimes liked to think, George was never merely parochial. In a quiet way, he had his finger on the pulse, even though he rarely strayed far from Orkney. So much did he seem to embody Orkney (both personally and in his wonderful, flinty writing) that, like Benjamin Britten in Aldeburgh, George's spirit still seems very much alive. He is buried in the remote kirkyard at Warbeth, a windswept spot overlooking the sea at Hoy Sound.

An equally moving monument can be seen at Lamb Holm. During the Second World War, Italian prisoners were set to work on building the Churchill Barriers. Lonely and isolated in a cold and alien climate, they set about constructing a small chapel. It was made from two Nissen huts and is simply known as the Italian Chapel. This was a labour of love and remains a very special testament to faith maintained in adversity. It is, too, all that remains of the original Camp 60. A man from Modena, Domenico Chiocchetti, drew freehand and then painted the frescoes as well as the interior. He stayed on to complete the work after the other prisoners were freed. In 1964, he returned to retouch some of his handiwork and had become, in the intervening years, an adopted Orcadian *in absentia*. He died in 1999 leaving behind him a legacy of great beauty, intimacy, and faith.

Connections, co-incidences, and memories: a friend of composer Elis Pehkonen, John Beardsmore-Marsden (Britten's one-time dentist), a walking encyclopaedia of twentieth century British music who owned a croft in Rackwick a stone's throw from Peter Maxwell Davies; a former Birmingham student,

Robin Cheer, who had been organist at St Magnus Cathedral; spending a day on Rousay being driven around by Mary Soames who, quite naturally and unpretentiously, stopped by the shore to sing to the selkies (seals) – seven of them appeared, bobbing up like black-capped swimmers, answering the singer crouched near the waves; and, most unexpected of all, meeting her neighbour John Vetterlein, harpsichord maker and astronomer, who had been a close friend of the late composer David Gow.

Creation great and small: the gigantic red cliffs at Rackwick and Yesnaby; the remains of the Neolithic village with its stone pillows at Skara Brae; the Ring of Brodgar standing-stones; the rhubarb leaves and tiny mauve roadside orchids. Innumerable riches, blessing and epiphany in equal measure. In fact, each time was not so much a visit, but more of a pilgrimage.

We left Stromness on the Saturday morning in a torrential downpour. As the *St Ola* carefully nosed her way out of the harbour, making its sharp turn into Hoy Sound past fog-drenched Hoy and out into the mint-green, churning Atlantic, there came an undeniable tug at the heart urging us to return.

As a coda to this section, the following are two tiny poems from *An Orkney Sequence*, written in celebration of these islands. Hamnavoe is the ancient name for Stromness.

Hamnavoe

At our feet, flagstones;
In the air, peatsmoke.
Cairns, skulls, brochs and bones:
All these things evoke

Soldier, merchant, saint.
All those voyagers on

That glittering crown,
The fierce, drowning sea:
Ice-cold witness to
War-song, history.

Maeshowe

Knobbly wart, inscribed ring:
Ancient growth, a memo
On a wide green hand.

Mary's seventieth birthday. Dingley Hill, May 1999.

42

Mum celebrated her eightieth birthday on the tenth of February 1999. It was a good day spent in the company of friends; but it was also bittersweet and surrounded by a certain amount of anxiety for her health was gradually failing, slowly though it was, in regard to mobility, heart and other problems. It was, therefore, imperative that she be rehoused in residential accommodation sooner rather than later. No one wants to be told this but her doctor informed her, as gently as he could, that she was becoming something of a liability to herself, wasn't she? She slowly nodded, sighed, and had to reluctantly agree that this was now the case. Mum had lived in Littlecross House in Greenway Bush Lane just off Coronation Road for twenty-two years. The prospect of moving to somewhere where she would no longer to be able to cook for herself and have her freedom curtailed was a shadow that fell and lingered over both our lives.

The previous Christmas had seen her come out of hospital and spend the festive season recuperating in a rehabilitation residence, whilst Mary and I spent it staying in Mum's flat and visiting her. She was as cheerful as it was possible to be given the circumstances. I was still on vacation and saw her back into her flat, but was becoming increasingly anxious and stressed with regard to her present circumstances and the omnipresent need to find residential, as opposed to merely warden-controlled, accommodation.

I was becoming short of breath, was finding it difficult to swallow, was walking at an almost manic pace (and I am a fast walker) and began to have terrifying panic attacks which, on the first two occasions, were so severe that I had to go, weeping profusely, to bed to try and sleep it off. I was meant to be looking after my mother, for Heaven's sake, not the opposite way round... I felt as if I had regressed to childhood when Mum took me in her arms and comforted me. I emerged from my bedroom some while later less distressed but very dazed with the feeling of having been drugged, which was of course not the case. For a time, these panic attacks were so disturbing and draining, both mentally and physically, that I seriously thought that I might become a near-alcoholic for it seemed to be the only thing that would calm me. Clearly, this was no solution, not even a temporary one.

Back in Oxford, I contacted a GP friend of Siani's who had developed a form of cognitive treatment to lessen or even wholly alleviate panic attacks. After a few visits, these one-to-one sessions began to work and I gradually became better. Although I had my moments of claustrophobia and escalating panic, I carried on my teaching and lecturing commitments and was, with the help of Mary, able to move Mum into her room at the residential home on the Wells Road in Knowle at the end of March 1999. Her attic room was clean, relatively comfortable, and spacious. As with the greater majority of these establishments, it provided food and warmth but was no substitute for her previous home environment. Some of the other residents, however, were companionable and friendly. The biggest fear was boredom in this alien house which was not a home.

I continued to visit Mum every month, spending the weekend with her as I had from my student days. We would go shopping and, if she felt strong enough, we would go out for trips in the car. These tended to decrease as she got frailer and her walking more torturous. On many Sunday afternoons (and increasingly with time), I would park the car, see Mum back to her room, stay awhile and chat or we would sit quietly in a companionable silence. Then I would have to leave and drive back to Oxford. This I hated, virtually leaving my mother imprisoned. I would walk out, look up to her window where she would be stood leaning on her stick or Zimmer frame, and we would forlornly wave at one another. I would try to smile broadly and give her an optimistic thumbs-up; then with a short honk of the horn I would drive off. I reflected that this must be what it was like to drive your son or daughter to their boarding school and then leave them. Only this was in reverse – I was looking after then, in effect, abandoning my mother.

We took it in turns to phone each other and have a long chat twice a week, on Wednesdays and Sundays. This broke the monotony for her and we would have a good old gossip about the usual things such as TV programmes, friends, etcetera. My old friends Ann and Philip Maycock came to the rescue, bless them. Learning that I would no longer have a base in Bristol, they immediately and unhesitatingly said that I must stay with them in their roomy house in Clifton on these monthly weekends – and so I did for nine years, Christmases and Easters included, until Mum's death in 2008. It was a sense of *déjà vu*, too, being back in the house where I had had so many piano lessons as a teenager. Their house in Manilla Road was also just around the corner from Christ Church where I had, all those short-trouser years ago, been a choirboy absent-mindedly fingering my chafing, starched ruff and trying to sing (and stay) in tune. Needless to say, I'll never forget that long-term gesture of support from them both.

That summer of 1999, Mary and I had our main holiday in a Cornish cottage in the village of Tredavoe, up in the hills between Newlyn and Penzance. The cottage had kindly been leant to us by musician colleagues in Oxford and their neighbours in Tredavoe were the artist John Piper (the Cornish one) and his wife Judith. We immediately took to John and his paintings, which were landscapes of the locality but painted with very rich yellows, ochres, and deep blues. As a result, his paintings gave off a warm glow. Later, he gave permission for two of his paintings to grace a CD of improvisations that George Haslam and I recorded. The title of the album was, appropriately, *Tredavoe Blue*.

It was a good, relaxing holiday, although I was still occasionally prone to a passing bout of anxiety and panic, especially if I was in a confined and/or very dark house. Our next memorable holiday, and a first for us, was when we went to the south of Ireland.

In January 2000, Roger's wife, Sue, died from breast cancer. She had undergone surgery and had suffered very badly for a couple of years. This left their two daughters, Michelle and Charlotte-Eve (my god-daughter), motherless and at a very vulnerable age, too. Roger, despite much sadness and stress, raised them single-handedly and with great devotion. Sue's funeral was at her Catholic church in Tiverton and her memorial service was held later that year in Jersey, where she spent her childhood and adolescent years. On both occasions I gave the eulogy, and Roger and the girls were surrounded by affectionate and loving friends who embraced them, both actually and metaphorically, in those dark and long days. But even so, the death of the other half is the most terrible of human rites that any of us have to negotiate. It is, of course, a journey that is neither optional nor negotiable. One must quarry through the darkness until that first, tentative glimmer of pale light. And even then, as I was to find, it is only the beginning.

43

But back to Ireland...

Remarkably, we had a mini-heatwave of about three days duration – in Ireland! Such things are rare and to be duly celebrated. This was our first acquaintance with Ireland and we loved it, the landscape and the people in equal measure, as well as the food such as the deep, dark-tasting soda bread which accompanied breakfast.

We crossed on the overnight sailing from Swansea to Cork, arrived early in the morning into a harbour adorned with pastel-painted houses – blue, pink, corn-yellow, and lime green – then drove to Kinsale where we sat outside having breakfast with wonderful Bewley's coffee and croissants. For the first couple of miles from the harbour, the hedges were strewn with fuchsias in profusion. The whole atmosphere was European, almost festive and distinctly un-English, which, with our Celtic roots, suited us down to the ground.

The only problem was staying awake. With the prospect of the ten-hour ferry crossing, we had taken seasickness tablets which certainly worked – almost too well for we were struggling to keep awake, especially whilst driving. Our first bed and breakfast was in Clonakilty. Then we drove slowly westwards taking in villages and towns such as Rosscarbery, Glandore, Skibbereen (of song fame), Schull, Ballydehob and then up to Bantry Bay, Glengarriff, Kenmare and then back east to Macroom and Bandon.

On our second visit, we decided to take the ferry from Fishguard to Rosslare and then head diagonally across the interior of the Republic via Clonmel, Cahir, and depressed Tipperary until we came to the city of Limerick. There we stopped off at the Hunt Museum to see a rare retrospective of paintings by Jack B Yeats, the brother of poet WB Yeats. Fine and colourful they proved to be, too.

Then onwards and upwards into County Clare where we stayed in Doolin, a thriving tri-partite village where traditional music is the backbone and the centre of gravity. It was here, in a small record shop, that we met Orla – Orla of the dark hair, sweet face, and stillness – who was interested to hear of our harpsichord playing. She gave us advice about taking the ferry to Inisheer, the inner of the three Aran Islands (which we did and the weather not only held, but was fine), and talked variously about the members of Planxty and The Bothy Band.

A day or so later (time is very flexible and elastic in Ireland), we met her with her daughter having dinner in a small, but good restaurant. We greeted each other, and as we shook hands or touched in some way, I received a very direct gaze from her eyes, a bolt of psychic energy from Orla as pure and as shocking as electricity; a kind of almost physical telepathy; an intuition or moment of total understanding, even love, perhaps. I composed myself and we settled down to our dinner, but I was shaken up, my mind a whirling vortex, although I was still able to eat. On our last evening in Doolin, we saw her again at one of the pubs.

For all we know, we may never meet again.

At a suitable break in the music, we got up to leave. Orla saw us, came over, and exchanged a few words.

Before you go, make this moment sweet again.
We won't say 'Good night' until the last minute.

We said goodnight and, in effect, goodbye; she gripped

my hand fiercely in a gesture of spontaneous, but reluctant farewell.

I'll hold out my hand and my heart will be in it.

Mary and I walked to the car; I looked at her and, in the fading light, there were tears in her eyes. I am sure that she had sensed the strong bond, that unfathomable connection, between Orla and myself.

Nothing was said and we returned to our lodgings, but that moment has continued to haunt me. Naturally, I had no intention of upsetting Mary, or Orla for that matter. But (and fortunately rarely) these rather bizarre occurrences seem to happen to us, involuntarily and not of our own making or, indeed, conscious willing.

On the ferry back to Fishguard, I felt utterly desolate, as if I had left part of myself behind in County Clare – or, at least, in Doolin. Perhaps, in some small way, I had...

It has been said (I have forgotten by whom) that the island of Ireland has, attached at various points, a plethora of magnets that serve to lure the first-time visitor to its shores, as well as enticing back for the umpteenth time the homesick exile. It is, in all probability, a rumour. On the other hand, it may well be true – this was our third visit, after all... That sheer sense of *mystery* and *otherness* which may be sensed is, nonetheless, all too apparent, especially if one is open to such things. Both those qualities seem to hang in the air around the village of Doolin in County Clare, as do the aromas of sewage wafting their way up from the stream under the bridge. The charms tend to outweigh the smells, though – at least when the wind is blowing the *other* way...

Thursday 30th June 2005

Stena ferry from Fishguard to Rosslare on the afternoon sailing. The conditions look reasonable, despite a slight sea mist that obliterates landmarks every few minutes. Amazingly, we contrive to be the first car in our queuing lane. The peace and quiet of this corner of West Wales is suddenly shattered, however, by the arrival of what looks to be three Hell's Angels on very powerful and impressive motorbikes. On closer inspection, however, their leathers are bedecked with numerous badges, but no wings or skull-and-crossbones motifs. We visibly relax and start to enjoy their jokey, good-natured banter, and realise that they are probably members of the Harley Davidson Club of Great Britain who are convening somewhere in Ireland and are already in holiday mood. The men are of a certain age and are running to fat, but their corporate enthusiasm is contagious and they are clearly in their element meeting up with old friends.

Our crossing was as calm as the proverbial millpond and our ferry docks in Rosslare spot-on its estimated time of arrival. As we nose into the harbour, a rainbow penetrates the clouds and we feel that this is both a good omen and a welcome. We then drive the hour or so to our overnight accommodation at New Ross before heading off the next morning in a westerly diagonal, passing through Tipperary, Limerick and Ennis. Unbeknown to us, all the largest lorries in Ireland have chosen this particular couple of hours to converge, nose-to-tail, on the already crowded town of Ennis. (We resolve to find an alternate route on our way back the following Wednesday...)

A return to the pretty village of Doolin for two nights' stay at Susan Daly's on the Friday and Saturday. We are welcomed by her daughter Kate and are just walking the hundred or so yards down from the farm track to the street, when Susan passes us in her car, stops and gives us a hug through the window. She is slightly stressed, for twenty-five American cousins are arriving the next day from Boston. With profuse apologies, she has to move us for our second night across the path to her brother's newly-built house; this is both comfortable and tasteful, but at only eight weeks old does not yet feel like a home. More pressingly, the bathroom window's glass is not frosted and directly overlooks the other houses... The laconically-chewing, American-style cattle have clearly seen worse, however, and decide to ignore us. Put it this way – it hasn't put them off their breakfast.

We manage to catch two music sessions in two out of the three pubs in the village, but are somewhat disappointed by the music-making which seems rather lacklustre and underpowered. Perhaps we heard such excellent playing last summer in these same pubs that we have been spoilt? Like jazz, it all depends on the *zeitgeist*, the spirit of the moment.

Apart from buying more CDs and popping in to say a brief (and with great difficulty), composed hello to Orla, I purchase a biography of Sean O'Riada, a composer, harpsichordist, scholar and lecturer, without whom the future of Irish traditional music in the 1960s and 70s would have looked entirely different – i.e. virtually non-existent. He was a legend in his all-too-short lifetime and his early performances lead directly to the formation of that Irish supergroup, The Chieftans.

We came to the pretty town of Westport in County Mayo. Described (erroneously) as a village, Westport is imposing, stylish and individual. More importantly from our point of view, we caught an excellent session at the rear of Matt Molloy's pub. Matt Molloy is not merely another traditional musician, but a legend. One of the finest flute-players to grace the traditional music scene, he performed with such seminal bands as Planxty, The Bothy Band and has been with The Chieftans now for many years. When not touring the world, he can be seen dropping in to play at his own pub. The evening we were there he was absent, but this was compensated for by an excellent duo of fiddle and accordion.

The back room was packed, but space was cleared to enable two young girls to dance a handful of jigs and reels. We talked to their parents and gleaned that they were from the United States from where apparently, the majority of Irish Dancing Champions now hail. They could have sworn that I was a long-lost cousin called O'Malley : "Not Jim O'Malley? That's spooky – sideways on, you look *just* like him. Are you *sure* that you don't have Irish blood?" I had to assure them that, though partly Cornish and Scottish, I was not Irish – at least, to the best of my knowledge. (I think they felt compensated by talking to Mary who is, of course, Welsh.) In common with many of their country folk, this family appeared to be ancestor-hunting – more to the point, Celtic-ancestor hunting!

Whilst at Westport, we thought we would attempt to climb the Holy Mountain, Crough Patrick, where the saint himself fasted and prayed for forty days and nights, in emulation of Moses and Jesus. Hiring stout, shepherd-style walking sticks, we prudently decided to climb only halfway, admiring the view of the 365 tiny islands in Clew Bay as we went. We then gingerly picked our way down the craggy paths and retreated to the very good cafe, where we bumped into a singer and her boyfriend from Dublin, with whom we had shared a table the previous night at Matt Molloy's. The entire experience was fairly extraordinary and brought about a genuine feeling of peace and tranquility for both of us.

In the afternoon we decided to drive inland through the mountains of Connemara, whose hills and valleys were pristine, whilst the small roads were devoid of traffic. Every now and again, the sunlight would catch and reflect several glistening mountain streams; the landscape through which we were slowly journeying seemed to resonate from some prehistoric era.

Onto the village of Leenane where the film of John B Keane's play *The Field* was made, starring Richard Harris and John Hurt, thence to Kylemore Abbey, a former Benedictine nunnery, but now a girls' school, complete with a walled Victorian kitchen garden and a one-time philanthropic owner, a Mancunian cotton merchant. With its dark, sombre brick and marble, Galway Cathedral was impressive, in a dour kind of way. A young organ scholar was playing Bach, but his interpretation was not being aided by the overly generous acoustic. We stepped outside and the sun was gradually dispersing the strata of clouds.

Our last full day (Wednesday) was spent journeying back across Ireland, but this time via Roscrea and Thurles, thus avoiding the congestion of Ennis and Limerick. On Thursday the 9am ferry departs absolutely punctually and the sea is smooth. As we return to the car-deck, we hear the odd muttered word about casualties in London, but nothing is clear... On a radio in a bookshop in Fishguard, more details begin to emerge, but it is not until we arrive home in Oxford and catch the extended evening bulletins on TV, that the horrors of that day fully begin to penetrate... rubble, twisted metal both above and below ground, fifty-two people dead...

Saturday 29th January 2005

The Barbican Centre, London: After an absence of some thirty years, the legendary Irish group Planxty have reformed and are playing three consecutive concerts. It is no exaggeration to say that this is, musically, a historic occasion. We travel up with Tessa and Donal and meet Jim and Jean Honeybone in the hall itself. Most of London's Irish community seems to be gathered here and emotions are running high with expectation – will they be able to recapture the old magic? The spotlights hit the stage and the boys (Christy, Andy, Donal and Liam, all grey-haired, now) stride onto the platform and the packed auditorium virtually erupts. They play beautifully, movingly and with the old mellifluousness and fire, as if their lives depend on it. With the rest of the capacity audience we give them a standing ovation, practically shouting ourselves hoarse. We leave on a high – an auditorium full of beaming, yet tearful faces. As Donal, who remembers them from the first time around commented, they were the Irish equivalent of The Beatles. On the journey home, we talk about Doolin, Milton Mowbay (home to the great piper Willie Clancy and the summer-school in his memory) as well as the coast of County Clare. I think we intuitively realise that the siren-song of Ireland is calling to us across the waters once more and that we cannot delay our return too long...

As things turned out, we never did visit Ireland again after our trip in 2005. We had planned to take the ferry to Rosslare and then drive up to Sligo and Donegal in the summer of 2007, but Mary had died in the February. It is not a trip to undertake by oneself; you need to delight and share in the landscape together, share small intimacies and jokes, share gestures and glances, as well as the practicalities of the driving.

Our last holiday was, in fact, spent on the Northumbrian coast, based at Alnmouth, where we explored Morpeth and all that area, listened to Kathryn Tickell, visited Durham and then my friends Stephen and Gillian Daw in Darlington, where we had a very convivial Italian lunch together. Sadly, as I write this, Stephen is in a care home suffering from Alzheimer's and is slowly failing. In purely humane terms it shouldn't be, but is, somehow, all the more potent and devastating when this terrible disease ravages the mind of a dedicated scholar.

44

The days, weeks and months quietly trundled on with teaching, lecturing, reviewing and occasional recitals and concerts. Full enough to be satisfying, yet also leaving room for seeing friends of us both, plus going to yoga and trying to fit in a couple of sessions a week at the gym. Yes, I had reached the age (middle age) when exercise was becoming a necessary corollary to a fairly sedentary lifestyle.

By February 2004, Mum's residential home was (for all the usual reasons) closing down, due to a lack of clients. I took her to view a handful of others in Bristol and Clevedon, but she was not impressed and we had reached an impasse. Serendipity was about to play a hand, however. One of the cleaners in the home on Wells Road knew the owners of, so she said, a very pleasant home called Rose Villa in Eagle Road, just off the main A4 road to Bath. She thought that it would suit my mother very well. After much to-ing and fro-ing and various assorted pieces of paperwork by the Social Services, I took Mum down to meet the owners, Julia and Philip who showed us the potential room that Mum would occupy, should she choose to go there. It was small, but homely and looked out onto a tiny courtyard containing a few plants. We talked this over and she seemed keen, almost delighted about the prospect of moving into Rose Villa. As one would with a small child, I tried to remain encouraging, but pointed out, gently, that the final decision was in the hands of the Social Services, for they paid for the great majority of my mother's care. I didn't want her hopes to be unnecessarily raised, then dashed. After frustrating delays and general bureaucratic dilly-dallying, they did, in the end, see fit to sanction Mum's move to Rose Villa and she moved into her new home in late February, nearly three weeks after her eighty-fifth birthday.

Everything about Rose Villa felt different from the previous establishment in Knowle: homelier, friendlier, diligent but more relaxed management, and some extremely nice and thoughtful carers who provided good meals and drinks at regular intervals. There was also a relaxing walled garden in which to sit and let the time, as well as the clouds, drift by. The original house, I gather, had been a nunnery; no wonder, then, that a feeling of peace and tranquility pervaded the place. In spite of her increasing frailties and serious mobility problems, Mum was, generally speaking, content in her new abode. As was Vernon, who had also come from the same home as my mother. A fellow Londoner, he liked his cigarettes and whisky and, for a time, used to play his organ in the dining room.

Carol, Carolyn, Dawn, Diane, Donna, Jane, Jenny and Tina. Those were the girls and ladies who bathed, cooked and attended to the residents. From our very first brief meeting (she was putting away a vacuum cleaner at the time), I particularly took a shine to Carol, whose gentle Somerset voice, easy and elegant walk, tied-back hair in a Mozartian bow and generally calm demeanour increasingly entranced me during the four or so years that Mum was there. She usually worked on Friday and Sunday evenings, so she normally 'framed' my monthly, weekend visits with her cheery welcomes and farewells which, over time, gradually became more intimate and protracted. When my mother was particularly low or weak, Carol's reassuring presence boosted my spirits. Not that she was without her own problems, for her husband Jim was in the Treetops nursing home in Keynsham with advancing dementia and Parkinson's disease.

It is a sobering thought that, without the need for her to work, plus the fact that my mother moved to Rose Villa when she did, that Carol and I would never have had any reason to meet. That old (non-black) magic called serendipity, was weaving its spell once more... and there's no such thing as coincidence, by the way; call it Fate or what you will, but don't deny it, for it is absolutely real. Little did I imagine in those days, however, that we would fall in love, let alone marry six years later! But I am moving on too far ahead.

Mum's residency at Rose Villa was interrupted at various junctures by emergency admittance to the Bristol Royal Infirmary. These were usually related to circulatory-cum-heart problems. On at least one occasion, I was rung up by her consultant saying that I should expect the worst, adding that she was virtually refusing to eat and had more-or-less given up the ghost – a phrase that tends to send shivers down my spine. Clearly, this wasn't her time, for she gradually rallied and recovered and was able to return home to Rose Villa, albeit in a weakened state. In these situations, I used to almost dread the phone ringing, for fear of what bad tidings an unfamiliar voice might bring. I began to understand why some members of the older generation (next-door neighbours in Ferry Road) refused to have a telephone installed. In their younger days, a ringing phone invariably meant bad news.

45

Bad news of an infinitely lesser hue was on my mind from the September of 2005. I would be fifty in early January and I wasn't looking forward to it. Illogical, ridiculous, vain even. Yes, all of those things, I realise now as then; but it didn't prevent lurking shadows of unease from periodically swirling around my brain and haunting me during the ensuing weeks.

By the day itself, I had half-heartedly resigned myself to the inevitable and even managed to enjoy a party at home with a good handful of friends. A little later, the photographs of me sat in a chair from my Clifton days, show me to be facing the camera with a subdued, almost wistful expression, which didn't seem to bode too well for the year ahead. Mary gamely made it through the evening, having been unwell since just after Christmas with a bad virus. Just as the last guests were leaving (Andrew, Rob and Sarah from The Mad Hatter Band), Mary collapsed against the hall radiator, knocking her head as she went down. The ambulance arrived and I followed in the car up to the John Radcliffe Hospital which was, luckily, only five minutes away – well, three if you really went for it up Jack Straw's Lane. She was seen promptly, had some tests and was released in the early hours and instructed to take things easy. Quite a birthday. Perhaps, I thought to myself (a born worrier, I admit) that my forebodings of the past few months had been justified... How little I knew and just how true those uneasy stirrings, those inner promptings, would become.

In June, with my co-operation, Birmingham Conservatoire laid on a belated fiftieth birthday concert of my music. This was held at lunchtime and consisted of me playing piano pieces by Graham Fitkin, Howard Skempton and myself. Also performed were premieres of *encore III* (conducted by Joe Cutler), *encore IX* and *Halcyon* for saxophone quartet. Friends such as Mary and Chris Lashmore-Davies drove up from Abingdon and composer John McCabe, who was examining at the Conservatoire that morning, then Birmingham University in the afternoon, kindly gave up his lunchtime to attend and offer support. It was a thoroughly happy occasion, topped by a very generous review by my old friend Chris Morley in *The Birmingham Post*.

I had attended rehearsals the previous afternoon and stayed

overnight in an hotel, where Mary was due to join me later in the afternoon. For some days she had been suffering stomach discomfort and severe constipation and she wasn't at all certain that she would be able to attend. She did appear, however, late the following morning in time for the concert.

In late August, I was down in Bristol visiting my mother. I cannot now remember if it was a Saturday or a Sunday. Whatever day it was, she was not feeling fit enough to be taken out in the car to have lunch. I walked the short distance from Rose Villa to the bottom of Brislington Hill and had lunch at The King's Arms. During this meal, I began to feel distinctly anxious and became increasingly unsettled. I didn't have a panic attack as such, but my ears were pounding, I felt constricted in my throat and utterly, morbidly desolate. In desperation, I walked around a local churchyard, my mind mechanically beating with the same terrible thought, a form of dark, pleading prayer, a huge Mahlerian *totentanz*: O Lord, dear God, please don't let either Mary or my mother die. At that moment, I suspected very strongly that I would not be able to cope with either of those eventualities. This seemed to have come entirely out of the blue; a heavy, suffocating velvet curtain that had descended, uninvited and unannounced. An inescapable blackness, where each second was elongated into a minute and each minute seemed to last for an hour, an eternity of emptiness. I walked back, shaken and very slowly, to Rose Villa and entered my mother's room, trying to appear calm and normal, so as not to alarm her.

For the remainder of that autumn I felt variously stressed and seemed to be undergoing odd bodily sensations such as sweating, muscle aches and generally flu-like symptoms. I was given some tablets that didn't, if I recall, work very effectively or possibly not at all. I was also involved in recording a CD over in East Anglia, whose producer was bullish and unhelpful, which only served to exacerbate my stress levels.

One Saturday in November, a former pupil of Mary's was being married (a civil ceremony) in a hotel north of Oxford. She had asked that Mary play both at the ceremony and background music before the reception. The night before, we both retired to bed, only to wake up in the small hours, feeling very queasy indeed. Neither of us was sick, but we felt rough and wondered how the hell we were going to manage to play at the wedding later the same day. Somehow we made it and Mary played very proficiently on my portable electric keyboard, both upstairs in the minstrels' gallery and later in the lounge. Fortunately, the staff were prevailed upon to move the hefty keyboard and amplifier. At the wedding breakfast, to which we were invited, the usual obligatory photographs were taken. Mary was wearing a dark red velvet top and I couldn't help noticing, later, that this contrasted with her wan and very white pallor.

Christmas came and went and we returned to Bristol to spend New Year's Eve with Ann and Philip in Clifton, as had been our custom for some years. It was a convivial evening and we all raised our glasses of champagne to toast in 2007 with the usual sentiments of health and happiness.

46

We drove back to Oxford later that New Year's Day and Mary mentioned, en route, that she felt as if she was going down with flu. She went to bed early that evening in the spare bedroom and I hoped that she would feel slightly better in the morning. She didn't have a good night, however. She had been sweating and thought that her ankle was hot and throbbing. Things had not improved over the next couple of days, her doctor was called and she suggested that Mary be taken to the Churchill Hospital to be screened for a possible deep-vein thrombosis. This was on my birthday, the fourth of January. We returned home, she was very tired and we decided to cancel going out to dinner. I brought in a take-away from our favourite Indian restaurant Qumins, and she ate a few lacklustre mouthfuls without finishing her meal.

By now she was on antibiotics, which appeared not to be making one iota of difference. Her night sweats were getting worse and she was becoming weaker; I was becoming increasingly worried, feeling impotent to really help and do something to alleviate whatever it was that was afflicting her. Paracetamol was failing to bring down her temperature.

On Monday the fifteenth, I reluctantly set off to teach in Birmingham on Mary's insistence, saying that she would be resting and would be alright. I made sure that I kept my mobile phone switched on. Old friends and teaching colleagues Tony and Oonagh dropped by and drove Mary to her appointment with her GP. Clearly, her GP was sufficiently alarmed to ring through to the Gynacological department of the John Radcliffe Hospital demanding that a bed be found for her. A voice at the other end seemed to be demurring – something about a shortage of beds and couldn't it wait until later in the week? The doctor crisply replied that she did not think that Mary might last that long. Tony and Oonagh drove her up to the John Radcliffe and Mary was admitted, carrying with her the blood sample that the GP had just taken. Our neighbour, Freda, alerted me to this development and I immediately travelled back from Birmingham and got to the hospital as quickly as possible. At this point, I was relieved that she was going to be properly looked after and I left, heaving a sigh of relief, almost feeling happy. Things would surely be alright now.

By Friday the nineteenth, things were far from alright and Mary's condition was declining at an alarming rate; to the extent, in fact, that Bryn summoned Rhodri and Adele from Durban, fearing that their mother might not make it through the weekend. Mary was due for more tests and X-rays, but was too weak to be moved from her bed – she lay on her side barely able to move or talk, while the whole family was convened around her bedside. Rhodri and Adele arrived and stayed with Bryn and Jayne near Goring. Contrary to what we had all thought, Mary survived the weekend and after a few days, was comparatively well enough to undergo more tests. The results of these tests were not wholly conclusive due to the amount of liquid present, which was masking key areas.

This liquid was, in fact, issuing from a large (and growing) tumour in the pancreas, although the primary site was thought to be the left ovary. We were stunned. What words are there at these times for either the patient or their loved ones? Strangely (and this must be a quirk of memory), I don't recall the doctors and nurses at any time referring to Mary's condition as cancer. Perhaps they did, perhaps they didn't. By now, the label (or a lack of it) was almost irrelevant. What we instinctively knew, I think, was that she probably had, at the most, only a few months left to live. If living, it was, indeed.

At the end of January, a bed was found for Mary in Sobell House, a wonderful hospice adjacent to the Churchill Hospital. She had spent nearly a fortnight at the John Radcliffe and they must have decided that they could do nothing further. So it was now palliative care – and then? That latter question I tried to put, at least for the moment, to the back of my mind. On the morning that she was transferred by ambulance, she sat in a wheelchair clutching an overnight bag. Her eyes and expression looked hollow, drained and pinched at the same time. Seldom, if ever, had I witnessed such emptiness and forlornness of spirit.

Initially she could walk the few steps to the en suite bathroom; then with the aid of a zimmer frame and, after a week or two, not at all. Meanwhile, her tumour was secreting watery fluid that was mixed with blood – a colour that resembled a grotesque rose. Her abdomen was becoming more distended and uncomfortable, but draining off the fluid into a bag helped to release some of the pressure. Then for a day or so, the stomach would resume a more normal contour, but only temporarily so... Sitting with her one evening, I noticed that the replaced bag had filled up with this liquid in a mere twenty minutes. A nurse came to empty it again and also to attach another bag. It wasn't long before, that too, was full.

During the last couple of weeks, Mary was becoming more nauseous and was given a syringe driver that administered anti-sickness drugs and morphine at regular intervals. This was not really having any effect and she was attached to a second syringe driver (which I later learnt, was a fairly rare procedure). She ate what she could, but this gradually diminished. Quietly cheerful and friendly volunteers came round the rooms, just prior to mealtimes, with trolleys of drinks, both soft and alcoholic. Occasionally, Mary would have a tiny sweet sherry that barely covered the bottom of the glass, but at least she was game for a drink. Quite often Siani and I would be offered one, too and, by that time, we felt that we deserved a glass of white wine.

A mother of one of Mary's pupils very thoughtfully visited with the present of a mini CD player. As news of her condition spread amongst friends and former teaching colleagues, Mary received many visitors though, latterly, the family and I had to ration them due to Mary's tiredness. Even in the last week,

Mary continued to receive visitors graciously and, amazingly, in a spirit of peace and contentment, between bouts of bringing up green bile so shockingly iridescent that it resembled the colour of an exotic lizard or a blob of paint from a Patrick Heron canvas.

The ambience of Sobell House was extraordinarily peaceful and serene, this atmosphere being further enhanced by the gently curving corridors (as on board a ship) and the high, airy ceilings. All was quiet, except for the occasional television or isolated murmurs of conversations with visitors and consultants. The loudest sounds were those of feet passing the rooms, in either a measured gait or in a hurry... In bleak reality, of course, this building was a ship of death, yet the voyage towards its destination was civilised, dignified and as calm as it was possible to be. The staff and its volunteers who manned the reception desk were never less than welcoming, helpful and sympathetic.

Cancer – the sideways-scuttling, cancrizans crab.

Cancer – that insidious bastard of a disease that looks so beautiful and multi-faceted under the microscope; evil, live deceptor.

Cancer – that insatiable, greedy feeder that demands more and more; that takes over the body, mind and (almost) the soul of a person.

Cancer – a deadly, mean-spirited, uncaring, volatile and voracious fucker.

Cancer – a thoroughly unscrupulous and dodgy geezer, who pounces when you least suspect it.

On one or two evenings, we would listen to excerpts of piano music on the CD player. Usually the great Arturo Benedetti Michelangeli playing Chopin – some of the Mazurkas or, Mary's favourites, the Ballade in g minor and the second Scherzo. We had, over the years, been privileged to see him play, solo, at the Barbican Hall in London. We now silently held hands, giving one another an occasional and affectionate squeeze, as Michelangeli's marvellous delicacy and power surged over and around us. Then she would ask me to stop the music as she was tired, just too tired. Around nine o'clock each evening I kissed her goodnight and gave a subdued wave to her (how could it be otherwise?) from the doorway of this strange room, that was not hers but that had, parodoxically, become all too familiar. For many nights, I drove home wondering whether I would see her alive the next day.

In the last three days, she lost the ability to speak; could, in fact, barely croak or whisper. She was, I think, already moving into another sphere, one where she could, without fuss, shed her earthly body and begin to embrace the realm of pure spirit.

On the Saturday morning, Siani, Bryn and I were sat around her bed saying words of comfort and holding her hand, but saying very little ourselves. Ominously, she had been moved nearer to the nurses' station. Someone opened the curtain and she gestured feebly and with a groan, indicating that the light was too much for her eyes. By this stage, bless her, anything and everything was too much. In the afternoon I had to sing in our church choir for some special festive service or other and left Bryn and Siani with their Mum. I returned after five o'clock, Bryn departed and Siani stayed on a while; I think that we had a glass of wine together and chatted intermittently, our minds being elsewhere and in a place that neither of us wanted to be...

About eight o'clock, I said to Mary, *sotto voce* in her right ear, that I really ought to go home as I was hungry and needed to eat. I was also weary with worry and fatigue. Although she must have been barely conscious, there was a faint smile of recognition, as if she was thinking, "That's typical of Tigger" (her pet name for me). I kissed her goodnight and the nurses asked me to be as alert as I could be during the coming night, as they would probably need to phone me.

That call awoke me at about ten past two. The nurse simply said that Mary's breathing had altered during the last few minutes and that I ought to come up as soon as I was able. I tried to dress hurriedly, but my limbs virtually refused to move quickly; it felt as if I was wading through heavy mud or treacle, to be honest. I cannot remember what I thought of or how my mind was functioning, if at all – it was, most likely, on a form of autopilot as I drove as quickly as I dared. I arrived at Sobell House, rang the night bell and was let in by a nurse with a very serious demeanour. This was approximately at 2.45am and it transpired that Mary had slipped away very peacefully about ten minutes earlier with this same nurse holding her hand. I had missed her transition, her gentle sliding from this world into the next, but she wouldn't have known that I was there, in all probability. Siani arrived at about ten past three, an hour's drive from Stanford Dingley in Berkshire. We silently held each other and hugged one another for some long moments. While the staff were attending to Mary's body, we sat down and drank tea, the comforting, stereotypical English reaction to situations of crisis. Then someone popped in and said that we were free to take a last look at her and remove any personal items. They had opened the windows wide, but there was still a terrible stench of putrefaction in the room, on which I commented. Siani, a nurse herself, merely observed that on many occasions it was far worse than this.

We gathered her personal belongings together, then kissed her, said a farewell out loud, and touched her forehead in a gesture of blessing and departure.

I realised that my churchyard premonition of almost exactly six months to the day had been fulfilled. Mary was seventy-seven, but we all thought that she would live until her late eighties or nineties, but it was not to be.

Nos da, cariad*; nos da…
Requiescant in pace… in pace… Ora pro nobis
* Welsh = Goodnight, love.

Siani drove back to Berkshire and I drove the few minutes down the hill to Marston. I climbed numbly into bed at around 4. 45am, setting the alarm for eight o' clock. I reasoned that I possibly wouldn't be able to sleep and I might as well go to church and sing in the choir for Eucharist as normal. As normal? Nothing would now be normal and, to paraphrase Yeats' words, everything had been "changed utterly". Yes – and *if* there was any beauty, even the tiniest modicum of it, it did indeed appear to be truly terrible.

I sang Eucharist that Sunday morning, although I could barely see the hymns for the tears which welled up ceaselessly. Jim Cocke announced Mary's death from the pulpit and there were many kind comments and supportive hugs from various members of the congregation afterwards over cups of coffee. I agreed to meet up with other members of the choir (Tom, Colin, Sheridan, etcetera) for a pub lunch – I really did not want to be alone.

But before that, I had to return to Sobell House to collect the death certificate at noon. With surprisingly little fuss and efficiency I was given this. Then one of the staff, a man, gently but firmly guided me with his hand in the small of my back, through a door, to view Mary in the mortuary. Her face and hands were beginning to turn blue and her forehead was marble-cool, if not quite cold, to the touch. Her face had a slight trace of a frown, as if death had disturbed a good night's sleep, but otherwise she had a peaceful countenance, in spite of the hollowed and shrunken contours.

From the day that she became ill, on New Year's Day, until the night of her passing was fifty-six days – eight weeks, bar one day.

Nos da, cariad; nos da, nos da…

Then I turned away, forever as it were, not glancing, Orpheus-like, back over my shoulder, but merely followed the man out into the bright light and surreality of this bizarre Sunday.

Sunday 25th February 2007: also Anthony Burgess' birthday and the day after Roger's fifty-second birthday. A death and two birthdays…

That evening I honoured an already-agreed dinner date with our friends Chris and Mary in Abingdon which, even in these circumstances, was of immense help and solidarity. Ironically, Abingdon would prove to have a further link – and within the next few days.

47

The funeral was arranged surprisingly quickly. Jim Cocke had tactfully suggested during the previous few weeks that a very good and reliable undertaker would be Nigel Carter of Abingdon. He was known to both myself and Bryn and it was agreed that this seemed to be a good plan of action. Nigel came to our house in Ferry Road and all the necessary arrangements were made, remarkably enough, for the Friday 2nd March of that same week. All the family and myself were in agreement that we didn't want to delay Mary's funeral any longer than was absolutely necessary. From the Monday to that Friday, I was busy, as were Bryn and Siani, with seeing to all the usual official documentation such as registering the death and sorting out details of the funeral service. Rhodri flew back from South Africa for the second time within five or six weeks and Mary's cousin Vida from Dolfor near Newtown, came to stay and support me for the days either side of the funeral.

Early on the Friday morning, Nigel Carter considerately rang me to see how I was coping. I felt very weak, as if I could barely walk and was at a complete loss but, of course, you don't admit to that either on the phone or in person. You know that what you and the family are going through is ghastly and a complete nightmare, but you have, perforce, to get on with it. In that (normally not hideous) phrase, the show had to go on. A funeral is a very public event and is, in that sense and however much one would wish it to be otherwise, a kind of show – albeit of a very formal kind.

All Saints' church was packed close to capacity, or so the array of faces seemed to indicate. Relations form Wales, neighbours, pupils, friends and ex-teaching colleagues all turned up in profusion to honour the life, work and memory of Mary; Mary the small, dignified lady with a quiet demeanour and immense fortitude, faith and love. As is so often the case on these occasions, the tone, though naturally solemn, also felt celebratory. In the hymns, which included *Angel voices ever singing*, one of her favourites, we sang our hearts out for her and to her. She had always liked the idea of angels, heavenly messengers, mediating between the human and the divine. There was also *Love divine all loves excelling* to the rugged but beautiful Welsh tune, not Stainer's more famous melody; and *Cym Rhondda*, in which the Welsh contingent, true to form, raised their rugby-honed voices to the roof in a *paean* of praise. Canon David Owen read a poem by Dafydd ap Gwilym, whilst Bob Evans read Psalm 23 in Welsh.

Afterwards, we made our way down to the small cemetery in Old Marston, where Mary was buried in an inconspicuous plot in the left-hand corner. As in life, she had always loathed being conspicuous. Amidst the dull hum of traffic on the nearby ring road, we departed in dribs and drabs to attend the reception, up the road and across the fields, at the Victoria Arms. The formalities now over, we all needed a few drinks and the chance to slightly wind down, greet old friends, make our thank-yous and generally raise a glass to Mary's memory. For the last time, then, *Nos da, cariad*.

I entered into unknowing,
yet when I saw myself there,
without knowing where I was,
I understood great things;
I will not say what I felt
for I remained in unknowing
transcending all knowledge

Those lines written by St John of the Cross seemed and still seem to me to sum up Mary's thoughts on the afterlife. Once, when asked what she thought lay beyond this life, Mary replied that she hoped that she would learn more, implying that she hoped, as we all do, perhaps, that her questions might be answered. I would like to think that this has happened, either wholly or in part.

For purely earthbound and almost selfish reasons, I, too, was in a state of unknowing and the vista at this time was far from pleasant. My faith wasn't wavering, exactly, but I did feel that God was being mysteriously and obdurately silent at the one time in my life that I needed Him most. What was happening, I realised was that, however tough the situation, my faith was being tested to the utmost limits. That Friday afternoon, we all drove over to Bryn's house at South Stoke for a family get-together. The next day, the Saturday, I saw Vida off and onto her coach at Gloucester Green, bound for Newtown. I was sorry to see her go, for her presence had been a source of real comfort and strength. I waved her off as cheerily as I could and then wandered around for an hour or two in Peacocks and Marks & Spencers, putting off the return to an eerily empty house. I was in a trance-like daze.

Some (still dazed) days later, I thought that it would be appropriate and proper to submit, with Mary's children's approval, an obituary notice to *The Oxford Times* and The *Oxford Mail*. The children agreed and so that is what I did. In one sense, perhaps, I was too close to undertake this task and yet in another sense I could, to an extent, speak on behalf of old acquaintances and colleagues. After a life has been extinguished we tend to need a resume and summing-up of that person's life; a form of bearing witness to them, I suppose.

Over the twenty-four years of our partnership, Mary had given me stability, support, a real home, a great affection and respect for the linguistic and literary heritage of Wales, the beauties of the Lleyn peninsula and the poetry of RS Thomas.

She had many more qualities and I can only hope that I was able to adequately reciprocate; although, of course, one always tends to feel inadequate.

With her Latin, Welsh, belly-dancing and most of all her gardening, Mary had, I think, achieved most of her ambitions. All except one, that is. She had hoped to visit the Welsh community in Patagonia and, possibly, some descendants of her ancestors. George, the saxophonist, had given her some maps and ideas of where to visit. She did, however, manage eighteen visits to South Africa in twenty-one years to visit her youngest son Rhodri.

Foolishly, perhaps, except for the week of the funeral, I didn't take any time off work, but soldiered on. Probably stupidly, I thought that that would be what Mary would have wanted me to do; indeed, what she most probably would have done herself in the same circumstances. This was, in theory, all very well. But I hadn't allowed for the fact that I was having huge difficulty in concentrating on anything, be it reading or even listening to music, which was rather alarming, never mind being sufficiently alert to help my pupils and students. I had bargained on feeling rough mentally, but not so much physically. Nonetheless, I ploughed on and socialised as much as I could, hating the idea of spending time alone. Pubs, jazz, up to London to see a revival of John Osborne's *The Entertainer* starring Robert Lindsay with Siani's brother-in-law Edward, the Ledbury Poetry Festival, over to Suffolk to stay for a few days with Elis and Pam – and so it went manically on, the list was endless. And that's how I wanted it to be, how I needed it to be.

By the time I came to the summer vacation, however, I was practically on my knees. I also had to start packing and to move house, for it was part of our mutual agreement (and her will) that, in the event of Mary's death, the house would be sold and split four ways, between myself, Bryn, Siani and Rhodri. This was fine and I had no qualms about this arrangement whatsoever, but I was completely exhausted and had trouble even working for an hour at a time, let alone being very effective or efficient. It was a very fraught time. There were, in the end, four large skipfuls of detritus from the loft and the garage. The family and a few friends proffered assistance which was invaluable; now all I needed was to find a flat that I could afford.

Before that, however, I needed some help to enable me to cope. My friend John Lanyon (nephew of the painter Peter, whom he never met) suggested that I make an appointment with his acupuncturist at the Oxford Natural Health Centre at the bottom of Rose Hill. By now, I was willing to try anything that might help. The first few sessions didn't really seem to kick in, but after the fifth one, I began to slowly notice a difference, even if I was still very fragile mentally. I kept imagining, for example, that I was going to be ill, lain up in bed and not able to cope by myself. I had even got as far as alerting one or two friends to this possibility, so that I might, if need be, come and stay with them... As a colleague of my own acupuncturist commented, "The trouble is, Richard, that you're trying to run on empty." Yes, that was about it; depleted, a husk, a spent shell. Any of those terms would, I surmised, have summed up my state at that time.

I did find a flat, in Nursery Close, just off Lime Walk in Headington, which was very convenient for church, amongst other things. It was a clean and comfortable two-bedroom flat with a small, but not overlooked patio garden and a fairly large, light kitchen. I moved in at the end of August and within a few days, with the help of one or two friends, I had unpacked the majority of cardboard boxes and hung a few pictures. It was beginning to look a bit more like home, even if it wasn't the one that I had been used to for the past twenty-one years. I tried to be positive and count my blessings. At least I had a roof over my head (quite a nice one), plus the first instalment of my share of Mary's legacy had arrived, which was really providential.

With the commencement of the Michelmas term, I was flung back into teaching and was still struggling with bereavement. If anything, it now seemed more acute than it had in those first early weeks. Things came to a head when I collapsed twice within the space of nine days in November, the second occasion of which I was taken by ambulance to the John Radcliffe, though I was later discharged the same day and told to rest. I thought hard about this and decided, very reluctantly, that I had better start taking some anti – depressive pills (Citalopram) which I already had, but had resisted taking. For about a month, the side-effects were bizarre and far from pleasant, but they gradually settled down as did my brain chemistry. A friend, another John, told me quite categorically that he wouldn't still be alive if it were not for the calming balm of Citalopram. He had, in fact, been desperate and was about to give it all up. I both sympathised and empathised with him as I was still tunnelling through the darkness, hoping against hope to catch a glimmer of light. That glimmer, then a small shaft, would arrive, but not in a manner that I might have expected or imagined.

The next section, though odd and deliberately fragmentary, quite distressing perhaps, attempts to give you some idea of how disassociated and peculiar I was feeling in those bleak months. My life, such as it was, appeared to be on hold and in a state of suspended abeyance.

48

no no out out of mind beside myself outside outside of myself floating

out of my mind high above only only shadow

yes fast breath

stomach an idling engine with choke fullypulled out
slow it all down
blurred eyes blurred brain
cannot think cannot listen cannot read no

no nom no more roar no focus on autopilot yes

whirling whirling black hole sucking everything in sucking all energy till nothing

no thing thing will live to sing

but but no strength anything everything is effort and at many

removes

so far away are you so you are
other side of thin veil so thin now all light no no darkness anymore

in His nearer presence all light all pulsing

but we are left here me left here I try but drifting
away towards again

cannot but

She does not want this for you, she is saying that she does not wish this pain that you are suffering. But you and we have no choice in this matter. It is a predetermined path which neither Mary or anyone else here can change. It was time, she had completed her Earthly journey; you must understand this. Mary wants you to understand this both in your heart and mind and to be happy for her, difficult though that now is for you. Light will come to you, though you may not think this possible at the moment; but, rest assured it will come, though not necessarily in the way that you will be expecting. Put your trust in God. We are only too aware of your grief and your many problems in the physical world, but we are with you, healing and protecting you. Now, dear one, God go with you and may His blessings be upon you and the light of the Lord enter into you and surround you in all your ways.

Roger and Richard, Devon, 2007.

BRISTOL AGAIN,
LOVE AGAIN

49

That small ray gradually brightened and grew bigger over the succeeding months, the darkness faded and eventually disappeared to a pinprick and was extinguished. Occasional ghosts rise to the surface of the memory (and that is right and proper), but they are not all painful – far from it, in fact.

All this was due to Carol who I had been unable to see for some weeks at Rose Villa. When I managed to pop down and see Mum, during the course of Mary's short illness, it was invariably for one day only or even just half a day at the weekend, when Carol was not on duty. She heard of Mary's passing from my mother and was shocked, for she had met her briefly, twice, served tea to her and liked her. Mum couldn't believe it, found it hard to take in the tragic information, either and was sad that she was no longer able to be around to help me. "Darling," she said one afternoon, "nothing will ever be as terrible as Mary's death." She really, of course, was meaning her own demise, whenever that would come. She was trying to comfort and strengthen me, bless her. In the next moment, she added, half seriously, half impishly, "Well, darling, I will do my very best not to peg out on you this year, too." She grinned, but meant it; and it was typical of her Cockney wit to diffuse a potentially difficult, possibly sentimental moment, with a dash of dry humour.

Carol's husband Jim had finally succumbed to his Parkinson's disease and dementia on 3rd July 2006, seven months before Mary's death. One day (was it a phone call or face to face?) she suggested that if I wanted to chat to her or share anything, then I would be most welcome and, perhaps, we could meet. We went for a drink and our first date was on the Easter Sunday evening at the Arnos Court Hotel, just past the cemetery and the television studios on the Bath Road. (So that's where TV producers go...) I was at the junction of Eagle Road, on the way to our rendezvous, when she drove past in her black Peugeot 206, waving merrily. It seemed like a good and propitious omen. I parked, greeted her with a kiss on the cheek and we went inside where I ordered a gin and tonic for her and a lager for me. Sadly, I couldn't drink too much as I had to drive back to Oxford later that evening to be up early for a recording session (recorder and harpsichord) on the bank holiday Monday in Buckinghamshire.

She looked lovely, even glamorous, but I nearly didn't recognise her, for at work she quite sensibly wore her hair up. This evening, however, she had freshly washed and curled it and I couldn't believe how long it was – at least halfway down her back! She was dressed in a pretty black and white blouse, a pale mauve jacket with black skirt and black shoes. She looked elegant, stylish and smart and I was proud of her and so pleased to be together, just the two of us, after a long absence of not seeing her, even fleetingly. We got through two gin and tonics and two lagers, respectively and then, very reluctantly, I had to set off down the M4. Carol was taking her mother Joyce abroad on holiday and I wouldn't see her until the end of May. It had been an evening of shared thoughts and closeness and I couldn't wait to see her again. The end of May seemed a long time ahead, however.

Halfway through the month, I received a lovely postcard from Carol in Mallorca. She thoughtfully included a very true, simple but beautiful sentiment which was applicable to the two of us: "Life is not measured by the number of breaths we take, but by the moments that take our breath away."

After she returned, our relationship intensified and moved up a gear. She invited me for dinner at the beginning of June and, in a small but meaningful and thoughtful gesture, laid the table with two dark red roses, one each in memory of my Mary and her Jim. We toasted each other and our respective late loves, listened to some music and spent an evening full of closenness and warmth.

June 16th was 'Bloomsday' and is always celebrated by the literary and musical members of the Oxford Irish community. There was a lively night held upstairs at the Port Mahon pub, with music by various local musicians including the traditional singer Mick Henry (a fount of knowledge in this area), guitarist Gerald Garcia, violinists and box players plus poets Tom Paulin and Bernard O'Donoghue reading poems and prose by Yeats and, of course, James Joyce. I mention this, not only because of my empathy with and love of traditional Irish music, but more personally and pertinently, because this evening formed an upbeat to the next day, when I drove down to Bristol and visited Carol for Sunday lunch. This day was especially memorable, for it was the first occasion on which we made love. We had waited for this moment, not rushed into it and when it seemed appropriate and right, we then savoured it.

By the beginning of July and the summer vacation, Mary's death had really hit me and I felt as if I was almost a ghost of myself, barely aware of what I was doing. Carol decided that I needed a short break, away from the house clearing, so took me down to Dorset for a few days, to a favourite haunt of hers, Burton Bradstock. She had known this area when her parents had had a static caravan high above the beach. We stayed in the one hotel there; it was comfortable, but had seen better days. The manager was a double of Basil Fawlty (only politer) and one of the elderly waitresses resembled Julie Walters as Mrs Overall. Never mind; the air was fresh, the scenery beautiful and the hotel was no more than a couple of minutes walk down to the beach. Next door lived the singer Billy Bragg. Those few days revived my spirits, if not my body and they felt like an unofficial honeymoon. After we returned to Bristol, we then drove back to Oxford where Carol stayed to help me host a farewell drinks party to say goodbye to Ferry Road. Without her help, I could not have coped. We tried to be discreet, but I am sure that some of my friends guessed that we were already romantically involved.

Which, in the opinion of some, was clearly too soon – too soon after Mary's death. Well, from their small-minded and blinkered perspectives, that may have been so. But to that ten per cent or so (and, if you are reading this, which I doubt, you will know who you are...), let me say this: a couple of weeks before her death, Mary said, quietly but firmly to me, that she really hoped that I would find someone else to love and to settle down with. My more broad-minded friends were delighted for both of us, openly said so and even went as far as to say that they thought that both Mary and Jim would be looking down (if that's what they do in the next world) and would be glad for us. There is no rationale or time limit to grieving and we each have to battle through as best as we can. For Carol and myself, we felt absolutely blessed that we could comfort and strengthen one another and, through our mutual grief, help our love to grow. That point of light was growing and, yes, would continue to grow.

The Florentine writer Dante, that colossus of the Middle Ages, brought his *The Divine Comedy* to a close with these illuminating and majestic lines:

But already my desire and my will
Were being turned like a wheel, all at one speed,

By the love which moves the sun and the other stars.

Yes – that was absolutely and exactly what I was feeling and what I needed, almost ached for, with all my heart and mind. And that kind of love occurs – bang! – out of the blue and happens to one totally involuntarily; you are placed in its path and resistance is wholly futile. It is both an unlooked-for joy as well as a privilege and a blessing. It does, in every sense, move one into fresh regions of experience and understanding, even if that understanding comes only later and retrospectively.

50

The owners of Rose Villa residential home were planning to take early retirement. This meant, therefore, that alternative accommodation had to be sought for the ten or so remaining residents, which included my mother. Ample notice had been given, but this still created various assessments and administrative headaches. The residents were also suffering headaches – to be moved, uprooted in your late eighties and early nineties is unsettling, to say the least. All this upheaval occurred in mid-December 2007. I felt then and still feel now, that the residents should have been left to have their Christmas in peace and familiar surroundings and be moved out in the early new year, but there we are...

Mum moved on December 19th to a bigger, less personal 'home' in Bishopsworth that had the option of a nursing section, which she looked increasingly likely to be needing, as her mobility was now virtually non-existent. There were more staff than at Rose Villa who, in the main, were perfectly pleasant and efficient, but the place was far less personal and, for Mum, the whole move was traumatic and fraught. She was never less than polite to the staff, but she didn't like her new en suite accommodation. The only thing to be said for it was that her window overlooked a peaceful bowling green, reminiscent of a stylised (and very English) scene from a David Inshaw painting. She was uncomplaining but...

Quite a proportion of the New Year was spent in hospitals, however. She had quite a tough time of it being fielded between the Bristol Royal Infirmary, the Bristol General and, at one point, Frenchay hospital where she needed a skin graft. On one occasion, she had only arrived back at the home for twelve hours, when she fell badly, twisted her leg and had to be re-admitted. The skin graft on her leg, ironically, became infected even though the operation was deemed necessary in the first place to prevent exactly that condition from occurring.

It was no small wonder that at the age of eighty-nine, Mum felt that she had had enough. Less than a year previously, she had admitted to me in a straightforward and non-morbid tone, that she didn't wish to live past ninety. Realistically, though, there had been a few false alarms before, so I never quite knew what to expect. And, as I have always felt, the big events at the beginning and end of our lives, are not in our own hands...

I drove down to Bristol for the weekend on Friday 9th. May. Carol and I visited her in the BRI that evening and she was in a lot of pain in her stomach and abdomen area. Mum was cogent but eating very little and had developed diverticulitis; she was in evident distress. We chatted to her for a while, hoping not to overtire her. Carol proudly showed Mum the engagement ring that I had recently bought her. Tired as she was, Mum very intently gazed at it and made murmuring noises of approval; she was finding difficulty in summoning up any energy to talk. In retrospect, we both observed that at that moment, my mother felt that Carol would look after me, that her own job, her life's work was done and that she could let go. Seeing her in this state was very difficult. We gave her a kiss and said goodnight as optimistically as we could and then headed straight for the pub opposite the hospital entrance – we had rarely needed a drink so badly.

As was my custom of many years, I stayed with Ann and Philip in Clifton. As was also our custom, we had some wine and I warned them that Mum's condition was not looking at all good. On the Saturday, I visited twice – in the morning, then in the evening, meeting up with Carol in the afternoon for some much-needed solace. One of the consultants called me in to a side office and gently warned me that they were not expecting Jennie to last much longer. She was cold to the touch, said the lady consultant and they thought that her organs were beginning to gradually close down. I sat with her and held her hand. At this distance, memories tend to blur, but I think that she was already slipping in and out of consciousness.

With a heavy heart and expecting the worst, I went again later that evening. She was already on her way to the next world, I suspect, but I talked to her, said prayers aloud to her (for a peaceful passing) and, clinging to the fact, the hearing is the last sense to atrophy, I thanked her for all that she had done for me, for all that she had given me and meant to me over my fifty-two years.

The nurses asked that I leave my mobile phone on during the coming night. This was a moment of pure *déja vu* for me of Mary's imminent death fifteen months before. Well, bless her, Mum had almost quippingly said that she would try not to die the same year as Mary and she had been true to her word. My phone did ring in the middle of the night: the nurse said that Mum had very gently passed away at 3.30am.

Thy kingdom come, thy will be done...

Mum died on Sunday 11th May, the Feast of Pentecost that year. She would have found this quite appropriate, the idea of fire being an agent of purification and renewal. I drove to the hospital and arrived at about 9am (it had seemed futile to go any earlier), saw her briefly and removed her few items of clothing. I then drove over to meet Carol at the nursery near Whitchurch, then we attended a service at St Margaret's Church in Queen Charlton where a prayer was said for my mother.

The funeral was held at Haycombe Crematorium on the outskirts of Bath on Friday 23rd. May at 2pm; the same resting-place, in fact, that Mum's mum was cremated back in January 1966. Reverend Jim Cocke came down from Oxford to officiate and although there were merely a dozen mourners, those present had all been part of my mother's life – from Grace, a neighbour in Littlecross House, who loyally visited her without fail every Friday morning in all three of her residential homes, to Eunice from Drama Group 7, two ladies from Southville Townswomen's Guild plus my oldest pal Roger from Tiverton as well as cousins Ann and John.

Ann Maycock read a poem by Elizabeth Barratt-Browning, her sonnet *How Do I Love Thee?* (which my father had given Jennie), there was a passage from the Book of Revelation and some John Donne.

The two hymns were *Crimond* and *Love Divine, All Loves Excelling* to Stainer's tune. Music, fore and aft, was the slow movement from Bach's *Concerto for Two Violins, BWV 1043*, Walford Davies' *God Be In My Head* and Duke Ellington's *Satin Doll*, this last being a longtime favourite. When I played to her, that gracefully swinging, yet punchy tune would be an invariable request.

Afterwards, we all repaired to The Compton Inn at Compton Dando. All in all, it had been a good and celebratory send-off to a multi-faceted life, as lived by my mother Grace Jennie Harris.

51

The week immediately following Mum's death proved to be a busy one, and not only for all the usual funereal reasons. I had two days of examining at the Birmingham Conservatoire to get through which I didn't feel I could cancel, although part of me felt exactly like doing just that.

More importantly and pressingly, I had to curate and oversee Mary's memorial concert at the Holywell Music Room. Sobell House had been so marvellous and supportive during Mary's illness, that I felt that it would be appropriate to not only have a concert in Mary's memory, but that the money raised should go entirely to Sobell House. In the previous February, a year since Mary's death, I met Lindsay Manifold, the charity co-ordinator at Sobell and she agreed with the proposal and thought that the project sounded a fine idea. I liaised with Lindsay over the intervening couple of months and organised who might be available and who might wish to play something in Mary's memory. In the event, there were no shortage of offers, but the last thing that I wanted was one of those ghastly concerts that doesn't know when to stop, however well-intentioned the participants.

We set the date for Friday 16th. May, five days before what would have been Mary's seventy-eighth birthday; Lindsay and her team of helpers diligently took on all the publicity and distribution. On the night itself, the Holywell was packed with familiar faces and the money raised was £1000 for the Sobell House Hospice. Lindsay and I were delighted at the response and I am sure that Mary would have been, too.

All the performers had known Mary in some capacity, either as pupils or colleagues or as friends and generously donated their services that evening. Violinist John Hounam opened the proceedings with a beautiful account of some solo Bach; also playing Bach were guitarist Ray Burley and myself on harpsichord performing one of our favourite movements, the slow movement from the organ *Trio Sonata in C*. Jazz pianist Pat Thomas delivered a surely-built and very organic version of Thelonius Monk's *Blue Monk*, whilst two new piano pieces by Laurence Crane and myself were given their premieres, played by the composers. There was also Irish music from Mick Henry and friends (including a spine-tingling version of *Si Bheag a's Si Mhor*) and Rebecca Money-Kyrle and her husband played duets for recorder and guitar. Oh yes, and Dvorak chamber music, plus Bernard O'Donoghue and Jenny Lewis reading their own poems. Mary would have relished each and every item in this moving, yet highly convivial tribute. Indeed, the whole evening felt somewhere between a feast and a wake; people paying homage, too, as they stepped up to make their offering, as it were. All in all, the whole thing was a marvellous celebration. It didn't overrun, it had made money and been thoroughly enjoyed by all those present. And, benignly presiding over us all with a broad grin that night, was the spirit of Mary herself, I felt sure, urging us on.

52

My mother had, as was so often the case, been (infuriatingly) right. Her death and funeral had, oddly and extraordinarily, been nowhere as bad as I had been anticipating. That occasion when she had said as much in the wake of Mary's death had proven true. I suppose I had been half expecting Mum's death for so long that, when the time came, I was almost prepared – at least, as far as anyone can be prepared for the passing of a parent. It was as if, somehow quite mercifully, things had seemed to be gradually slipping away from her. At the end, she had achieved a sense of calm and of equilibrium, qualities that had always eluded her in earlier decades. And now, I must make a new life; for both myself and Carol, for the two of us together.

It had become increasingly painful to have to separate from each other on Sunday evenings when I had to drive back to Oxford. From both our perspectives, it was financially unrealistic to try looking for a house in Oxford. We agreed, therefore, that it would be much better for me to be based in Bristol. I was driving down most weekends, anyway; I commuted by train to Birmingham once a week, so the whole scheme was not really much different, just turned around.

So that is exactly what I did. I moved out of my rented flat in Nursery Close in the middle of August 2008 and moved, courtesy of Luker Bros, of Headington, into Carol's comfy bungalow in Whitchurch. The flat had been a godsend for nearly the whole bizarre year, but now I needed to take a leap into the unknown and commit myself to Carol. To be frank, I had no qualms about the move; indeed, I was looking forward to starting a new life together, where we would support one another. And, in term time, I would be able to see and stay with some of my old friends in Oxford. A fresh page was being turned, a new (and very necessary) chapter begun. I had returned to the city of my birth – not so much completing a circle; rather, describing an elliptical orbit, perhaps.

In the summer of 2009, Carol's garage was converted into a music studio for me and, in due course, Andrea Goble delivered the double-manual harpsichord which he had stored since the previous year. This same summer, Carol's mother Joyce became ill with cancer. She had had a mastectomy ten years previously, all was thought to be well, but they had not entirely removed it all. She had been in remission, essentially, but now it had returned. Joyce had an X-ray which revealed a lesion in her back and now, during this summer, she was suffering from stomach problems. She had chemotherapy treatment which exhausted her and she gradually began to lose her lovely hair, which was her pride and joy. Joyce was not vain, but she always took pains with her hair. A replacement wig was found which looked virtually identical and she accepted this state of affairs reluctantly, but with good grace.

Cancer: marauding, lurking fraudster...

Cancer: that obscene, bastard *ritornelli*...

Cancer: a truth that will lie in wait for all too many of us, no matter how many prayers are said, how many candles lit in dark churches...

Cancer: encroacher of skin and bone, destroyer of vital organs; an invader intent on conquering all in its path...

Cancer: serial killer. When and where will it strike next...?

Joyce was told by her oncologist that she had "a window of opportunity." Mere medical rhetoric? She and the family decided, reluctantly, to open that small window, but... She was slightly better for three weeks over the Christmas, celebrated her birthday on the seventeenth of January as best she could, even paid her respects to a hotel Sunday lunch. Then it was downhill, that window was slowly closing and the light fading. The staff on her ward at the Bath Royal United were dedicated, warm and loyal to her needs. It was, for me, a replay of watching Mary die, for Joyce's cancer was pancreatic, too. *Encore, encore, déjà vu.* But it was new and infinitely hideous for Carol and her brothers Steve and Mike, to behold.

A hospital is the unwanted hotel, the wrong and uncalled-for room service that no-one, least of all us, has rung down to reception for.

Tuesday 9th March, 2010

I had returned from playing golf (trying to play golf) with Philip. There was a hastily scribbled message from Carol on the coffee table. Joyce had suddenly worsened and Carol was at the hospital in Bath. I drove over as quickly as I could. Steve was there and Mike had been, but had now left. Carol stayed at her Mum's bedside while Steve and I went down to the cafe for a sandwich and a coffee. We brought up a sandwich for Carol which she ate, momentarily letting go her mother's hand. And in that briefest of moments, Joyce slipped away. Her eyes and breath had stilled, but it was so gentle, that it was impossible to know when she had passed over; in fact, we had to ask a nurse to corroborate the fact that it was so. Her passing had been incredibly serene. As considerate as ever, we thought. Typically, Joyce hadn't wanted to bother us, hadn't wanted to make a fuss or alarm us unduly. A cherished wife, mother and future mother-in-law had been lifted from us and that window had irrevocably closed. As Steve commented, we were all orphans now.

Fast-forward four months to a far happier event. Carol and I married on 10th July 2010 in St Margaret's Church, Queen Charlton, the village near Keynsham where Carol had been born. She arrived absolutely punctually at 2pm, bless her, Steve gave her away and Roger was my best man (he has always been that, actually) and the whole afternoon was memorable – and I don't even like weddings. I had always been of that opinion until my own wedding; an attitude that, I suspect, is shared by many men. Even better, every single thing went according to plan and there were no hitches. We got hitched without a hitch, so to speak. The only element missing were our respective mothers and fathers.

Even the photographer didn't draw the whole business out unnecessarily, then we were driven off to the wedding breakfast at The Old Manor Hotel in Keynsham. Out in the garden, Derek the photographer suddenly pointed and said, "Look!" Roaring overhead were the Red Arrows on their way to an airshow. It was an unlooked-for bonus and we hadn't even hired them! We stayed overnight at the hotel and our room in the eaves was incredibly hot and humid. At about five am we gave up trying to sleep and re-read our cards and opened presents over a cup of tea. It all felt slightly naughty, rather like a very young child's Christmas morning!

Ten days later we stayed for a couple of nights in a boutique hotel on the edge of the New Forest; then in late August, we had our honeymoon proper, travelling down to the south of France by train (Eurostar to Paris and then SNCF to Brive) and staying in the Dordogne.

And that, thus far, is my life and as far as I can go with this. Except to say that I am blessed to be married to Carol, a bubbly, funny, kind and thoughtful lady. That we found one another and rescued each other is solely down to my mother – if she hadn't moved to Rose Villa at that particular time and if Carol had not needed work… well, we would never have been thrown together. That's quite a scary thought, isn't it?

The author's wedding to Carol, July 2010.

POSTLUDE

53

His story…

History

My story…

Mystery…

Mist… airy…

What if?

I have always thought that was a valid and fascinating question. What if I/we/they had done X and not Y? Were able to do X, Y or Z now and/or in the future?

The asking of that very question seems to help keep us fresh and young, in body, mind and spirit. I have tried my best to be truthful both to myself and to those who appear in my story. Inevitably, I have left out events and people that should have been included – to them my apologies, but, as one writes, certain things rise to the surface and while others do not.

I think that Rayner Heppenstall was right (see dedicatory page) – that we are, by and large, fictitious yes, even to ourselves as well as to our loved ones, however frustrating and hurtful that must appear. But it is, surely, the truth? (If you haven't read any Heppenstall, give it a go – he is wonderfully astute and observant, as well as being an economic writer – drily mordent, too.)

Memoirs… memories… repository of memories…

Perhaps my title should have been 'The Days of *My* Vanity'? But, come to think of it, even that italicisation might appear vain, certainly to some of you readers. (Funny how writers always presume an audience, a readership, isn't it?) 'Our' has more of a collective ring to it, I suppose. It also suggests that we are in this whole strange and barely-understood business together – which is certainly true, no denying that.

Ah, the old questions… and there you are, reader, wanting an orderly ending! Which, of course, I will not provide. Which, more accurately, I *cannot* provide, because we are not tidy, neat, rational beings. But do we really require or want neatness, rationality and tidiness…? The answer is probably yes – to balance all the chaos and crap that is routinely hurled at us (and, to be fair, that we in our turn hurl at others…). And yet, I still prefer to leave things open-ended. For any sense of resolution, I think we will have to look beyond ourselves and out to another dimension, to seek and anticipate both those immensities as well as intensities that we are not, in all probability, anywhere near ready to contemplate either mentally or in psychical reality.

With that cheering yet realistic thought I take my leave. Oh, yes – one last thing – thank you for your time, interest and patience in reading this book. Maybe some of it will have struck a chord? Chords have, after all (and for obvious reasons) been an important, on-going aspect of my life.

As for the rest (what remains, what is to come) well, who knows…? As TS Eliot remarked, "For us there is only the trying; the rest is not our business". I would go along with that – indeed, raise a glass or two to it…

The composer Francis Poulenc (1899–1963) once confessed that his personality was a mixture of playboy and monk, the one then the other being in the ascendant. He could be very naughty and impish, yet underneath was a strong faith and seriousness which gave way on various occasions to deep depression. I can empathise with all of that, indeed have a tendency towards those same traits myself.

"Let's be lucky!" as my old pal John Wain used to say; or equally valid, Spike Milligan's manner of signing-off his letters, "Love, Light and Peace", followed by a large, generous signature in black felt pen.

Cheers! *Salut*! *Salute*! *Slainte*! *Iechyd Da*! *Gesundheit*! *Ebiba*! *Gambe*!

Enough of this nonsense. Bye-bye...

54

Ending 1

By way of a postscript, I append an alphabetical selection of adjectives, some of which may be apposite or relevant in describing the contents of this foregoing memoir. Take your pick...

amusing, annoying, anodyne; bitchy, bucolic, brave; candid, caustic, creative; demonstrative, delectable, deranged; emotional, ebullient, esoteric; fabulous, flatulent, ferocious; garish, gauche, grumpy; hectoring, humane, humorous; impish, innocent, irritating; jesting, jocular, juicy; karmic, kindly, knowing; loving, lachrymose, luminous; maddening, mellifluous, mundane; nebulous, negative, nervous; oratorical, odious, outrageous; petulant, pedantic, playful; querulous, quiet, quizzical; radical, ramshackle, revelatory; scurrilous, stupefying, surreal; teasing, tender, terrific; ubiquitous, unequivocal, unctuous; vacant, vicious, vital; wacky, waspish, wearisome; xenophobic; yammering, yawn-inducing, youthful; zany, zealous, zippy.

NB: Please circle those of the above that you feel are appropriate.

Disgruntled or delighted readers may wish to append their own real or invented adjectives here:

Or, if you prefer, read ending 2…

55

Ending 2

On a lighter note…

If you have stayed with it thus far, I think that you deserve a joke, if not a drink. (This one is for you, Roger, by the way and I first heard it told by Carol's mother, Joyce, who always relished a ripe anecdote.)

A VAT inspector visits a lady at her place of work and wishes to clarify the nature of her business.

"I'm a prostitute," says she, quite openly and without embarrassment.

"I can't put that down. It's an illegal occupation," retorts the inspector, visibly frowning.

She thinks for a moment.

"I know. Put me down as a poultry farmer."

"A poultry farmer?" enquires the inspector, thinking that this woman is a bit of a case.

"Well – I have raised an awful lot of cocks in my time,"

replies the lady with a smile. "And," she continued, "some of them *were* bloody awful, too."

Leave 'em laughing, eh?

Today is Tuesday 23rd August 2011 and, after two summers work, this memoir is, as far as I am concerned, complete. Setting these events down has been a journey of not only remembering, but self-discovery and *re*-discovery too. The thing that surprised me most was the fact that the act of writing itself (clattering on the keys) was a great enabler, helping to trigger half-forgotten, half-buried memories. Not for the first time, either, have I been amazed by the apparently limitless capacity and resources of the mind.

Now... not only 'bye', but buy...

Acknowledgements

My many and grateful thanks go to the following individuals who have all helped in the making and production of this book, without whom, etcetera, etcetera:

Sian Dismorr (nee Howell-Pryce); my editors Helen Hart and Sarah Newman of SilverWood Books; Rachel Hemming-Bray who started me writing in my schooldays; Roland Phillipps of John Murray for permission to use a line from George Mackay Brown's poem *A Work for Poets* as my title; Roger Prideaux for simply, but always, having been in my life and sharing memories of our schooldays; my late and beloved partner Mary Howell-Pryce who gave me so much; my wife Carol who does likewise; Will Wain for permission to reprint John Wain's poem *In the Beginning*. The greater part of section 35 on John Wain first appeared in *Oxfordshire Limited Edition* in June 2004. Every effort has been made to contact copyright holders.

Lightning Source UK Ltd.
Milton Keynes UK
UKOW050432280312

189732UK00001B/14/P